Teaching and Learning Patterns
in School Mathematics

Ferdinand Rivera

Teaching and Learning Patterns in School Mathematics

Psychological and Pedagogical Considerations

 Springer

Ferdinand Rivera
Department of Mathematics
San Jose State University
San Jose, CA, USA

ISBN 978-94-007-2711-3   ISBN 978-94-007-2712-0 (eBook)
DOI 10.1007/978-94-007-2712-0
Springer Dordrecht Heidelberg New York London

Library of Congress Control Number: 2012948335

Printed on acid-free paper

Springer is part of Springer Science+Business Media (www.springer.com)

The human mind is desperate to
find patterns. ...
Pattern implies meaning.
                    (du Sautoy, 2008, p. 97)

Although behavior and development appear
structured, there are no structures. Although
behavior and development appear
rule-driven, there are no rules. There is
complexity. There is a multiple, parallel, and
continuously dynamic interplay of perception
and action, and a system that, by its
thermodynamic nature, seeks certain stable
solutions. These solutions emerge from
relations, not from design. When the
elements of such complex systems cooperate,
they give rise to behavior with a unitary
character, and thus to the illusion of
structure. But the order is always executory,
rather than rule-driven, allowing for the
enormous sensitivity and flexibility of
behavior to organize and regroup around
task and context.
                    (Thelen & Smith, 1994, p. xix)

Contents

Chapter 1
Introduction

Fundamental Notions of Patterning and Pattern Generalization

Beam Patterning Task: Below are four stages in a pattern. Each stage has two rows of squares, a top row and a bottom row.

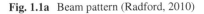

Stage 1   Stage 2   Stage 3   Stage 4

Fig. 1.1a Beam pattern (Radford, 2010)

1. *Interviewer (I): Jennifer (J, Grade 2, age 7), can you draw and show me how stage 5*
2. *would look like?*
3. *(J starts counting the squares in stage 4. She then draws stage 5 as shown in Fig. 1.1b.)*
4. *I: Okay, how did you know?*
5. *J: Coz I counted this one [points to stage 4] and I*
6. *like added a couple more.*
7. *I: Okay, how come a couple more?*
8. *J: When I counted [stage 4], it was 1, 2, 3, 4, 5, 6,*
9. *7, 8, 9 and if you put like if 9 was here*

F. Rivera, *Teaching and Learning Patterns in School Mathematics:*
Psychological and Pedagogical Considerations, DOI 10.1007/978-94-007-2712-0_1,
© Springer Science+Business Media Dordrecht 2013

Fig. 1.1b J's constructed
stage 5

10.   [*referring to her constructed stage 5*], *then you put more.*

11. *I: Okay how do you know how many more?*

12. *J: Coz the ... 9 is less, so you put more.*

13. *I: So it could be lots more? Few more? Doesn't matter?*

14. *J: A few more.*

15. *I: Okay, so what would come next in stage 6?*

16. (*J draws stage 6 as shown in Fig. 1.1c.*)

Fig. 1.1c J's constructed
stage 6

17. *I: Okay, what about stage 10? Can you draw for*
18.   *me stage 10? (J draws stage 10 as shown on*
19.   *the right.)*

20. *I: So how would you explain how you knew what*

21.   *to draw first like that one* [*referring to stage*
22.   *10*]?

Fig. 1.1d J's constructed
stage 10

23. *J*: *It was like this one [referring to stage 6] but then I added like ... like 5 more.*

24. *I*: *Okay, and how did you pick 5?*

25. *J*: *Coz 5 is a lower number.*

26. *I*: *A lower number? Than what?*

27. *J*: *Than the [pause] I forgot the next one.*

28. *I*: *Okay, what would you do for stage 25? You're gonna tell a friend that this is what*
29.   *stage 25 would look like. This is how you would draw it.*

30. *J*: *I'll draw like 50 squares?*

31. *I*: *Okay, why 50 squares?*

32. *J*: *Because ahm when you said the big number, then another big number has to come*
33.   *next.*

34. *I*: *Okay, then what if it was like stage 100? Then what would you do?*

35. *J*: *Then it'll be more like more than 100.*

36. *I*: *More than 100? Then how many little squares total would you have?*

37. *J*: *400.*

When expert generalizers process school patterning tasks such as the *Beam Pattern* in Fig. 1.1a, they oftentimes generate structures that enable them to extend the stages and predict outcomes in a convenient manner. Also, their interpreted structures are consistent in all aspects (e.g. shape and count) within and across stages beginning with the first stage. Further, because they "see" relationships rather quickly, they tend to produce several different, but equivalent, responses. If we compare the thinking of expert generalizers with that of 7-year-old Jennifer in the above interview episode, we are provided with an opportune moment to reflect on what beginning learners need to understand about what it means to engage in *patterning* activity. Jennifer was in second grade when she was asked to extend and explain the pattern in Fig. 1.1a to several more stages. The clinical interview took place near the end of the school year immediately after a design-driven 1-week classroom teaching experiment on patterning.

For Clements and Sarama (2009), *patterning* basically involves constructing and being predisposed to establishing mathematical regularities and structures in both ordered and unorganized data. They write:

> *Patterning is the search for mathematical regularities and structures.* Identifying and applying patterns help bring order, cohesion, and predictability to seemingly unorganized situations and allows you to make generalizations beyond the information in front of you. Although it can be viewed as a "content area," patterning is more than a content area; it is a process, a domain of study, and a habit of mind. (Clements & Sarama, 2009, p. 190)

Jennifer's patterning in the above interview episode seems to be nowhere near the description that Clements and Sarama stipulated in the above quote. What she appears to have, in fact, is a global sense of her pattern on the basis of her responses in lines 5–6, 14, and 32–33 in which she briefly described growth in protoquantitative terms, albeit in an inconsistent manner. In lines 5–6, for example, she "added a couple more" squares in each row of stage 4 (Fig. 1.1b) without taking into account how the previous three stages were also changing in terms of the number of squares that were being added from stage to stage. Also, her responses conveyed inconsistent notions of growth relative to the same pattern. While she was aware in line 14 that she needed "a few more" squares to construct an unknown "near" stage (e.g. stages 5, 6, and 10 required the addition of 4, 3, and 4 squares, respectively; Fig. 1.1b–d), however, with a "far" stage she simply hypothesized its outcome in lines 32–33 to be "another big number" (e.g. stages 25 and 100 would have 50 and 400 squares, respectively).

Rivera (2010a) describes *pattern generalization* in the following manner below.

> When students perform a *pattern generalization*, it basically involves mutually coordinating their perceptual and symbolic inferential abilities so that they are able to *construct* and *justify* a plausible and algebraically useful structure that could be conveyed in the form of a direct formula. (Rivera, 2010a, p. 147)

Thus in patterning activity learners infer structures on patterns, which means to say that patterns do not have any inherent invariant, stable, and essential property[1] other than what is imposed on them in the first place. However, the inferential abstracting process[2] fundamentally requires the coordination and convergence of several cognitive, cultural, and other factors (e.g. linguistic, neural) that influence both perceptual and symbolic abilities. Among expert patterners, for example, they might easily perceive a structure consisting of a corner square and n diagonal pairs of squares for each known stage in the pattern (Fig. 1.2) as a result of prior experiences on similar patterns. Also, assuming that they have a rich conceptual understanding of variables, they might be able to construct an algebraic generalization that, say, takes the form $T = 2n + 1$, where the variable T corresponds to the total number of squares in stage n. In justifying the formula, they might explain it deductively and empirically. In a deductive context they might begin with the formula and the known instances as premises in order to logically conclude that the succeeding stages in the pattern must be true via a proof of mathematical induction. Or, they could visually and, thus, empirically, demonstrate the reasonableness of the structure as their way of establishing its consistency by analogical reasoning, as shown in Fig. 1.2.

In Jennifer's case, while she perceived a growing pattern, drew stages, and verbally described them all in approximate terms, she still was unable to construct

---

[1] This characterization of structure in generalization is consistent with Davydov's (2008) definition of generalization, "(g)eneralization involves searching for some invariant property within a class of objects .... The general, as something recurring or stable, is a definite invariant of the various properties of a given type of object—i.e. it is essential. In many works, the terms 'general' and 'essential' are used interchangeably: 'To identify attributes as essential, they must be found to be general or common to a certain set of objects but not to some other set of objects'" (p. 74).

[2] In this book, we share Davydov's (2008) view regarding the strong link between generalization and abstraction, as follows: "Generalization is regarded as inseparably linked with the *operation of abstraction*. Singling out some essential quality as a general or common one means abstracting it from other qualities. This enables the child to transform the general quality into an independent and special object of subsequent actions (the general quality is labeled by some word). *Knowledge of the general, since it is the result of making a comparison and recording the result using a word,* is always something abstract, extracted, thinkable" (p. 75; italics added for emphasis).

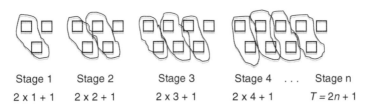

Stage 1   Stage 2   Stage 3   Stage 4   ...   Stage n

$2 \times 1 + 1$ $2 \times 2 + 1$ $2 \times 3 + 1$ $2 \times 4 + 1$ $T = 2n + 1$

Fig. 1.2 An analytical-driven structural generalization for the Fig. 1.1a pattern

and justify a direct formula. Certainly with young learners their level of expressive ability is likely going to be gestural, pictorial, and/or rhetorical (verbal) in nature and their justification empirical in form in the sense following Hershkowitz (1998), that is, "to understand, to explain, and to convince" (p. 29).

Two Basic Issues in Patterning Activity

In light of the foregoing initial characterization of the processes involved in patterning activity, individual learners are confronted with at least two very difficult tasks, as follows.

First, they need to perceive differently and, as a matter of fact, in a mathematical way. For instance, they may focus on aspects in a pattern that they think may either change or remain invariant within and across the given stages. Doing this may help them perceive possible differences and similarities. But matters are far more complicated than they are on the surface because of the human predisposition or natural tendency to primarily pay attention on what one finds significant to see, a phenomenon we refer to as *perceptual diversity*. That is, especially in patterning activity, what one considers meaningfully invariant and/or changing may likely be unrecognizable or trivial to another.

Second, especially among elementary students, they need to acquire the mathematical practice that a pattern with only a few known stages will most likely behave according to an imposed general expression drawn from an interpreted structure, which is then projected onto both the unknown and far stages of the pattern. Borrowing a few terms from Strevens (1008), we refer to this particular practice as the need for a *regularity explanation* relative to the *high level phase* of structuring that follows the *concrete phase* of extending the pattern. Here, we also emphasize the compelling roles we accord to both the prediction of outcomes (extensional activity) and the formal requirements that are needed to construct a regularity explanation in patterning activity.

While the above second task can be addressed, certainly in no easy terms, via the notions of abduction and induction (i.e. truth generation and testing, respectively; see Fig. 1.3) and deduction (i.e. truth preservation via proof), research knowledge is still needed that will more or less establish a stable trajectory of progressive abductions, inductions, and deductions on patterns of varying levels of complexity (e.g. oscillating to linear to nonlinear). The learning trajectory proposed by Clements and Sarama (2009) in the case of repeating patterns (for children ages 2–7 years) is an exemplar of this kind of work (see footnote 5 in Chap. 2). We also need converging research evidence that identifies shared skills among children and adults who successfully abduce algebraically useful structures. Further, stemming from very recent exciting work with lower elementary students (ages 7–8 years), they tend to produce more algebraically useful structures than recursive relations (e.g. "add 2 squares" from stage to stage in Fig. 1.1a; see Chap. 5) in the absence of tables of numerical values. However, with older children and adults (middle school students whose ages range from 11 to 13 years, undergraduate students, and inservice teachers), the reverse pattern is evident at least in the initial phase of their patterning process. What do these findings mean both from psychological and pedagogical perspectives? Additionally, what factors shape the manner in which individual learners construct their regularity explanations, including how they acquire the relevant formal requirements in pattern generalization? To what extent can we claim that such formal requirements are acquired naturally or learned in some meaningful sequence?

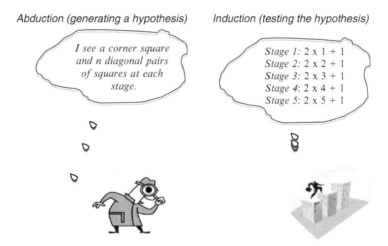

Fig. 1.3 A complementary abuction-induction processing illustration of Fig. 1.2

Regarding the first task, *perceptual diversity* is still an open problem. While research findings appear to converge on the view that the relevant high-level strategies and skills are learned especially in purposeful teaching experiment contexts, there are and will always be students who are and will be unable to model them appropriately on different tasks involving different domains. For example, Emma, an eighth grader (age 13) who was involved in Rivera's (2011) 3-year longitudinal study on patterns and algebraic thinking that started when she was in sixth grade, effectively decomposed the stages in her constructed linear pattern into two parts that enabled her to establish an algebraic generalization (Fig. 1.4a). In fact, she employed the same structuring process on all patterning tasks that were presented to her during the clinical interview that took place near the end of the school year. However, she felt frustrated when she tried to use the same strategy in dealing with a triangular pattern that had a quadratic structure. Figure 1.4b shows how she tried to initially cope with the triangular pattern on her own without any teacher intervention. Later on, when she engaged in joint activity with an expert adult, she became aware of a different way of looking at the pattern, which enabled her to establish a direct formula through a figural compensatory process of adding and taking away the same number of squares (Fig. 1.4c). Emma's situation is typical in all mathematics classrooms.

Consequently, any single conceptual framework that purports to explain pattern generalization processing is bound to be insufficient. What we thus need is a dynamic framework that is sensitive to different patterning situations. Further, since all patterning tasks are subject to perceptual diversity and different levels of representational competence, singular frameworks that attempt to model a unidirectional, hierarchical, and rigid emergence of patterning skills are also likely going to conceptually implode because they will not be able to explain all complex factors that shape pattern generalization processing.

A Semi-Free Patterning Task: Continue the pattern to stage 5 given the first two stages below in a growing pattern of squares. Then find a direct formula.

Emma (Grade 8, age 13 years) looks at stages 1 and 2 then constructs stages 3 through 5, as shown below.

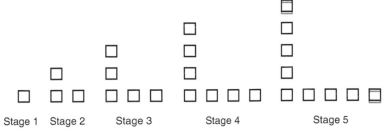

| Stage 1 | Stage 2 | Stage 3 | Stage 4 | Stage 5 |

Emma's Algebraic Generalization: $s = n + n - 1$

Explanation:

38   This is stage 1 [*referring to the one square*]. This is stage 2 [*the column of two squares*]. This

39   is stage 3 [*the column of three squares*] and this is stage 4 [*the column of four squares*]. And

40   then so ahm when I figured that, I try to see what's left. So if it's 1 [*the remaining square on*

41   the row of stage 2], if you subtract the stage number from 1, you get 1. If you subtract 1

42   from the stage number [*stage 3*] you get 2 [*the two remaining squares on the row of stage*

43   3]. If you subtract 1 from this stage number [*stage 4*], you get 3 [*the three remaining squares*

44   on the row of stage 4].

Fig. 1.4a Emma's structuring process involving the growing L-shaped pattern

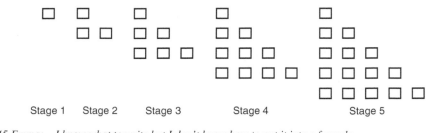

Stage 1   Stage 2   Stage 3   Stage 4   Stage 5

45 Emma: *I know what to write but I don't know how to put it into a formula.*
                 Like so if
46   *there's n and then you add all the numbers before it. Like if it's 5, you*
                 put n
47   *1, n – 2, n – 3, and n – 4. But I don't know how to put that in a*
                 formula.
48 FDR: *So if it's stage 6, if you use your formula, it is?*
49 Emma: *It's n plus n – 5 plus n – 4 all the way to 1.*

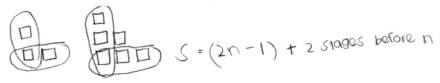

Fig. 1.4b   Emma's initial structuring process of the triangular pattern

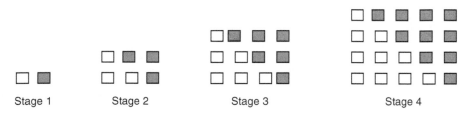

Stage 1   Stage 2   Stage 3   Stage 4

Fig. 1.4c   Joint structuring process involving the triangular pattern in Fig. 1.4a

Additional Considerations Regarding Patterns, Structures, and Generalization

In this section we further clarify the terms *patterns*, *structures*, and *generalization*. At the very least, we shall fundamentally assume that all patterns in school mathematics convey relational structures or, simply, structures. Every structure needs to be cohesive, general, and accurate, that is: cohesive in the sense that there is a single rule that can determine all the necessary outcomes; general in the sense that it can explain the most number of stages possible; and accurate in the sense that there is a precise goodness of fit between a hypothesized or predicted output and the actual output (cf. Strevens, 2008, p. 19). Whenever possible, we also desire simple structures. For example, Emma's initial structure of her pattern in Fig. 1.4b is not as simple as her other structure in Fig. 1.4c.

While the explicit external representations of patterns convey some kind of an internal structure in the sense of being embodied objects, their causal potency (Rogers & McClelland, 2008) is, in fact, interpreted. Their meaningfulness emerges only when they are interpreted as objects-in-context, that is, they are seen in relation to an interpreted structure, a relation-driven arrangement, which links the elements together in some way.

Thus, central to students' fundamental understanding of patterns in school mathematics involves the necessity of inferring an interpreted (high-level) structure that can explain and instantiate a replicable regularity (Papic, Mulligan, & Mitchelmore, 2011, p. 238), which can then be captured, contracted, and condensed symbolically by a single mathematical rule, preferably a function that depict the necessary features. Implicit in the nature of explanations or justifications is either an expectability or a subsumption criterion, which means to say that either the interpreted regularities in patterns are expected to behave according to the inferred structures or the perceived uniformities are instances of laws and general relationships and principles that make them meaningful mathematical objects in the first place.

There are many different kinds of patterns in the school mathematics curriculum, and they can be represented either numerically or figurally. Table 1.1 lists some of the patterns that K-12 students will encounter throughout their mathematical experiences in the classroom. These patterns are, in fact, explored in this book in some detail. Across such patterns, students are expected to develop the habit of formulating a generalization, which basically involves identifying basic or common blocks that make up the individual stages and developing a mathematically valid explanation that link all the stages in some sensible but rigorous manner.

Table 1.1 Different kinds and examples of patterns in the school mathematics curriculum

Kinds of Patterns	Arithmetic Examples	Algebraic Examples
Constant Patterns	A A A A A ...	Horizontal Line Models
Oscillating (Repeating) Patterns	A B A B A B ...	Piecewise Models, Trigonometric Models
Increasing Patterns	1, 3, 5, 7, 9, 11, ... Figurate numbers	Linear and Exponential Models, Some Polynomial Models over Some Specified Domains
Decreasing Patterns	12, 10, 8, 6, 4, ...	
Mathematical Algorithms	Operations Involving Numbers	Operations Involving Expressions
Mathematical Concepts	Compensation, Decomposition	Transformations of Functions
Other Recursive Patterns	Fibonacci Sequence, Tower of Hanoi Pattern, and Recursive Patterns in Discrete Mathematics	
Other Spatially Drawn Patterns	Some Geometry Relationships (Fractals, Pythagorean Theorem, Interior Angle Sum Theorem in a Triangle, Rigid Motions)	

"Mathematics," du Sautoy (2008) writes, "is sometimes called the quest for patterns" (p. 15). The taken-as-shared practice that comes with such a quest involves making generalizations about them, and students learn the skill in different ways using several multiple and in many cases parallel approaches. At the end of the road, however, they need to learn that valid (hypostatic) generalizations replace the stages or condense them into either an expression or equation that can be used later to make predictions about future outcomes in an efficient manner. Like categories in everyday life involving sets of objects of the natural kind forming, constructing, and naming them all require hypostasizing regular and stable characteristics without having to inspect each object, which is cumbersome and simply impossible to accomplish.

The same everyday experience is true when we ask students to establish generalizations involving sets of mathematical objects. For example, Emma's algebraic generalizations in Fig. 1.4a, b enabled her to deal with the far stages such as stage 25, 100, and 1,055 on the basis of her structural generalizations alone. Beyond the calculations, her algebraic generalizations conveyed how she mentally conjured those stages, which would be too time-consuming to construct on paper. Emma's understanding of an algebraic generalization more or less reflect expert patterners' perspective with regard to expressing generalities. In Fig. 1.2, their generalizations describe how they see the structures of their pattern in both aspects of shape and count. One unresolved issue in pattern generalization is the extent to which learners can be provided with sufficient opportunities that will enable them to comprehend that basic intent, which implicitly suggests the need to develop appropriate instruction and effective orchestration so that they see generalization as being both a process (i.e. a way of calculating) and a concept (i.e., conveying an interpreted structure of a collection of stages).

Peirce offers the following definition of generalization:

> Generalization, in its strict sense, means the discovery, by reflection upon a number of cases, of a general description applicable to all of them. This is the kind of thought movement which I have elsewhere called formal hypothesis, or reasoning from definition to definitum. So understood, it is not an increase in breadth but an increase in depth. (Peirce, 1960, p. 256)

Thus, a generalization is a signpost that we are getting deeper on matters involving the definiteness of our conceptions of the known things that can then assist us in how we might handle the unknown things. For example, Emma in Fig. 1.4c began to see triangular shapes as configural subsets of their corresponding rectangular arrays, which enabled her to justify the direct formula that emerged from her actions. Another example is taken from Rivera's (2011) second-grade class (mean age of 7 years) that explored notions relevant to even and odd numbers. Figure 1.5 shows the written work of several students' generalizations regarding the parity sum of two odd numbers. Initially, they learned about even numbers in the context of having exact pairs of circles. Working in pairs, they compared even and odd numbers by consistently drawing on their perceptual and conceptual experiences with circle-pairs. Consequently, establishing generalizations about the parity of the sum of two whole numbers also occurred naturally, that is, within the context of their experiences with circle-pairs. For them, even sums meant "hav[ing] a friend, a partner, and a buddy" and with "no one [that] is left out," that in fact reflected their representational experiences with even numbers. In a Peircean context, the depth that was evident in their written work in Fig. 1.5 could also be seen as a derived effect of their basic understanding of parity. When they redrew their two separate sets of drawn circles (each representing an odd number) together and saw that the total represented an even number, that enabled them to frame an explanation that was sufficiently generalizable and appropriate at their grade level. Their depth explanation was, of course, empirically supported by repeated testing involving different paired sets of circles.

The structural generalizations that Emma in Fig. 1.4c and the second-grade students in Fig. 1.5 produced model the way in which Strevens (2008) talked about *depth* in relation to the "explanatory enterprise in science," that is, "science is said to be deep just when it provides understanding" (p. 136). Peirce's association of generalization with "increase in depth" appears to have that same goal, which is aimed at understanding as it is routed and conveyed in some valid structure. Thus, any structure that co-emerges from a generalization is, borrowing Strevens's words, "the end point of the supreme and sublime explanatory maneuver" that "transform[s] the raw material [i.e., the objects comprising the stages in a pattern] into something [that] provides understanding: abstraction" (Strevens, 2008, p. 137).

Parity Sum Problem: A. Name two odd numbers. Illustrate them using circles. Is the sum even or odd? How do you know for sure? B. Name another two odd numbers. Illustrate them using circles and check to see if the sum is even or odd. How do you know for sure? C. Complete the sentence: The sum of two odd numbers is always _____. How would you convince a friend that your answer is correct?

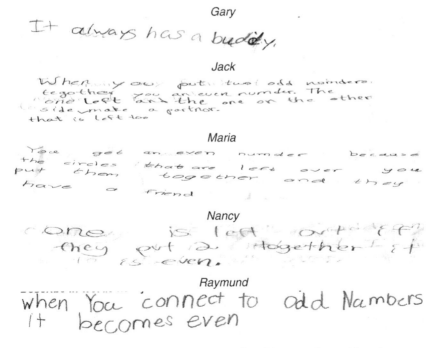

Gary

It always has a buddy.

Jack

When you put two odd numbers together you an even number. The one left and the one on the other side make a partner. that is left too

Maria

You get an even number because the circles that are left over you put them together and they have a friend

Nancy

one is left out if they put a together if is even.

Raymund

when You connect to odd Nambers It becomes even

Fig. 1.5 Second-grade students' responses on the parity of the sum of two odd numbers

Increasing depth via generalization can also be accomplished in several other different ways. Constructing and justifying equivalent structures for the same pattern is one powerful suggestion since the determination of valid relationships is central to both actions. Current research evidence on patterns, in fact, supports the emerging view that the construction and justification aspects in patterning activity work hand in glove. That view aligns well with the following forceful argument raised by Otte (2011) in the paragraph below.

> School mathematics is algebra but does not conceive of algebra in relational terms, considering it rather as generalized arithmetic. School algebra does not have real variables and school mathematics identifies meaning with verification and is not interested in generalization. There have also been less "anti-didactic" approaches to algebraic thinking, however, Davydov, for example, always had emphasized the timely and proper transition of children to the ability to orient themselves in the relations of quantities and figures themselves … as an essential condition of [their] understanding of mathematical thought and he therefore proposed to begin mathematical teaching with an introduction of these relations themselves. (Otte, 2011, p. 316)

Establishing depth via the practical activity of generalized arithmetic in which generalization is viewed as basically changing constants to variables (cf. Kline, 1980) and justification equated to the empirical process of verification does not seem to match the same depth as establishing a generalization in relational terms. Figures 1.2, 1.4c, and 1.5 illustrate the latter perspective. In Fig. 1.2, the pattern stages were initially seen as comprising of two additive configurations (i.e. a corner square and a $2 \times n$ rectangular array), which explains why the direct formula evolved as such in symbolic form. Emma in Fig. 1.4c saw a growing rectangular array with dimensions n and $n + 1$ that when halved produced the figural stages in her constructed pattern. The students' generalizations in Fig. 1.5 were derived from their actual experiences on earlier tasks A and B. When they drew two odd numbers on paper using small circle pieces, some mentally inferred, while others drew circles and arrows to show that all the drawn circles matched perfectly in pairs.

In other words, each algebraic generalization emerged in an attempt to capture an interpreted relationship within and across stages in patterns of objects, which does not appear to have the same intent as, say, an algebra-within-arithmetic practice of setting up a table of values, engaging in pattern spotting, and eventually obtaining a direct formula as a consequence of merely replacing numbers with variables. Current research and practices are not clear about and rather unwilling to decide in terms of which perspective to value more than the other. It is also worth noting Radford's (2001) view that there is more to variable-based generalizations than merely substituting variables for numbers. That is, the presence of variables in students' generalizations does not necessarily mean that they understand them as being general and algebraic. Algebraic generalizations, at the very least, need to be interpreted objectively as "disembodied placeholders," "generic numbers," and "unknown quantities" beyond their original sources in concrete contexts. Unfortunately we still lack sufficient research knowledge regarding ways in which learners can effectively transpose their conceptions of independent variables in patterning situations from being ordinal (i.e. indexical, positional, deictically based) in source to being cardinal in the evolved form (i.e. as numbers that are "capable of being arithmetically operated").

Exploring a Complex Theory of Graded Pattern Generalization

Skype (S) was in the same second-grade class with Jennifer who was also asked to obtain a pattern generalization for the Beam Pattern in Fig. 1.1a in a clinical interview setting that took place after a teaching experiment on growing figural (linear) patterns. In the 1-week experiment, the students explored linear patterns to help them develop the habit of noticing and paying attention to parts in figural stages that appeared to them as being common and shared across the given stages. Once those parts have been identified, they colored those parts with the same color from one stage to the next and then used a different color to shade the remaining parts. Next, they extended the given stages to two more near stages (oftentimes stages 5 and 6) before dealing with the task of either drawing or explaining to a friend how certain far stages (e.g. stage 10, 25, and 100) were to behave on the basis of their inferred abductions.

50 I: Your job is to figure out what comes next, stage 5 [in the Beam Pattern, reproduced below].

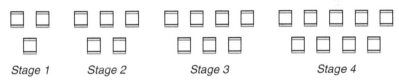

| Stage 1 | Stage 2 | Stage 3 | Stage 4 |

51 S: Okay. [He draws stage 5 on paper. See Figure 1.6a. Notice the extra square in the top row.]

Fig. 1.6a Skype's constructed stage 5

52. *I: Okay, so how did you know what to do?*
53. *S: Because here [referring to the bottom row of stage 4] it has 4 and that I added 1 more.*
54. *And right here [referring to the top row of stage 4] I added 1 more. And this [top row]*
55. *[in stage 4] one has more [in comparison with stage 3]. And the top row has more*
56. *[pointing to the top rows in stages 1, 2, and 3] and the bottom row [pointing to the bottom*
57. *rows in stages 1, 2, and 3] has less.*

57. *I: Okay, so can you show me what comes next in stage 6. [He draws stage 6 on paper. See*
58. *Fig. 1.6b.]*

Fig. 1.6b Skype's constructed stage 6

59. *I: Okay, and how do you know how many to put?*

60. *S: I just added 1 more on each side [referring to stage 6] and then right here [referring to the*
61. *top row of stage 5] has less than this [referring to the top row of stage 6].*

62. *I: Okay so when you said you added 1 extra [square] on each side, could you explain that a*
63. *little more on this drawing [referring to stage 5]?*

64. *S: Hmm. Like you added another 1 right here [on the right corner of the top row in stage 5]*
65. *and another here [on the left corner of the top row in stage 5]. Then you just add 1 more*
66. *right here [on each corner of the bottom row of stage 5].*

67. *I: Okay, and how did you know how many to put here [referring to the entire stage 5]?*

68. *S: Because over here [stage 5] it gets bigger and bigger [points to stages 1, 2, 3, and 4].*

69. *I: Okay, so what about stage 10. Could you explain to me how to make stage 10, give me*
70. *instructions so that I could draw it, how would you explain it?*

71. *S: Hmm, you need 10 on the bottom and 11 on the top.*

72. *I: Okay, and what about stage 25?*

73. *S: 25 on the bottom and 26 on the top.*

74. *I: And a hundred? What about stage 100?*

75. *S: 100 on the bottom and 101 on the top.*

When the interviewer asked Skype to check whether his constructed stages 5 and 6 (Fig. 1.6a, b) were consistent with the verbal description he offered for stages 25 and 100, he redrew them and produced the figural stages below.

Fig. 1.6c Skype's new stage 5

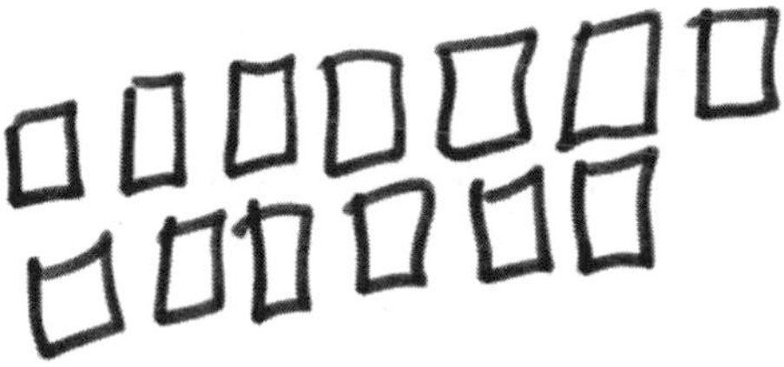

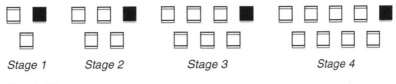

Fig. 1.6d Skype's new stage 6

In a follow up interview that took place the following day, Skype was presented with the modified Beam Pattern shown in Fig. 1.7a below.

Stage 1   Stage 2   Stage 3   Stage 4

Fig. 1.7a Modified beam pattern

Following the same protocol, the interviewer asked Skype to first extend the figural pattern to stages 5, 6, and 7 (see Fig. 1.7b). When the interviewer asked him to explain his pattern, he reasoned as follows:

Stage 5   Stages 6 and 7

Fig. 1.7b Skype's extensions of the Fig. 1.7a pattern

76. *S: Right here [referring to stage 4] it has 4. You add 1 more [referring to the top row in stage*
77. *3]. And then you add 1 more right here [referring to the bottom row of stage 4 in*
78. *comparison with the bottom row of stage 3].... Then in stage 5, there's 5 [squares] here*
79. *and 1 black square [referring to the top row], and then 5 [squares] right here [referring to*
80. *the bottom row].*

81. *I: Okay, great! So what would stage 10 look like if you just explain it to me?*

82. *S: 10 on this side [using stage 5 as a point of reference and pointing to the top row] and 10*
83. *on this side [the bottom row].*

84. *I: And what about stage 25?*

85. *S: 25 on the top and 1 black one and 25 on the bottom.*

86. *I: And what about stage 100?*

87. *S: 100 on the top and a black one and 100 on the bottom.*

Skype in the context of the two preceding interviews established two algebraically useful structural generalizations for the same pattern. While his incipient generalizations were verbal, they nevertheless enabled him to determine unique outcomes relative to the two patterns. In symbolic form, his first generalization could be converted to the formula $T = n + (n + 1)$, where the terms appear in that order, n assuming both the stage number and the number of squares in the bottom row, $n + 1$ the number of squares in the top row, and T the total number of squares. His second generalization $T = n + 1 + n$, where the terms also appear in that order, n assuming both the stage number and the size of the two equal rows of unshaded squares, and the constant, 1, referring to the black square. What is interesting to point out at this stage is the nature of emergence of Skype's generalizations, which actually foregrounds a number of interesting considerations that we shall explore in greater detail in the remaining chapters. Foremost among these considerations involves Skype's natural predisposition toward function-based thinking that enabled him to quickly state outcomes for certain far generalization tasks. Where research is rather gray is the extent to which young learners understand their rhetorical direct formulas as conveying characteristics of functions. Researchers who work with elementary school students notice that they appear to have an innate or intuitive understanding of functions due to their ability to construct direct formulas. Certainly, the more interesting question involves how this connection is actually established. The presence of explicit equations or verbal descriptions does indicate some preliminary understanding of functional relationships, but it is not sufficient.

Another important issue is related to algebraic language. Skype in second grade was classified as an English learner. However, his lack of verbal competence in the English language did not deter him in conveying an algebraically useful (verbal) generalization. Skype drew on other semiotic resources that enabled him to represent and convey his two pattern generalizations. For example, his drawings clearly reflect a figural understanding of the key relationships in pattern generalization. His drawn pictures such as the ones shown in Figs. 1.6c, d and 1.7b shows a rather well-defined relationship between stage number and outcome and between two stages in the patterns. Further, having had no formal knowledge of, and instruction in, variables did not prevent him from expressing his structural generalizations. A few recent patterning studies at the elementary level have already introduced students to variables as a way of supporting the generalized arithmetic perspective. However, successful situations with young learners like Skype provide an existence proof that variable-based generalizing in the elementary school mathematics curriculum can still be optional. What seems to be more important than introducing variables involves the nature, trajectory, and quality of the mathematical relationships that are constructed. In other words, algebraic variables as they pertain to pattern generalization can be routed in several different ways depending on a number of factors, and that generalizations that are perceived in valid relational terms seem to hold much more promise and meaning in developmental accounts of growth in variable understanding than traditional generalized arithmetic views that seem to equate variable understanding with variable use.

Both Skype and Jennifer began their process of generalization globally by employing a few familiar and age-appropriate protoquantitative terms such as more, more than, less, big, and bigger. However, Skype's perceptually drawn inferences were certainly more refined and exact than Jennifer's. In the first part of the interview, he employed a series of horizontal/vertical and local/global analogies in helping him establish how stages were related to one another. For example, in lines 53–55, he inferred a relationship that was local and horizontal, where each of the two rows in a succeeding stage increased by 1 square from the preceding stage. In lines 56–57, he then inferred a relationship that was global and vertical, where there were more squares in all the top rows than in the bottom rows. In line 68, he inferred another relationship that was global and horizontal, where the stages appealed to him to be "getting bigger and bigger." Finally, in lines 71–75, he abduced a relationship that was local and vertical, that is, depending on the stage number, the bottom row corresponded to the stage number and the top row was 1 more than the number of squares in the bottom row. In the second part of the interview, Skype also exhibited a series of analogies. In lines 76–78, he inferred a relationship that was local and horizontal (add 1 square to each of the two rows from stage to stage). In lines 78–87, he inferred a relationship that was local and vertical (two equal rows of unshaded squares and a black square).

The beginning responses of Skype and Jennifer seem to convey that they are at the same entry level of abductive processing in generalization. Research is needed that can extrapolate how and why succeeding deviations take place differently among learners. What inputs (cognitive, cultural, neural, linguistic, etc.) does Skype utilize which enable him to produce more well-defined structural generalizations than the ones offered by Jennifer? More generally, what mechanisms can explain differences and similarities in pattern generalization ability? Further, especially considering older students (see, for e.g., Emma's thinking relative to Fig. 1.4a, c), research has not fully explored the extent to which they use either rules or constructive actions in pattern generalization, which tend to influence the inferential nature and representational content of their generalizations. The main point that we highlight in this paragraph are those perceptual and representational choices that learners make and other relevant cognitive inputs that they tap in performing a pattern generalization, which may not be hierarchical, unidirectional, and transitional in character but dynamic, multidimensional, graded, and continuously evolving through predictable and unpredictable factors that shape individual perceptual and representational abilities. Consequently, such choices beg the question of usable pedagogical implications. For example, how can instruction be effectively designed and orchestrated so that is sensitive to this complex characterization of pattern generalization?

The preceding accounts might also have impressed the view that Skype fully transitioned in establishing algebraically useful structural generalizations and that Jennifer retained her global approaches in dealing with other patterns. The truth of the matter is that both successfully conveyed valid algebraically useful structures in the case of the Cross Squares Pattern in Fig. 1.8a (Fig. 1.8b shows Jennifer's extensions). Further, both Skype and Jennifer constructed incorrect extensions in the case of the Triangular Circles Pattern in Fig. 1.9a (Fig. 1.9b shows Skype's constructed extensions). These findings and their implications are discussed in greater detail in later sections in the book. However, it suffices for the time being to note the complexity of factors that influence pattern generalization among K-12 learners.

In this book, we make a case for graded pattern generalization, a view that deemphasizes stable transitional shifts in favor of parallel or nonhierarchical and distributed processing actions or choices that inevitably lead to the natural occurrence of different types and qualities of pattern generalization. Depending on the task, in fact, including a host of cognitive, neural, sociocultural, and classroom-related factors, pattern generalization draws on a complex net of parallel choices or actions, where every choice or action seems to depend on the strength of ongoing connections that learners establish themselves.

Cross Squares Task : A square has four corners or vertices. Below are three stages in a growing pattern of squares.

Stage 1	Stage 2	Stage 3

a. How might stage 4 look like? How about stage 5? Explain your figures.

b. If we extend the pattern based on the preceding stages, how might stage 10 look like? Either draw it or explain to me.

c. How might you explain to a friend how he or she might build stage 25? How about stage 100?

Fig. 1.8a   Cross squares pattern task given to Grade 2 students

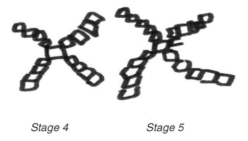

Stage 4   *Stage 5*

Fig. 1.8b   Jennifer's constructed stages 4 and 5 of the pattern in Fig. 1.9a

(Same Protocol in Fig. 1.9) Below are stages in a growing pattern of circles.

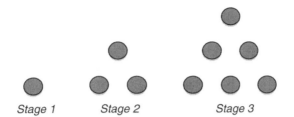

Stage 1   Stage 2   Stage 3

Fig. 1.9a Triangular circles pattern task given to Grade 2 students

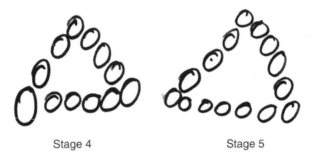

Stage 4   Stage 5

Fig. 1.9b Skype's constructed stages 4 and 5 of the pattern in Fig. 1.9a

Figure 1.10 is a specific example of a nonhierarchical parallel distributed processing network that we explore in greater detail in Chap. 4. The example models Skype's thinking relative to the Beam Pattern in Fig. 1.1a as indicated in lines 51 through 87 above when he was asked to obtain a plausible generalization in a clinical interview session. Our model of a general network consists of three major layers that work together in some way as soon as students are confronted with a patterning task. Each layer consists of units. The input layer consists of units that pertain to the given and already available information regarding a given patterning task. The hidden layer consists of units that emerge from relationships that occur between the relation layer and representation layer. The relation layer consists of units that provide the contexts in which an individual learner interprets a pattern, which might refer to, say, a name, a property, a behavior, and other qualities that characterize the input units. We note that on their own as objects, the units in any layer have no internal relationships other than what learners infer between and among the individual layers. Together they provide learners with the necessary basic stimulus for pattern generalization performance. Some of the relation units convey abductive constraints that allow individual learners to see a pattern in different ways, which then influence the nature of the emergent hypothesis or structure for the pattern. For example, abductive constraints might involve interpreting stages in a novel pattern as instantiations of an already established pattern in which case the same label and formula will be used to develop complete propositions about the novel pattern. The *representation layer* refers to the perceptual, linguistic, numeric, and other symbolic units that describe patterns in various formats. Some of these units include verbal descriptions, gestures, pictures, and algebraic representations. The hidden units can be seen in terms of being more or less subjective or personal factors that are not directly influenced by either the input or context units and yet provide assistance in making decisions about which output units to choose. The *output layer* refers to single-unit descriptions of configurations or parts that describe plausible structures of a pattern that is undergoing generalization. The units include both general (e.g. protoquantities) and more specific descriptors. Except for the input and relation layers, the other layers consist of units that can interact with each other.

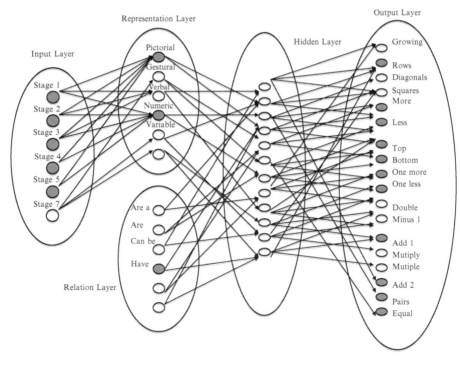

Fig. 1.10 Example of a parallel network model of a pattern generalization task

Skype's pattern generalization in lines 50 through 75 exemplifies an instance of parallel processing. The input units comprising stages 1 to 5 activated the output units such as top and bottom rows, adding a square on each row, more squares on the top row than on the bottom row, and one more square on the top row than on the bottom row. The additional input unit of color (black and white squares) further assisted him in generating a different structural generalization in lines 76 through 87 in which case he activated the units corresponding to equal rows and the addition of one square. The hidden layer assisted in propagating the activity forward to the output layer. Further, the activation of both pictorial and numerical units under the representation level indicates how he also perceived and manipulated the pattern in at least two ways. Choice was determined on the basis of the strengths of the connections that he established between and across the units with the connection weights continuously adjusting themselves in small amounts, an indication that a mapping was taking place between the units in the input layer and the appropriate units in the output layer.

Certainly connections can change depending on the type of task being dealt with in patterning activity. Also, frequent exposure on similar structuring tasks trains the network to activate the appropriate connections. What is nicely conveyed in a parallel distributed model is the property of being a continuously changing and evolving network, which means that the reality of manifesting different kinds of, and approaches to, pattern generalization is taken as given to the system. For example, Jennifer's manifestation of several pattern generalization strategies above in relation to the different tasks presented to her in a clinical interview context can be explained by the different activations of connections between units and layers in her parallel processing network, which produced structural generalizations in some cases and global generalizations in others. It is likely that changing the learning context from individual to joint activity (e.g. Jennifer and Skype collaboratively working together) might mean generating a different sequence of activations as a consequence of their interaction.

Overviews of the Remaining Chapters

Chapter 2 deals with issues of depth that are relevant to the concept and process of generalization. In the first two sections, we clarify the following useful terms that are now commonly used in school-based patterns research: abduction; induction; near generalization and far generalization; and deduction. We then explore nuances in the meaning of generalization that have been used in different contexts in the school mathematics curriculum. In the closing section, we begin to discuss initial implications of the findings in the chapter on our proposal of a theory of graded pattern generalization that we explore in some detail in Chap. 4.

In *Chap. 3*, we provide an interpretive synthesis account drawn from 20 or so years of research studies on pattern generalization that were conducted with younger and older students in different parts of the globe. In this chapter, we also explore an organizing framework that takes into account various aspects of pattern generalization that emerged from the interpretive synthesis account. Central to the organizing framework are the inferential processes of abduction, induction, and deduction that we discussed in some detail in Chap. 2. In this chapter, we explain other equally important (and overlapping) dimensions of pattern generalization, namely: natures and sources of generalization; types of structures; ways of attending to structures; and modes of representing and understanding generalizations. We also remain consistent in articulating the complexity of pattern generalization due to differences in, and the simultaneous layering of, processes relevant to constructing, expressing, and justifying interpreted structures. Much effort has been made to include all the relevant published research articles on the topic. Also, since we aim for maximal inclusiveness, our synthesis includes research on patterns that have been done in other countries. For example, just a few years ago Portugal introduced patterns as a unifying theme in their countrywide modification of their school mathematics curriculum. Countries such as Taiwan, Thailand, and Lebanon recently reported results of several patterning studies that were conducted with older children and adults.

Chapter 4 deals with the theory of graded pattern generalization. Theories and findings in cognitive science, in particular, those that deal with the theory of parallel distributed processing (PDP), will be used to explain the notion of emergence and structure formation from a distributed and multimodal perspective. We then contrast an emergent structure from other well-known points of view of structures in cognitive science, namely, symbol structures, theory–theory structures, and probabilistic structures. Next we expound on the theory of PDP in semantic cognition in some detail and close the chapter with a discussion of the implications of the PDP theory on pattern generalization processing that matters to mathematical learning. In the closing discussion we also address the need to modify some of the elements in the original PDP model based on cognitive factors that bear on the pattern generalization processing of school mathematical patterns. Here we demonstrate the usefulness of a PDP network structure primarily as a thinking model that enables us to describe the complexity of many students' pattern generalization processing not in terms of stable and permanent transitions from, say, arithmetical to algebraic generalizations but as parallel and graded, adaptive, and fundamentally distributive among, and dependent on, a variety of cognitive sources.

The proposed theory on graded pattern generalization fundamentally claims that generalization is not a simple account of shifts or transitions in skill or ability (e.g. from the use of recursive relations to function formulas) as it is more about parallel and distributed connections involving several factors that influence the emerging shape of a generalization. The theory also seeks to explain differences in students' generalization processes in terms of the types of task that are presented to them. For example, while it might be easy for a student to obtain a function-based generalization for the pattern in Fig. 1.1a, the same student might demonstrate difficulty in obtaining a function-based generalization for the pattern in Fig. 1.9a. The theory can then be used to explain the subtle influence of pattern complexity and familiarity that causes the student to resort to a recursive rule. One principle of the PDP theory is that it is a learning system, which means that with more experience, the student will eventually choose function-type generalizations. But choices are always available and never fade as connections can be reactivated anytime depending on the nature and complexity of a patterning task being dealt with.

In *Chap. 5*, we focus on pattern generalization studies that have been conducted with elementary school children from Grades 1 through 5 (ages 6 through 10 years) in different contexts. We should note that a huge chunk of data that is reported and discussed in this chapter has been drawn from the author's longitudinal studies with intact classes of Grades 2 and 3 students in the USA. We infer the graded nature of young children's pattern generalization states by drawing on their constructed structures and incipient generalizations, which involve the use of various representational modes such as gestures, words, and arithmetical symbols that convey their expressions of generality.

Chapter 6 deals with the graded pattern generalization processing of older children and adults. Graded pattern processing occurs along several routes depending on the nature and complexity of a task being analyzed. The four documented routes that are highlighted and discussed have been drawn from a number of empirical sources and are structured rather flexibly in some way in order to capture the actual manner in which students' graded pattern generalization processing and conversion can in fact change in emphasis from manipulating objects to relationships (and possibly back to objects) in numerical or figural contexts (and possibly both). We also discuss older students' understanding of (linear) functions, which be interpreted as an instance of generalizing extensions that emerge from their experiences in pattern generalization activity. Readers are certainly encouraged to compare older and younger children's pattern generalization strategies. For example, one interesting finding concerns the disposition of older children to process patterns by drawing primarily on a variety of numerical and additively recursive strategies. Even among adults, numerical generalizing strategies appear to be more dominant and unnecessarily complex than those strategies offered by elementary school children. Among younger children, however, the entry level of their incipient structural generalizations does not appear to be additively recursive but additively functional. In other words, their natural ability to use a combined global-particular sensing strategies seems to support structurally justifiable generalizations of the algebraic kind, unlike older individuals who tend to choose more object- than relationship-driven strategies that frequently yield variable-based generalizations that in many cases they are oftentimes unable to justify beyond the verification of particular cases by numerical substitution. Examples of an object-dependent strategy involve the use of trial and error or a systematic guess and check from a table of values as a way of setting up a direct formula may or may not be able to justify for reasonableness.

In Chap. 7, the conclusion, we extend the nature of patterns from figural and numerical sequences to mathematical concepts and processes that involve generalization. For example, learning the algorithms for combining whole numbers in the elementary grades is a fundamental matter of generalization involving methods. In this chapter, we discuss in some detail relationships among patterns, generalization, arithmetic, functions, and graded forms of algebraic thinking (nonsymbolic, pre-symbolic, and symbolic). The overall intent of this book on pattern generalization is once again noted, which is about exploring ways in which patterns may be used to help democratize students' access to structural thinking. Consequently, we articulate its central role in the development of algebra, a subject that Kaput (2008) notes has "deep, but varied, connections with all of mathematics" (p. 15).

Acknowledgment This work has been supported by a Career Grant from the National Science Foundation under Grant Number DRL 0448649 awarded to me between 2005 and 2012. I take full responsibility for all the views and opinions expressed in this book. My sincere thanks to all my program officers who allowed me to pursue work in this research area. A warm thanks as well to Joanne Rossi Becker, SJSU colleague, who collaborated with me in the early foundational stages of this work. I am grateful to all my students and their teachers, from first to eighth grade, who generously shared their thinking on patterns.

Chapter 2
Contexts of Generalization in School Mathematics

Square Frog Pattern: Consider the pattern below.

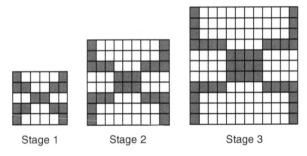

Stage 1   Stage 2   Stage 3

Fig. 2.1a A growing square frog pattern

  a. How does Stage 4 look like? Either describe it or draw it on graphing paper.
  b. Find a direct formula for the total number of gray square tiles at any stage. Explain your formula.
  c. How many gray square tiles are there in Stage 11? How do you know?
  d. Which stage number contains a total of 56 gray square tiles? Explain.

1. *Diana (D; Grade 7, age 12 years): Well, basically you always, like, to this number here, to this*
2.   *part here [referring to Stage 2 in Fig. 2.1a], you added 1 [square on top] and on this side*
3.   *you add 1 [square] to make it longer [referring to the growing legs on each corner]. You*
4.   *always add 1 to everything to make the legs longer. Instead of like 2×2, you make it 3×3.*
5.   *And for this one, too [the middle rectangle], instead of 1×2, you make it 2×3. [She then*
6.   *writes the following direct formula:* $x(x+1)+(2x+1)=n$.]
7. *Rivera (R): Okay, so tell me what's happening there. Where did this come from,* $x(x+1)$?
8. *D: This, the little square,* x *times* $x+1$.
9. *R: So where's the* x *times* $x+1$ *here [referring to Stage 3 in Fig. 2.1a]?*
10. *D: Like 3×3, or 3×4.*
11. *R: So where's the* $2x+1$ *coming from?*
12. *D: This, I mean I can look at it like two times* $(x+1)$ *minus 1 but I just made it, like, 3, 3, and 1*
13.   *[referring to Stage 3 in Fig. 2.1a], so* $2x+1$. *[Note that she initially saw that each leg had*

F. Rivera, *Teaching and Learning Patterns in School Mathematics:*   25
Psychological and Pedagogical Considerations, DOI 10.1007/978-94-007-2712-0_2,
© Springer Science+Business Media Dordrecht 2013

14.   *two overlapping sides that shared a common corner square.*]

15.   *R: But this 2x+1 is just for this side [referring to one leg], right?*

16.   *D: For all of the legs, oh [she adds a coefficient of 4 to her formula], $x(x+1) + 4(2x+1) = n$.*

17.   *R: Okay, so are you happy with your formula?*

18.   *D: I think I could simplify it. I'd like to see what happens if I simplify it. [She then simplifies her*
19.   *formula to $x^2 + 9x + 4 = n$.] 4 would be these [the corner middle squares], I'm pretty*
20.   *sure. 9x would be, oh, yes, I see it. I see how it works. There's an x squared here [referring*
21.   *to the rectangle, which she saw as the union of an x by x square and a column of x by 1 (=x)*
22.   *squares] if you see one square here and the 9x would be these legs [referring to the*
23.   *(x+1)st column of the middle rectangle and the eight rows and columns of legs with*
24.   *dimensions x by 1 minus the four corner middle squares]. Plus 4 would be the center of each*
25.   *leg [the four corner middle squares. (See Fig. 2.1b for a visual description involving Stage*
26.   *3 of Fig. 2.1a.)*

Diana (age 12 years) was in seventh grade when she participated in an all year teaching experiment on generalization and algebraic thinking at the middle school level. In a clinical interview that took place near the end of the school year, which was about 6 months from the time she initially learned the concept and process of pattern generalization in class, she obtained two algebraic generalizations for the Square Frog Pattern in Fig. 2.1a. Her two equivalent pattern generalizations capture the sense in which we interpret Peirce's (1960) basic meaning of generalization, which involves constructing a general description that applies to all the

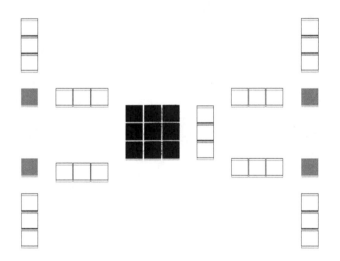

Generalization 1: x^2 refers to the number of squares in the middle black square
9x refers to the number of squares in all 9 unshaded rectangles
4 refers to the gray corner square tiles
$x^2 + 9x + 4 = n$, n corresponds to the total number of squares in stage n

Generalization 2: $x(x + 1)$ refers to the number of squares in the x by $(x + 1)$ middle rectangle
2x + 1 refers to a corner leg consisting of two groups of x squares and a corner square
$x(x + 1) + 4(2x + 1) = n$ refers to the total number of squares in stage n

Fig. 2.1b Visual demonstration of Diana's generalization using stage 3 of the Fig. 2.1a pattern

cases in a given collection. Within the scope of her interpreted structure that she imposed on all the stages in her pattern, Diana's algebraic generalizations signified an increase in depth (Peirce, 1960) or understanding (Strevens, 2008). That is, instead of merely seeing an increasing number of gray squares, her algebraic generalization conveyed an interpretive understanding of structures that were regular and stable and consisted of properties that were invariant and essential to the pattern. Also, her curiosity regarding the simplified form of her direct formula in line 16 further deepened her understanding and appreciation of the different stable subconfigurations that comprised her interpreted structure (lines 18–25). But, is generalization tantamount to merely constructing structures with uniform, regular, and stable features? Further, are there domain-specific requirements in constructing a generalization? For example, what constitutes a generalization in arithmetic that deals with number relations and figural patterns? Do we employ the same or a different characterization of generalization in the case of school geometry that deals with spatial relationships and schematic diagrams?

In this chapter, we discuss issues of depth that are relevant to the concept and process of generalization. In the next two sections, we clarify the following useful terms that are now commonly used in school-based patterns research: abduction; induction; near generalization and far generalization; and deduction. We then explore nuances in the meaning of generalization that have been used in different contexts in the school mathematics curriculum. In the closing section, we discuss preliminary implications of the findings in the chapter on our proposed theory of graded pattern generalization that we explore in some detail in Chap. 4.

Abduction, Induction, and Deduction in Generalization

Table 2.1 lists the characteristics of the three types of inferential reasoning that come into play when expressing a generality. At the outset, abduction involves initially generating a hypothesis or narrowing a range of hypotheses that then undergoes verification via induction. Further, abduction is the source of original ideas and is oftentimes influenced by prior knowledge and experiences, unlike induction that runs an abductive claim by testing it over specific cases in the hope that possible errors are corrected along the way with more data. Deduction, unlike abduction and induction, primarily establishes the necessity of a single valid conclusion and, like induction, does not generate any original ideas (Peirce, 1934). Certainly, a justification can be routed in several different ways. In elementary and middle schools, for example, figural and numerical demonstrations that explain by highlighting the relevant features (Knuth, 2002)—that is, empirical structural arguments—are much more meaningful and appropriate than statement-to-reason and rigidly logical proofs that are used at the high school level. However, across grade levels, students need to acquire an understanding of the implications of a "deductive argument," that is, conclusions as effects of the explicitly stipulated hypotheses, the causes.

Table 2.1 Inferential types and their characteristics

Inferential type	Inferential form	Intent	Inferential attitude	Sources	Desired construction	Verification and justification
Abduction	From result and law to case	Depth (intentional)	Entertains a plausible inference toward a rule; generates and selects an explanatory theory—that "something maybe" (conjectural)	Unpredictable (surprising facts; flashes; intelligent guesses, spontaneous conjectures)	Un/structured	Structured via induction
Induction	(From result and more cases to law)	Breadth (extensional)	Tests an abduced inference; measures the value and degree of concordance of an explanatory theory to cases—that "something actually is operative" (approximate)	Predictable (examples)	Structural based on abduction	Empirical (e.g., enumeration, analogy, and experiments)
Deduction	From law and case to result	Logical proof	Predicts in a methodical way a valid result—that "something must be" (certain)	Predictable (premises)	Structural (canonical form)	Steps in a proof

Consider the following three statements below that have been extracted from Diana's generalization of the figural pattern shown in Fig. 2.1a.

Law (L):   All the stages relative to the pattern in Fig. 2.1a follow the direct formula $x^2 + 9x + 4 = n$.

Case (C): Stages 1, 2, 3, and 4 are specific cases of the given pattern.

Result (R): Therefore, stages 1, 2, 3, and 4 follow the rule $x^2 + 9x + 4 = n$.

Deduction assumes a general law and an observed case (or cases) that then logically infers a necessary valid result that does not have to depend on real or empirical knowledge for verification (Goswami, 2011). Cases are specific occurrences or instantiations of the general law. When we switch the three statements above in two different ways, we obtain the canonical structures for abduction and induction, which are ampliative and invalid from a deductive point of view. Figure 2.2 visually captures the fundamental differences among the three inferential types.

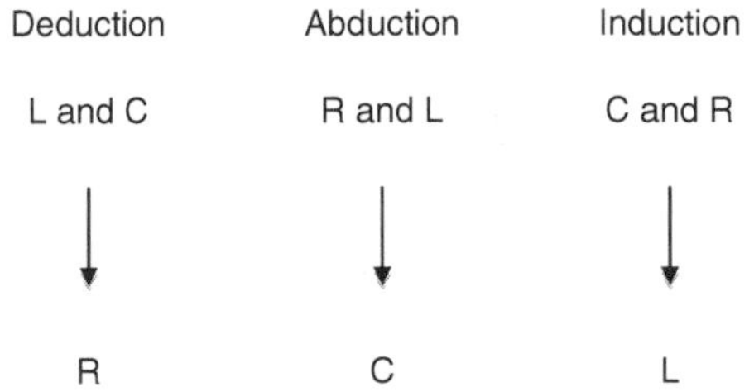

Fig. 2.2 Differences among the three inferential types

Deduction	Abduction	Induction
L and C	R and L	C and R
↓	↓	↓
R	C	L

From a psychological perspective, students need to learn to anticipate inferences that are sensible and valid in mathematical activity. For Peirce, it is context that determines the type of inference that matters despite our naturally drawn disposition[1] toward "perpetually making deductions" (Peirce, 1960, p. 449). Further, while context matters, students also need to consider the limitations of each inferential process. Following Polya (1973), deduction, on the one hand, exemplifies demonstrative reasoning, which is the basis of the "security of our mathematical knowledge" (p. v) since it is "safe, beyond controversy, and final" (ibid). Abduction and induction, on the other hand, exemplify plausible reasoning, which "support our conjectures" (ibid.) and can be "hazardous, controversial, and provisional" (ibid.). Despite the constraints, however, Peirce and Polya seem to share the view that all three inferences are epistemologically necessary. For Polya (1973), while "anything new that we learn about the world involves plausible reasoning," demonstrative reasoning uses "rigid standards [that are] codified and clarified by logic" (p. v). Polya's view is rather confined to how we come to understand and explain the nature of mathematical objects, but Peirce formulated his inferential process by drawing on

---

[1] As an aside, kindergarten students (ages 5–6 years) in the absence of formal learning experiences appear to consider deductive inferences as being more certain than inductive ones and other guesses (Pillow, Pearson, Hecht, & Bremer, 2010).

the nature of scientific practice. That is, doing science in fact involves the use of abduction, the fundamental source of the emergence of ideas. *Pace* Peirce (1934):

> All ideas of science come to it by way of abduction. Abduction consists in studying facts and devising a theory to explain them. Its only justification is that if we are ever to understand things at all, it just be in that way. (Peirce, 1934, p. 90)

Abduction

Perceptual-like clues provide one possible source of abductive claims (Paavola, 2011). When students investigate specific stages in a figural pattern, for example, they guess and produce plausible interpretations that depict perceptual judgments relative to the stages in the pattern. Consequently, some of these plausible observations evolve into hypotheses, thus, abductions. In particular, when Diana initially encountered the Fig. 2.1a pattern, her perceptions "forced themselves" upon her that she could not control or change at will (Paavola, 2011, p. 305). The steps below outline a percept-based "formula that is similar to abduction" (p. 305), which captures Diana's pre-deductive approach in support of her emerging algebraic generalization.

> A well-recognized kind of object, M, has for its ordinary predicates P[1], P[2], P[3], etc., indistinctly recognized. The suggesting object, S, has these same predicates, P[1], P[2], P[3], etc. Hence, S is of the kind M. (Paavola, 2011 p. 305)

Diana's abductive reasoning in lines 1 through 16 relied on the given three stages that enabled her to interpret an abductive claim about the pattern (i.e., the form) $x(x+1)+4(2x+1)=n$. She then specialized in stage 3 as her way of pointing out the basic structure of her abductive claim, which also enabled her to establish the membership of stage 3 (and later stage 4) in her pattern.

Performing abduction can also mean establishing iconic-based inferences (Paavola, 2011). Icons, unlike percepts, are pure possible forms of the objects they represent or resemble. For example, when my second-grade students learned about even numbers as a set, they more or less used the following abductive process below.

$$\left.\begin{array}{l} P1 \\ H1 \rightarrow P2 \end{array}\right\} \text{An iconic relationship between P1 and P2}$$

P1 and P2 are similar (iconically)
∴ Maybe H1 (or something that is similar to H1)
(Paavola, 2011, p. 306)

Initially the students investigated single-digit even whole numbers that enabled them to abduce the stable feature that produced perfect pairs of dots. In the next set of activities, they investigated two-digit even numbers. Figure 2.3a shows two examples of student work in which they coupled dots together in their own way. In the third and final phase of their abductive processing, they either named or described a category for such two-digit whole numbers and concluded that they were all even on the basis of an iconic resemblance that they interpreted across several instances. Figure 2.3b shows Nikki's analysis of the even parity of the whole number 22. Her verbal description "counting by counting by 2" captured the sense in which she (mentally) grouped circle dots by twos.

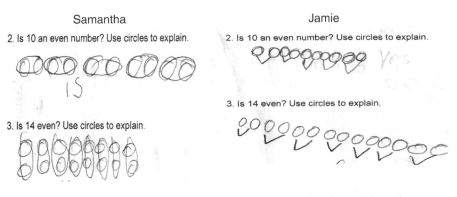

Fig. 2.3a Examples of second-grade student work on the even parity of two-digit numbers

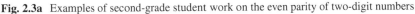

Fig. 2.3b v-grade Nikki's work on the even parity of the whole number 22

We note the following three important points about abduction, as follows.

First, Thagard (1978) notes that an abductive process involves developing and entertaining inferences toward a law that is expected to undergo testing via induction, hence, producing an inference about a case. However, for Eco (1983), "the real problem is not whether to find first the Case or the [Law], but rather how to figure out both the [Law] and the Case *at the same time*, since they are inversely related, tied together by a sort of chiasmus" (p. 203). Diana's thinking in lines 1 through 6, for example, models this simultaneous search for a law (i.e. the direct formula for all stages in the pattern) and a case (e.g. stage 4) that satisfies the law.

Second, Josephson and Josephson (1994) added to the concept of abduction the condition of being an "inference that yields the best explanation," which revises the structure of abduction in the following manner below:

> Case: *D* is a collection of data (facts, observations, givens).
> Law: *H* explains *D* (would, if true, explain *D*).
> Strong Claim: No other hypothesis can explain *D* as well as *H* does.
> Result: *H* is probably true.

Fig. 2.4 A strong abduction (Josephson and Josephson, 1994)

Adler (2008) identifies the following additional criteria in the construction of a strong abduction: simple, conservative, unifying, and yields the most understanding (p. 19). In pattern generalization activity, as well as in most cases in everyday contexts, a strong abduction is a desired condition. Lee's (1996) well-known phrase, *algebraically useful*, in relation to pattern generalization is a strong abduction in that all interpreted structural generalizations involving numerical and figural patterns ought to be conveyed in the form of a direct expression or a closed formula. Diana's formulas in Fig. 2.1b and the students' verbal expressions in Fig. 2.4 represent algebraically useful formulas that model strong abductions. The recursive response "add two circles" in relation to the pattern in Fig. 2.4 is an abductive claim, however, it is not a strong abduction on the basis of the preceding discussion. The recursive expression, in fact, could not be reasonably used to predict the outcome of a distant stage number (e.g., stage 97).

Third, abductive hypotheses provide explanations or justifications that do not prove. Instead, they provide explanations or justifications that primarily assign causal responsibility in the following sense below.

> Explanations give causes. Explaining something, whether that something is particular or general, gives something else upon which the first thing depends for its existence, or for being the way that it is. . . . .. It is common in science for an empirical generalization, an observed generality, to be explained by reference to underlying structure and mechanisms. (Josephson, 2000, p. 7)

Induction

Induction tests a preliminary or an ongoing abduced inference with the goal of supporting a (most reasonable) law that link both the known and projected cases together. By testing an abductive claim over several cases, induction determines whether the claim is right or wrong. So defined, a correct induction does not produce a new concept that explains (i.e. an "explanatory theory"), which is the purpose of abductive processing. Instead, it seeks to show that once the premises hold (i.e. the case/s and the result/s), then the relevant conclusions (i.e. the law) must be true by enumeration (number of observed cases), analogy (i.e. structural or relational similarity of features among cases), or scientific analysis (through actual or mental experiments) (Hibben, 1905). In the case of enumeration, in particular, the goal is not to establish an exhaustive count leading to a precise numerical value, but it is about "produc[ing] a certain psychological impression ... brought about through the laws of association, and creat[ing] an expectation of a continuous repetition of the experience" (Hibben, 1905, p. 184). In all three contexts of inductive justification, inductive inferences do not necessarily yield true generalizations, however, "in the long run they approximate to the truth" (Peirce, 1869, p. 207).

We illustrate the significance of induction in 20 second-grade students' (age 7 years) thinking relative to the Triangular Pattern shown in Fig. 2.5a. The task was presented to them in a clinical interview setting that took place immediately after a weeklong teaching experiment on patterns. Figure 2.5a was meant to be an ambiguous figural pattern, which meant that the students could extend it in several different ways. For example, eighth-grader Emma's work in Fig. 1.4b involves a construction that reflects a quadratic structure. In the interview with the second-grade students, the three initial stages were presented together on a single sheet of paper in order to avoid any undue influence from the interviewer. The interviewer then asked them to extend the pattern to stages 4 and 5 before skipping to stages 10 and above. Figure 2.5b shows stages 4 and 5 that 10 of the 20 students constructed relative to the pattern.

The statements in Fig. 2.5c reflect three incipient generalizations for the pattern in Fig. 2.5a that the students extended to two more stages as shown in Figure 2.5b. The statements implicitly conveyed abductive claims regarding plausible structures for the pattern that all ten students initially inferred on stage 3 alone. Then on the basis of their inferred abductions, they extended the pattern to stages 4, 5, 10, and above. The constructed extensions in Fig. 2.5b, c, by our definition, represent the inductive verification phase that usually accompanies and supports an abductive claim. However, the dilemma, which applies to all the ten students who produced the same generalization shown in Fig. 2.5c, is that none of them tried

Triangular Pattern Task): Below are stages in a growing pattern of circles.

Stage 1   Stage 2   Stage 3

1. How does Stage 4 look like? Can you draw it for me?
2. How does Stage 5 look like? Can you draw it for me?
3. If we skip stages, how might, say, Stage 10 look like? If you were to tell a friend how your pattern looks like, say, stage 10, how would you tell him what to do?

Fig. 2.5a Ambiguous triangular pattern task given to Grade 2 students

Stage 4   Stage 5

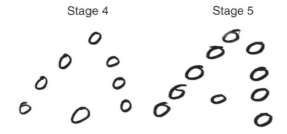

Fig. 2.5b Extended stages 4 and 5 relative to the Fig. 2.5a pattern

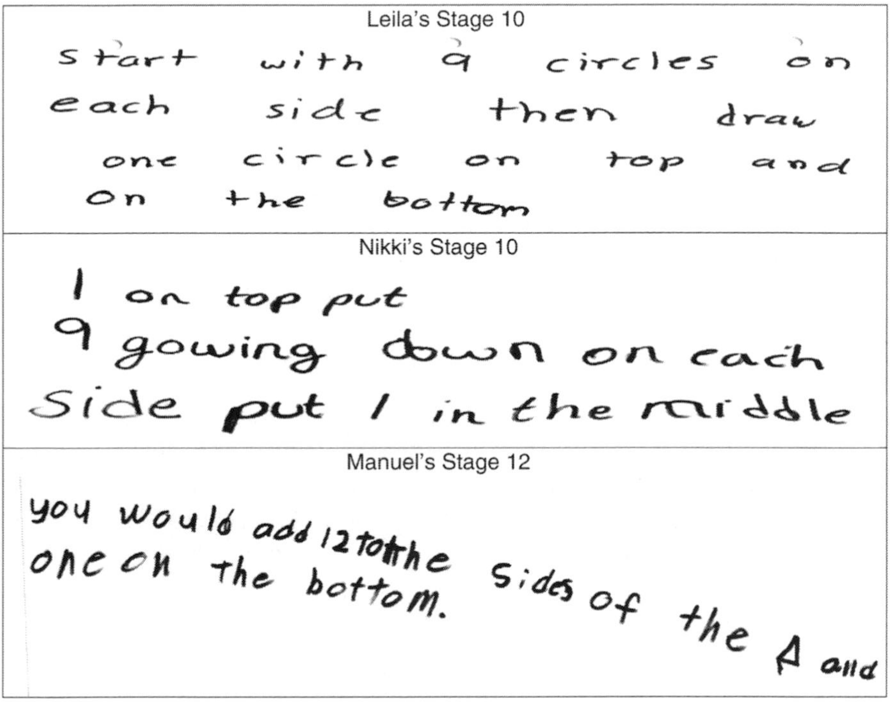

Leila's Stage 10
start with a circles on each side then draw one circle on top and on the bottom
Nikki's Stage 10
I on top put 9 gowing down on each Side put I in the middle
Manuel's Stage 12
you would add 12 to the one on the bottom. Sides of the A and

Fig. 2.5c Incipient generalizations based on Fig. 2.5b

to test the abductive claim on the initial two stages of the pattern. Diana in Fig. 2.1b, perhaps being older, performed induction on all three given stages in lines 1 through 16 that allowed her to correct her initial algebraic generalization in line 6 to the one shown in line 16.

Abduction and Induction Together

From the preceding discussion we take it as given that abduction is a requirement for induction.[2] Even in the most naïve and complex cases of inductions, say, number patterns with no meaningful context other than the appearance of behaving like objects in some sequence, learners initially tend to produce an abductive claim as a practical coping mechanism, that is, as a way of imposing order or structure that may or may not prove to make sense in the long haul.[3] For example, Becker and Rivera (2005) report that among 22 US Grade 9 students who established a generalization for the Growing Cross Pattern in Fig. 2.6 without the benefit of an intervening classroom teaching experiment on patterns, 13 of the 23 generalization strategies were numerically motivated (and the remaining strategies being figural). The numerical strategies ranged in complexity from a random trial-and-error method to more systematic methods (e.g. employing table-based finite differences; extending rows or columns in a table by recursion; using an incorrect method of proportionality; cf. Chap. 6). The brief interview transcript below demonstrates a random trial and error process. Because student S did not see any relationship between the pattern stages in Fig. 2.6 and the numbers that S generated from them, S explained his direct expression $4n + 1$ via numeric-driven patterning (i.e. pattern spotting), as follows.

27. *I started off with more like 2 and that didn't work so then I tried to make 5 work and I*
28. *did the same thing with 2, 3, and 2 and then when I tried it with 4, and I tried to figure*
29. *a number to make 5 so I add 1, and I tried it on 2 and it still gave me the number.*

S employed guessing as an abductive mechanism. His initial series of abductive claims (i.e. seeing 2s, 3s, and 5s in lines 27 and 28), however, underwent refutation and evolution via induction that enabled him to make corrections along the way.

Another consequence of the preceding discussion involves the so-called *inductive leap*, which involves establishing a generalization from concrete instances to a

---

[2] Certainly, there can be an abduction without induction (i.e. abductive generalizations). Some geometry theorems, for example, do not need inductive verification. We do not explore these situations in this book in light of our interest on patterns. However, it is useful to note the insights of Pedemonte (2007) and Prusak, Hershkowitz, and Schwarz (2012) about the necessity of a structural continuity between an abduction argument process and its corresponding justification in the form of a logical proof. That is, a productive abductive process in whatever modal form (visual, verbal) should simultaneously convey the steps in a deductive proof.

[3] Polya (1973, pp. 17–22) recounts the story of Euler's numeric-driven generalization of the infinite series $\sum_{n=1}^{\infty} \frac{1}{n^2}$ by initially establishing an analogical relationship between two different types of equations (i.e. a polynomial P of degree n having n distinct nonzero roots and a trigonometric equation that can be transformed algebraically into something like P but with an infinite number of terms). Euler's abductive claim had him hypothesizing an anticipated solution drawn from similarities between the forms of the two equations. Upon inductively verifying that the initial four terms of the two equations were indeed the same, Euler concluded that $\sum_{n=1}^{\infty} \frac{1}{n^2} = \frac{\pi^2}{6}$.

Growing Cross Patterning Task: Marcia is using black and white square tiles to make patterns.

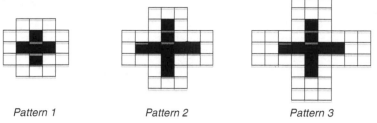

Pattern 1   Pattern 2   Pattern 3

1. How many black tiles are needed to make Pattern 4?

Marcia begins to make a table to show the number of black and white tiles she is using.

Pattern Number	1	2	3	4
Number of White Tiles	16	24		
Number of Black Tiles	5	9		
Total	21	33		

2. Fill in the missing numbers in Marcia's table.

3. Marcia wants to know how many white tiles and black tiles there will be in the tenth pattern, but she does not want to draw all the patterns and count the squares. Explain or show another way she could find her answer.

4, 5, & 6. Using W for the number of white tiles and P for the pattern number, write down a rule or formula linking W with P.

Using B for the number of black tiles and P for the pattern number, write down a rule or formula linking B with P.

Now, using T for the total number of tiles and P for the pattern number, write down a rule or formula linking T with P.

Fig. 2.6 Growing cross pattern task administered to Grade 9 students

conclusion that seems to contain more than the instances themselves. On the basis of the characterizations we have assigned to abduction and induction, such a leap is no longer an issue since the leap itself is settled by abduction. Hence, criticisms that in effect cite "hazardous inductive leap" as an argument in relation to erroneous mathematics assessment questions such as the one shown in Fig. 2.7 is more appropriately and fundamentally a problem of abduction.

It is also worth noting that neither abduction nor induction can settle the issue of *reasonable of context*. For example, the patterning situation in Fig. 2.8 can have a stipulated abduction and an inductively verified set of outcomes based on an interpreted direct expression. However, as Parker and Baldridge (2004) note, "there is no reason why the rainfall will continue to be given by that expression, or *any* expression," which implies that the "question cannot be answered" (p. 90). Other contexts that do not necessarily lead to reasonable and sensible generalizations include the stock market and gas prices.

A certain pattern begins with 1, 2, 4. If the pattern continues, what is the next number?

A. 1

B. 2

C. 7

D. 8

Fig. 2.7 An example of an erroneous generalization problem

It started to rain. Every hour Sarah checked her rain gauge. She recorded the total rainfall in a table. How much rain would have fallen after *h* hours?

Hours	Rainfall
1	0.5 in
2	1 in
3	1.5 in

Fig. 2.8 An example of a patterning task with an erroneous context

Deduction

While abduction and induction provide support in the construction of a generalization, a valid deduction basically demonstrates necessity. *Pace* Smith (2002): "(R)epeated co-instantiation [via induction] is not the same as inferential necessity" (ibid, p. 5). In patterning activity, learners employ abduction and induction in order to obtain a reasonable algebraic generalization. A deductive closure then can occur in at least two ways depending on grade-level expectations.

Elementary and middle-school students can (implicitly) form a deductive claim. However, they are more likely to provide an empirical (numerical or visual) structural explanation than a formal deductive proof as a way of justifying their generalizations. For example, Diana conveyed her algebraic generalization relative to the pattern in Fig. 2.1a in deductive form, where her premises reflected a coordination between her direct formula and stages 1 through 4 of the pattern that enabled her to conclude necessary shared membership among all (known and projected) stages on the basis of her premises. In her justification, she employed stage 4 to explain how her algebraic generalization captured the structure that she interpreted to be true across stages. The second-grade students' explanations on the even parity of the sum of two odd numbers shown in Fig. 1.5 also model the use of an empirical argument. Hence, in these two instances of empirical structural justifications, the students' explanations have been drawn from their empirical experiences with the available instances.

High school students and adults can formulate a deductive claim and provide any of the following types of justification that overlap in some situations: an

*Based on the figure below, Let us illustrate
why −3 x 2 = −(3 x 2) using properties of
integers. − 3 x 2 = −(3 x 2) means pull 3
groups of 2 cubes on the positive region to
the negative region.*

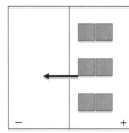 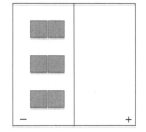

$$
\begin{aligned}
-3 \times 2 \; = \; & (-3 \times 2) + 0 & & \textit{Additive Identity Property} \\
= \; & (-3 \times 2) + [(3 \times 2) + -(3 \times 2)] & & \textit{Additive Inverse Property} \\
= \; & [(-3 \times 2) + (3 \times 2)] + -(3 \times 2) & & \textit{Associative Property} \\
= \; & [(-3 + 3) \times 2] + -(3 \times 2) & & \textit{Distributive Property} \\
= \; & 0 + -(3 \times 2) & & \textit{Additive Inverse Property} \\
= \; & -(3 \times 2) & & \textit{Additive Identity Property}
\end{aligned}
$$

Fig. 2.9 An empirical justification of $-a \times -b = -(a \times -b)$

empirical structural argument; a logical deductive proof; or a mathematical induction proof. Figure 2.9 illustrates how a group of 34 US Algebra 1 middle school students (mean age of 13 years) empirically justified the fact that $-a \times -b = -(a \times -b)$ by demonstrating a numeric-based argument following a statement-to-reason template (Rivera, 2011, pp. 126–130). Here, it is useful to note that when the numbers in the empirical argument shown in Fig. 2.9 are replaced with variables, the argument then transforms into a logical deductive proof in which case the steps follow a logical "recycling process" (Duval, quoted in Pedemonte (2007, p. 24)), that is, the conclusion of a foregoing step becomes the premise of a succeeding step from beginning to end. Figure 2.10a shows a mathematical inductive proof of a classic theorem involving the sum of the interior angles in an *n*-sided convex polygon that has been drawn from Pedemonte's (2007) work with 102 Grade 13 students (ages 16–17 years) in France and in Italy. The "multimodal argumentative process of proof" (cf. Arzarello, 2008; Prusak, Hershkowitz, & Schwarz, 2012) evolved as a result of a structural continuity between a combined abductive-inductive action that was performed on a dynamic geometry tool, which focused on a perceived relationship between the process of constructing nonoverlapping triangles in a polygon and the effects on the resulting interior angle sums, and the accompanying steps that reflected the structure of a mathematical induction proof. The work shown in Fig. 2.10b has also been drawn from the same sample of students that participated in Pedemonte's (2007) study. Unlike Fig. 2.10a, the analysis that was exhibited in Fig. 2.10b shows a structural discontinuity between a combined abductive-inductive action,

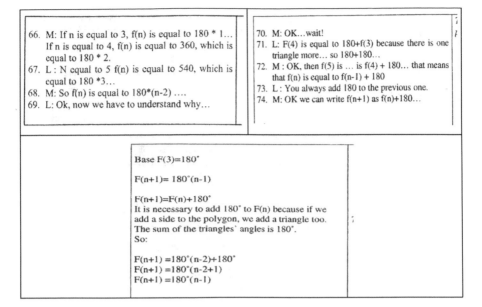

66. M: If n is equal to 3, f(n) is equal to 180 * 1...
    If n is equal to 4, f(n) is equal to 360, which is
    equal to 180 * 2.
67. L : N equal to 5 f(n) is equal to 540, which is
    equal to 180 *3...
68. M: So f(n) is equal to 180*(n-2) ....
69. L: Ok, now we have to understand why...

70. M: OK...wait!
71. L: F(4) is equal to 180+f(3) because there is one
    triangle more... so 180+180...
72. M : OK, then f(5) is ... is f(4) + 180... that means
    that f(n) is equal to f(n-1) + 180
73. L : You always add 180 to the previous one.
74. M: OK we can write f(n+1) as f(n)+180...

Base F(3)=180°

F(n+1)= 180°(n-1)

F(n+1)=F(n)+180°
It is necessary to add 180° to F(n) because if we
add a side to the polygon, we add a triangle too.
The sum of the triangles' angles is 180°.
So:

F(n+1) =180°(n-2)+180°
F(n+1) =180°(n-2+1)
F(n+1) =180°(n-1)

Fig. 2.10a A mathematical induction proof drawn from a process-driven abduction and induction (Pedemonte, 2007, pp. 37–38)

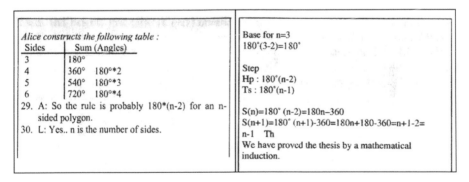

Alice constructs the following table :

Sides	Sum (Angles)	
3	180°	
4	360°	180°*2
5	540°	180°*3
6	720°	180°*4

29. A: So the rule is probably 180*(n-2) for an n-sided polygon.
30. L: Yes.. n is the number of sides.

Base for n=3
180°(3-2)=180°

Step
Hp : 180°(n-2)
Ts : 180°(n-1)

S(n)=180° (n-2)=180n-360
S(n+1)=180° (n+1)-360=180n+180-360=n+1-2=
n-1 Th
We have proved the thesis by a mathematical
induction.

Fig. 2.10b Example of a result-driven abduction and induction with an erroneous mathematical induction argument (Pedemonte, 2007, p. 36)

which primarily focused on the results or outcomes in a table of values, and steps that might have produced either a valid empirical justification or a logical mathematical induction proof.[4]

---

[4] See Pedemonte and Reid (2011) for a more refined analysis of different types of abductive action that support and hinder the construction of empirical arguments and deductive proofs.

Near and Far Generalization

The task structure shown in Fig. 2.5a involves several aspects that are worth noting. At the very least, the patterning task comes with a few initial stages that appear in a visual format. In this book we shall call them figural stages in order to emphasize their "simultaneously conceptual and figural" (Fischbein, 1993, p. 160) nature. That is, taken together, the stages represent objects or elements that might make sense in a certain interpreted structure. Hence they are not merely pictures of objects but exhibit characteristics that are associated with diagrammatic representations (Rivera, 2010a).

Items 1 and 2 in Fig. 2.5a are considered near generalization tasks, while item 3 exemplifies a far generalization task. Mainly for labeling, organizing, and reporting purposes, we set all near generalization tasks in a pattern to range from stage 1 to stage 9, while far generalization tasks span stage 10 and over. Dealing with at least one near generalization task first helps students in formulating an initial abduction that they can inductively verify rather easily. Stacey (1989) also notes that obtaining outcomes on near tasks can be accomplished by constructing diagrams, making a table, or counting. Beyond the procedural strategies, however, an initial abduction can express what students interpret to be a core unique unit of the pattern, which they can induce on all the near stages.[5] Consequently, a tentative generalization emerges. Repetitive induction over a few initial stages provides them with a secure sense of coping and dealing with the tentative generalization that is emerging to be rule-governed in some way. Following Varzi (2008), (correct) inductive action implicitly assumes the following two conditions that are needed to be satisfied in order to "succeed in guessing the [pattern]" (p. 285), which can be evaluated with near generalization outcomes: (1) a tentative abduced generalization for a pattern is able to establish a unique structure in order to correctly extend the pattern of choice and (2) the stages in the pattern is not generated but rule-governed.

Unlike most near generalization tasks that can be handled rather conveniently, dealing with a far stage in a pattern oftentimes represents a moment of perturbation to individual learners. At this stage in their generalizing process, they begin to test the projective power and validity of, including convenience in using, the tentative generalization. Repetitive success in verifying the correctness of all far generalization items

---

[5] Clements and Sarama (2009) note that children from ages 2–7 years developmentally progress in their understanding of, and expertise in, patterns in the following manner: being pre-explicit patterners of everyday things, actions, etc. at age 2; being recognizers of simple repeating sequences of objects and consecutive counting numbers at age 3; being fillers (or fixers) and duplicators of repeating patterns at age 4; being extenders of repeating patterns at age 5; being core unit recognizers of repeating patterns at age 6; and being numeric patterners of growing patterns at age 7. My overall interpretation of this progression deals with transitions in elementary students' ability to express an interpreted, stable, and unique core unit from the implicit (nonverbal, gestural, aided by concrete objects) to the explicit (verbal with and without aid of concrete objects) stage. I deal with this issue in some detail in Chaps. 5 and 6.

undergoing testing enables them to smoothly transition into the encapsulation and justification phases of generalization in which case a final expression of generality emerges. That is, the expression is seen in terms of being both an and a process, where the object (i.e., the formula) conveys what they interpret to be an appropriate structure for the pattern and the process (i.e., the individual coefficients, terms, and indicated operations in the formula) refers to figural and arithmetical of the established formula in determining any exact outcome at any stage in the pattern.

Various Characterizations of Generalization

In this book on patterns, we take it as given that all the inputs and the relations(s) in which they are drawn involve specific or particular stages, cases, or instances of objects that can be meaningfully interpreted as patterns in some way by individual learners. All patterns are then processed via generalization, which Polya (1957) describes in terms of a reflective passage from the particular to the general, as follows:

> [Generalization is the] passing from the consideration of one object to the consideration of a set containing that object; or passing from the consideration of a restricted set to that of a more comprehensive set containing the restricted one. (Polya, 1957, p. 108)

The passage of consideration from a particular member to the entire set can mean a number of possible actions. For Davydov, it refers to a *conceptual general-ization*[6] that involves "search(ing) for a certain *invariant* in an assortment of objects and their properties and a designation of that invariant by a word" (Davydov, 1990, p. 10) in which case the search involves both abductive and inductive actions. Once a label has been associated with the invariant, it is then "used to identify other objects as belonging to the given class" (Davydov, 2008, p. 74). Consequently, such generalizations yield useful structures or "systematizations" that enable individual learners "to be able to 'see' the general in each particular and individual case" (Davydov, 2008, p. 75). Viewed from a linguistic tool perspective, labels as generalizations allow individual learners to engage in: further comparison and abstraction; uniform relational processing across different situations; and further conceptual structuring (Gentner, 2010).

Kaput (1995) in the following paragraph below captures the sense in which an abductive generalization reflects an increase in depth (in a Peircean sense) via the commonalities, patterns, procedures, structures, and other relationships that indi-vidual learners generate and construct.

---

[6] We share Davydov's (2008) view that "(g)eneralization is regarded as inseparably linked with the operation of abstraction" (p. 75). Hence, in this book, abstraction is treated as an operation that constructs conceptual generalizations.

Generalization involves deliberately extending the range of reasoning or communication beyond the case or cases considered, explicitly identifying and exposing commonality across cases, or lifting the reasoning or communication to a level where the focus is no longer on the cases or situations themselves but rather on the patterns, procedures, structures, and the relations across and among them (which, in turn, become new, higher level objects of reasoning or communication). (Kaput, 1995, p. 136)

Mason's (2002) thoughts in the paragraph below, which describe an inductive action with an abductive intent, provide an appropriate follow up on the views of Davydov and Kaput regarding the meaning of generalization. When carrying out an induction becomes too difficult to implement—that is, it does not generalize—it signals the need for another round of abduction. The spiraling process is repeatedly performed until a strong abductive claim emerges. Such a process models how a strong abduction is sometimes viewed to be a type of eliminative induction (cf. Adler, 2008).

Whenever I encounter a generality, I find myself testing it against particular cases. If I am trying to decide *whether* the general assertion is true, or *when* it is true, I consider special, often extreme cases. The purpose of trying out particular cases is not just to seek a counter-example, but to attend to *how* the calculations are done, with an eye to seeing if they generalize. This is exactly what students are expected to do when learning a new technique: do some exercises *in order to see how the technique works* [in general] (not just to "get the answers"). (Mason, 2002, p. 108)

Drawing on Mason and Johnston-Wilder (2004), a possible closure in the passage from one to all involves constructing succinct notational expressions that can be used to "draw out further conclusions which may be particular or general" (p. 132) and are primarily mathematical and minimally context-based. In Davydov's (1990) case, such expressions are designated by names or labels on the basis of the invariant properties that have been singled out, and the names are then used and applied to identify objects that belong together. For Ellis (2007), such expressions fall under the category of reflection generalizations, which also include definitions, and results drawn from previous generalizations. Further, the notational expressions or "final statements of generalization" (Ellis, 2007, p. 198) reflect (stable) relationships that are evident to the learners who construct them. Holland, Holyoak, Nisbett, and Thagard's (1986) category of condition-simplifying generalizations capture the essence of such succinct and final general statements that result from, say, ignoring and dropping unnecessary conditions or taking the intersection of two or more conditions.

In the paragraph below, we gain a full sense of Mason and Johnston-Wilder's (2004) characterization of generalization and the special role they accord to specialization.

A related and extended version is "seeing the general through the particular, and the particular in the general" [*inspired from Whitehead (1911)*] (p. 138). Generalization is certainly present when thorough examination of a number of cases, often sequential in some manner, a common pattern is detected, …. But generalization often takes place on the contemplation of a single example. (Mason & Johnston-Wilder, 2004, pp. 132–133)

Thus, the process of generalization initially involves recognizing a common pattern that occurs over a span of several particular stages, which is explicitly investigated and constructed on a single example via specialization. Specializing, in other words, conveys both an intended generalization and an instantiation of that generalization. Radford, Bardini, and Sabena (2007) further characterize the nature and emergence of specialization in three different generalizing situations. At the very least, they articulate the shared view that a single example, as a particular, "must become a sign for something else" (p. 5). The particular, then, transforms into a generalization in the following situations that reflect moments of specialization: (1) when it is seen generically as an object that represents and substitutes for all the objects in its class; (2) when it is used metaphorically as a way of talking about the general; and (3) when it is seen dynamically as an instantiation that is endowed with a specific and general structure.

Harel and Tall's (1991) definition of generalization, that is, "applying a given argument in a broader context" (p. 38), captures the sense in which Peirce (1960) introduced the term *generalizing extension*, which he distinguishes from generalization. While the latter basically involves comparing inputs (stages, instances, cases, objects) in the same class, the former applies to what has already been generalized to new classes of objects. Hence, extension addresses an increase in breadth and assumes "all that the [generalization] did, and more too" (p. 256). Ellis's (2007) definition of generalization in the paragraph below includes both aspects of generalization and generalizing extension, including the emphasis on "what students themselves see as general [and, hence, actor-oriented]" (p. 198).

> (G)eneralization is defined as engaging in at least one of three activities: (a) identifying commonality across cases, (b) extending one's reasoning beyond the range in which it originated, or (c) deriving broader results from particular cases. The actor-oriented perspective guided the development of this definition in two ways. First, generalization is viewed as a dynamic rather than a static process. Second, evidence for generalization is not predetermined but instead is found by identifying the similarities and extensions that *students* perceive as general. (Ellis, 2007, p. 197).

Ellis suggests the following actions that support generalizing extension: (1) expanding to a larger range of cases beyond the original source; (2) developing a global analysis upon decontextualization; (3) performing operations on the relevant cases leading to the construction of new cases; and (4) using the same pattern as a way of producing new cases.

We raise an interesting point concerning the nature of explanations or justifications relative to generalizations and generalizing extensions. While induction as a verification tool applies to both of them and empirical-based structural argumentation and mathematical induction are useful strategies to further support generalizations in a deductive situation, generalizations, on the one hand, are constructed from true premises that yield conclusions that are at best "more probable, i.e., if the premises are true, then the conclusion is more likely to be true than false" (Smith, 2002, p. 35). Further, and following Israel (2006), since generalizations are drawn from abductive arguments that have been confirmed by repeated induction, they might be conceived as being *rationally explainable in the right context*, which means to say that "it is *possible* to explain" the patterns via their generalizations in practical terms without necessarily possessing them. This happens when the interpreted structures appear to have "lawlike" characteristics that make them extremely impossible to be violated in some way. Israel (2006) puts it rather forcefully in the following manner below.

> (W)e need to recognize that what we "project" are generalizations rather than properties. Whether a generalization is projectible or not depends on the context ... because it depends on the entire "web of belief," including the epistemic values of reflective equilibrium, coherence, simplicity, and the like that should be counted as part of the total "web." (Israel, 2006, p. 276)

There is no contradiction between generalization and properties that are constructed from the stages in a pattern through, say, specialization. Any learner can certainly establish invariant properties of objects in a class that can then lead to the formation of generalizations. However, the learner projects his or her generalizations on both the examined and unexamined (or extended) objects in the same class, which rely on his or her total web that comprises his or her context.

Generalizing extensions, on the other hand, are constructed within *subsumptive* and *unifying constraints*. That is, in some cases, a new object from another class might be shown to be an instantiation of an, and, thus, subsumed under the established general pattern or structure (Williams, Lombrozo, & Rehder, 2011, p. 1352). In some other cases, several different, but relevant, objects could be unified under a single generalization (Williams & Lombrozo, 2010). Both subsumptive and unifying explanations facilitate transfer and broader generalizations.

Mason, Stephens, and Watson's (2009) attentional states in structure discernment and formation provide additional abductive actions that describe various phases in the passage from the particular to the general. Depending on learners' mathematical experiences, they can manifest one or more of the following states:

I.   Holding wholes;
II. Discerning details;
III. Recognizing relationships;
IV. Perceiving properties as generalities that could be instantiated in particular contexts, and;
V.   Reasoning drawn from the properties.

(Mason et al, 2009, p. 11)

Holding wholes involves a global sensing of plausible features in an emerging pattern, describing them, and forming images that will be subject to further analysis. *Discerning details* involves determining, examining, and describing the interpreted features in detail in terms of which ones change and which others remain invariant within and across stages in the pattern. At this state, the images formed tend to be more analytical than descriptive. *Recognizing important conceptual (functional) relationships* plays a crucial role in establishing covariation, correlation, and causality. Abductions at this state are analytical and conjectural and oftentimes lead to expressions as objects that convey functional relationships. *Perceiving properties* involves articulating stable or invariant characteristics of the pattern and clearly delineating them from other details that vary. At this stage, there is also an attempt to assess the extent of applicability to a wide range of classes.

Reasoning marks the phase of deductive argumentation and generalizing extension (cf. Watson, 2009).

While Peirce (1960) makes a distinction between generalization and generalizing extensions, Davydov (2008) noted differences between empirical and theoretical generalizations.[7] Generalization, at the very least, is a "human thinking activity" that "unites" the "sensible and rational," "visual and discursive thinking," and the "concrete and abstract" (Davydov, 2008, p. 74). Empirical generalizations, on the one hand, employ abductions and inductions as ways of forming concepts and names by abstracting the essential or stable features of a class of objects through formal-logical schemes. They, however, do not yield deep internal characterizations as their essences are linked with the "external properties of objects—with their appearances" (Davydov, 2008, p. 77). The preceding characterizations of generalization exemplify empirical generalizations, which Davydov classifies as rational cognitive activities that aim at understanding. That is,

> [i]ts basic function is to classify objects – to construct a rigid scheme of "determinants." ... [Empirical generalizations and understanding] presuppose two paths: the path "from the bottom up" and the path "from the top down." In the first, an abstraction (concept) of the formally general is constructed, but this is essentially incapable of expressing, in mental form, the specifically concrete content of the object. On the path "from the top down," this abstraction becomes imbued with visual images of the corresponding object – it becomes "rich" and contentful, but not as a mental construction – rather, as an aggregate of descriptions and concrete examples that illustrate it. (Davydov, 2008, p. 78)

Theoretical generalizations aim at reasoning or dialectical thinking; it goes beyond "empirical dependencies" (Davydov, 2008, p. 93) and (empirical) understanding by articulating individual objects' "concreteness as a unity of different definitions that the understanding considers to be strictly separate" (ibid, p. 78) and by "studying the nature of concepts themselves" (ibid, p. 79). Further, in theoretical or internal dependencies, Davydov points out,

> one thing is a method for manifesting another within a certain whole. This transition of thing into thing, the sublation of one thing's specificity when it is transformed into its own "other" – i.e., their internal connections – is the object of theoretical thought. This kind of thought is always dealing with real, sensibly given things, but discerns the process of their mutual transition, their connection within a certain whole and in the dependence on that whole. Marx wrote, "It is the work of science to resolve the visible, merely external moment into the true intrinsic movement." (Davydov, 2008, p. 93)

Thus, abductions and inductions in theoretical generalizations are mediated actions within a system that counter empirical-based abductions and inductions, which primarily depend on sensory observations and processes such as repeatability,

---

[7] Certainly this view should be seen in Davydov's (2008) larger perspective in which school curricula should aim for higher level theoretical consciousness and cognition beyond, and not merely, the formation of roots of empirical consciousness and cognition. While the empirical grounding is "important," nonetheless, "at present [is] not the most effective way of developing [students'] minds" (p. 73).

resemblance, and differentiation. The "whole" that constitutes the *concrete* in theoretical generalizations "exists through the connection of individual things [i.e., the unity of the diverse]" (ibid, p. 93) and "brings together things that are dissimilar, different, multifaceted, and not coincident, and indicates their specific weight within this whole" (ibid, p. 93). Suffice it to say, theoretical generalizations construct and transform ideal mental objects (vs. empirical objects) and that the relevant abductions and inductions provide support by

> Idealizing the experimental aspects of production, at first giving them the form of a sensible, object-oriented cognitive experiment, and later on the form of a thought experiment realized through a concept. (Davydov, 2008, p. 94)

Scientific modeling exemplifies the process of theoretical generalization, where models are viewed in terms of "mentally conceived or materially realized systems that, by representing or reproducing the objects of study are capable of replacing them so that studying the models provide new information about the objects" (Shtoff, 1966, p. 19; quoted in Davydov, 2008, p. 94). Constructing models in relation to some target object involves an abstracting process in which connections and relations between the elements in a model convey the essential qualities of the object.

The preceding discussions indicate the central role of the inferential trivium—abduction, induction, and deduction—in various characterizations of generalization, albeit overlapping in many aspects. While the starting point of a general claim is abductive inference, the progressive evolution of a final generalization involves a dynamic interplay among the trivium. Hence, from both psychological and pedagogical standpoints, there is benefit in assessing whether a learner's problem in a pattern generalization task deals with abduction, induction, or deduction. Simply claiming that the learner cannot generalize does not clarify which aspect of the inferential process he or she finds difficult. Considering the preceding characterizations of generalization, it now seems possible to operationally assess the source(s) of students' difficulties. Some of these possible sources are the following:

• Conceptual difficulties in establishing an abductive claim;
• Conceptual difficulties in transitioning from an initial to a strong abductive claim;
• Conceptual difficulties in inductively verifying the reasonableness of an abductive claim on either a near or a far stage in a pattern;
• Procedural difficulties in carrying out an induction;
• Conceptual difficulties in framing and justifying a relevant deductive argument.

Vinner (2011) offers a different, and oftentimes neglected, view of generalization. In the following paragraph below, he draws on Maslow (1970) in order to articulate other (noncognitive) dimensions (e.g. curiosity, needs and desires) that manifest themselves in unpredictable ways as soon as individual learners begin to generalize. At the very least, Vinner notes that while similar examples can yield generalizations, the nature of such generalizations is that they tend to be "intuitive," "immediate, spontaneous, rely on global impressions and not analytical," which might explain why they "quite often fail" (Vinner, 2011, p. 253).

> We can assume that in our minds exists a tendency to generalize. It can even be considered as *a need to generalize*. In some cases, we are unaware of it. However, we can be driven by it without being aware of it. Maslow (1970) considers *"curiosity, cognitive impulses, the needs to know and to understand, the desires to organize, to analyze, to look for relations and meanings as an essential part of human nature."* If we accept this claim and we also accept another general claim that the *needs* that drive us have physiological ground, we have enough justification to assume that there is a certain mechanism in our mind, which drives us to generalize. I would like to call this mechanism the generalization schema. (Vinner, 2011, p. 252)

Thus, a generalization scheme, which can fail due to, say, overgeneralization, is separate from analytical thought processes such as using counterexamples to further establish validity and evaluate for correctness. In terms of abduction and induction, Vinner's notion of a generalization scheme falls under abductive processes and the analytic thought processes refer to inductive processes. Complications in generalizing actions can be traced to the influence of individual curiosities, impulses, needs, desires, and other factors (e.g. memory, neural connections, verbal/object/spatial driven cognitive styles, complexity of figural objects being analyzed) that cannot not be categorized under any of the three inferential processes. Also, in Fig. 1.10, the parallel network model for pattern generalization (p. 22), the hidden layer of units is not directly manipulable, which can further contribute to individual differences in perceiving the general. The hidden layer of units consists of the relation and representation layers and combinations of units drawn from the two layers.

Figure 2.11 is a visual summary of the ideas that have been presented so far with arrows indicating their relationships with one another. In the next section, we will explore the implications of the complex model in our proposed theory of graded pattern generalization. What remains to be clarified involves the nature of the input-relation pairs that matter to pattern generalization especially in the beginning phase of the process. In this book, we frame it in cognitive and sociocultural terms. We address the sociocultural dimension first.

All input and relation units are culturally mediated objects. The input layer of units consists of stages in a pattern, which are symbol-mediated and loaded with intentional meaning that began at the moment of construction. The relation units tell how the input units are conceptually perceived (e.g. they are instantiations of X, they exemplify Y, they have property Z, etc.), which initially rely on culturally mediated activity (e.g. classroom interaction). While it is true that individual learners are ultimately responsible for interpretively constructing structures on patterns as a way of transforming them into meaningful mathematical objects, they nevertheless obtain "analytic clues" (indirectly) from the larger community in terms of how the inputs and their relationships might be perceived and (figurally) apprehended.

We also share Vygotsky's (1962) view that the primary function of generalizations as signs that are endowed with meanings is to communicate (say, an intended structure), that is, in Davydov's (1990) words, "the sign-meaning-communication system [i]s a unit of human behavior and of all of the mental functions that

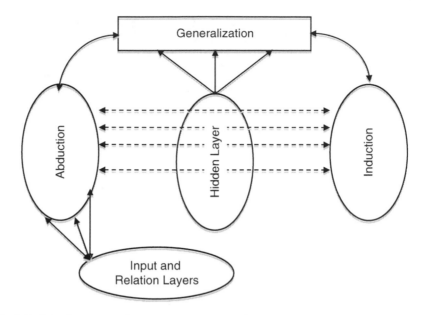

Fig. 2.11 Visual summary of pattern generalization actions

implement that behavior" (p. 175). For Luria (1976), and Vygotsky (1962) before
him, words and categories exemplify generalizations that pertain to classes of
objects. However, such generalizations emerge as "verbal acts of thought" whose
meanings are rooted in individual learners' reflections of their corresponding
sociocultural realities. Consequently, differences occur and exist due to differing
"systems of psychological elements that govern such reflections" (Luria, 1976,
p. 49). In a similar vein, Dörfler (1991) characterizes "generalizing as a social-
cognitive process" that despite the seemingly individual nature of the process "is
always conditioned and mediated socially, as it uses and depends on means
attained and prepared by society, like language" (p. 63). Thus, the context of the
formation of words and categories, that is, generalization, reflects social factors
that shape, reorganize, and restructure their conceptual meanings. Meanings
change and evolve over time because "the psychological processes that govern
the use of words are themselves subject to change chiefly through socioeconomic
factors" (Luria, 1976, p. 50). For example, children's general knowledge regarding the different forms of geometrical objects evolves from being situational and
preverbal (i.e. graphic-based impressions drawn from individual perceptions
based on interest, everyday relationships, and practical operations) to taxonomic
and verbal (i.e. logical and reflective of theoretical and abstract operations that

are learned in schools).[8] For Luria, the situationist context of generalization "is based on an individual's practical experiences," while the taxonomic context is a reflection of "the shared experience of society conveyed through its linguistic system" (p. 52). Further, he notes that

> (t)his reliance on society-wide criteria transforms graphic thinking processes into a scheme of semantic and logical operations in which words become the principal tool for abstraction and generalization. (Luria, 1976, p. 52)

Suffice it to say, the relation units are subject to change, say, through more formal learning experiences in the classroom.

Insofar as the cognitive dimension matters, the input units as objects are initially apprehended based on cognitive style, where cognitive style refers to "a stable dimension that delineates consistencies in how individuals process information across tasks" (Anderson et al, 2008, p. 189). In both neuroscience and mathematics education research, for example, problem solvers have been categorized to be verbalizers or visualizers, numeric or figural generalizers, concrete or operative thinkers, etc. Anderson et al. suggest at least three categories of cognitive styles, namely: verbal deductive; spatial imagery; and object imagery. For example, Fig. 2.12b–d exemplify three different cognitive style responses on the geometry problem shown in Fig. 2.12a. Verbalizers tend to draw on language and exhibit logical deductive reasoning. They use rules and definitions in making sense of object relationships. Object imagers as one type of visualizers tend to mentally (re)construct fixed but detailed images of objects and their shapes. Spatial imagers as another type of visualizers tend to dwell on complex spatial transformations (e.g. different orientations) of, and relationships within, images. In their empirical study with 186 US Grade 7 students (ages 12–14 years; 98 males; 88 females), they found that spatial imagers and those who employed a combination of verbal deduction and spatial imagery were by far more successful in geometry problem solving than object imagers. With respect to the implications of cognitive style in pattern generalization, individual learners are likely to manifest different ways of apprehending the input units, which should then influence the choices that are made and the connections that are established relative to both the relation and representation layers.

Especially in patterning situations where the input units are expressed as figural objects, the complexity of their shapes can potentially affect a generalizing process.

---

[8] See Luria (1976, pp. 53–98) for details of his experimental studies in which he obtained the same patterns of generalized thinking schemes among different groups of adult subjects. In his closing remark relative to the studies, he notes how the "evidence assembled indicates that the processes used to render abstractions and generalizations does not assume an invariable form at all stage of mental growth" but "are themselves a product of socioeconomic and cultural development" (p. 98). Further, he stresses the possibility of transforming from situational, concrete, and practical to theoretical and abstract ways of generalizing via an evolving language whose meanings are enriched via, say, more education, new experiences, and new ideas.

In a simple experiment that involves comparing perimeters of certain figural objects, the 18 participants (mean age of 27.3 years; 10 males; 8 females) in Stavy and Babai's (2008) study appeared to be distracted by features such as area and complexity of shapes. Areas, of course, do not matter in perimeter problems, but they nevertheless influence the calculation of lengths. Complex figures (e.g., irregular over regular shapes) necessitate a high cognitive load due to the large amount of information that needs to be processed.

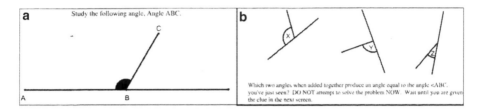

Fig. 2.12a Geometry problem and question screens

c
Verbal Clue Screen.

Which two angles (X, Y, or Z) when added together produce an angle equal to the angle <ABC?

Angle <ABC on the first screen is equal to 120°.

Rule of geometry: Two angles are supplementary when they add up to 180°.
For example, an angle of 70° is supplementary to 110° because 70° + 110° = 180°.

Angle X is supplementary to 65°.

Angle Y is supplementary to 90°.

Angle Z is supplementary to 150°.

Fig. 2.12b Verbal deductive screen

d

Shape Memory Clue Screen 1.

This is the angle from the first screen.
On the next screen you will be shown the three choice angles. You will need to
determine which two of the three choice angles will form the angle below when added
together.

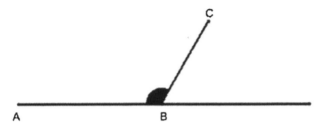

Shape Memory Clue Screen 2.

Which two angles (X, Y, or Z) when added together produce an angle equal to the
angle <ABC, you've just seen?

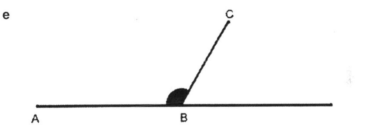

Fig. 2.12c Object imagery screen

e

Which two angles (X, Y, or Z) when added together produce an angle equal to the
angle <ABC, shown above?

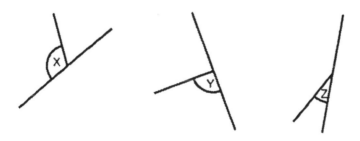

Fig. 2.12d Spatial imagery screen

Reflections on and Implications for a Theory of Graded Pattern Generalization

Expressing generalities is a complex phenomenon. Teachers certainly know this and it is old news. What seems new is that we are now able to describe and deal with the complexity that in this book we describe in terms of a mechanism called graded distributed processing. While earlier characterizations of generalization allude to some kind of a passage from the particular to the general and an extension from one domain or object to another domain or object, they do not fully capture the underlying complexities that students experience when they establish and justify a generalization. At the very least, the input and the hidden units exercise significant influence in abductive and inductive actions that can of course be controlled with more learning, albeit not easily so in some cases. Students' cognitive style and complexity of task features are also likely to influence initial perceptions of the input units. Luria's (1976) case studies provide sufficient evidence that illustrate ways in which individual learners' "modes of generalization" are "shaped by social, economic, and cultural conditions unlike our own" (p. 98) that tend to reflect, privilege, and validate institutional ways of generalizing. Ellis (2007) in her characterization of generalization has noted this dynamic (vs. static) dimension, which is really the case. However, the actor-oriented perspective (i.e. what individual students see as general) needs to be expanded to reflect the distributed context of generalization. Diana's thinking about the pattern in Fig. 2.1a and the students' joint activity in Fig. 2.10b exemplify instances of emergence in situations other than themselves that are, as a matter of fact, shared, culturally embodied, and institutionally acceptable. That is, they needed to attend to, construct, and internalize an appropriate general knowledge, which occur individually and socioculturally at the same time.

The model in Fig. 2.11 foregrounds the influence of the hidden layer that is not directly manipulable, which demonstrates the complexity of psychological and sociocultural factors that influence choices and connections in the input, relation, and representation layers. Vinner has alluded to desires and curiosities as additional noncognitive factors that can also influence the initial connections among the units that feedforward to the hidden layer. Further complications in the representation layer can also influence the emerging connections. One such complication, for example, is neural-based. The consistent neuroscientific finding called triple coding (Dehaene, 1997; Dehaene & Cohen, 1995) can influence an emerging general content (e.g. invariant shape of a figural pattern, exact cardinalities of outcomes), especially among elementary students. Triple coding has been neurally established in the number processing of older children and adults and consists of the following representational formats or codes: an auditory verbal or linguistic code that recalls automatized arithmetical facts (e.g., multiplication table) stored and remembered as strings of words; a visual or symbolic code for recognizing, say, the Hindu-Arabic notations that activates the need to perform arithmetical and other symbolic operations; and a language-independent analog magnitude or quantity code, the famous mental number line, that deals with numerical comparisons, approximate arithmetic, novel operations, conceptual relationships between numbers, and spatial judgments of relative sizes. Delays, impairments, or a lack of convergence among the three representational codes in triple coding can affect the manner in which individual learners establish shape and count, two aspects that are important in pattern generalization.

Figure 2.11 conveys a simple model of a parallel distributed processing (PDP) view of pattern generalization. We explore PDP in greater detail in Chap. 4, however, it is worth noting a few points at this stage. The nonlinear character that is evident in the diagram captures the sense in which individual learners are naturally predisposed to performing generalization in several different ways and modes at the same time on the same task, which implies the possibility of graded pattern generalization routes. Central to PDP are the connections, the repository of knowledge, which means that a stated emergent generalization could be interpreted as a matter of choice in which one route wins over all other possible routes (e.g., a pattern generalization that yields a closed formula over other different forms of pattern generalization). However, performance depends on the nature and complexity of a task being analyzed. Hence, there are no permanent or invariant processes, transitions, or conceptual shifts, only graded. With more learning, say, via purposeful classroom teaching experiments, adjustments in connection weights between and among the units can occur with familiar patterns yielding greater activation than unfamiliar or nonroutine ones. An initial generalization multipath or grade might reflect a recursive relation (e.g., "keep adding x objects from one stage to the next stage"). But it is also likely, especially among beginning learners, that a chosen multipath or grade is one that already yields an algebraically useful pattern generalization. Furthermore, depending on an individual learner's prior knowledge, several different kinds of algebraically useful generalizations can be constructed simultaneously. We pursue these issues in greater detail in Chaps. 5 and 6 with empirical data drawn from younger and older children and adults. McClelland et al. (2010) capture the sense in which we conceptualize a PDP approach to pattern generalization, as follows:

> No restriction to a set of possible structure types; no idealized type is represented, no decision on selecting one structure over another; learning is the gradual refinement and elaboration of knowledge based on each new experience. (McClelland et al 2010, p. 353)

Depending on a complexity of factors that influences learners in either individual or collective context, it is simply not possible to give a teleological account of or predetermine how they will perform on any pattern generalization task. Here, the subtlety of the implications of a graded perspective on generalization is important. There are, indeed, manipulable and nonmanipulable factors that exert influence on how individuals perceive the input units in a pattern. Hence, it is not the task per se, which has oftentimes been seen as "the" issue, but the factors and connections weights among the factors that influence generalization processes. Without a doubt, continuous learning also helps as McClelland et al have noted in their statement above.

Having clarified all the relevant terms, we explore in the next chapter several theoretical frameworks that suggest different types and levels of pattern generalization.

We also provide a synthesis of at least 20 years of research studies on pattern generalization that have been conducted with younger and older students in different parts of the globe. In this chapter, we propose an organizing framework that takes into account various aspects of pattern generalization that emerged from the interpretive synthesis account. Since we aim for maximal inclusiveness, our synthesis includes research on patterns that have been done in other countries. For example, Portugal recently introduced patterns as a unifying theme in their countrywide modification of the school mathematics curriculum. Countries such as Taiwan, Lebanon, Turkey, and Thailand have recently reported results of patterning studies that have been conducted with older students, which share many similarities with various reported findings drawn from students in, say, the United States, Canada, and Australia.

Chapter 3
Types and Levels of Pattern Generalization

Triangle Patio Task: This is stage 1 in a pattern consisting of triangles and a square.

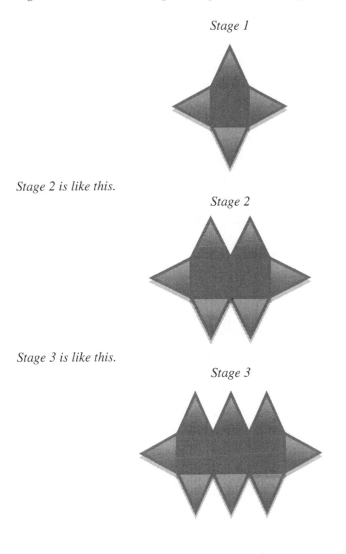

Stage 1

Stage 2 is like this.

Stage 2

Stage 3 is like this.

Stage 3

F. Rivera, *Teaching and Learning Patterns in School Mathematics:*
Psychological and Pedagogical Considerations, DOI 10.1007/978-94-007-2712-0_3,
© Springer Science+Business Media Dordrecht 2013

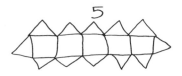

Fig. 3.1a Ricky's constructed stage 5

1. *Interviewer (I): Can you draw stage 4 for me? How about stage 5? (Figure 3.1a shows third-*
   grade student Ricky's ["R," age 8 years] stage 5.)
2. *I: Alright, can you describe your pattern for me?*

3. *R: Ahm, for (stage) 5, there's 5 squares and (points to the figure and gestures in a*
4. *circular manner) I put triangles on each side.*

5. *I: Okay now say that more specifically this time. So 5 squares and then what? How*
6. *many triangles?*

7. *R: There are 12 triangles.*

8. *I: And how did you get 12 triangles?*

9. *R: Ahm by counting by twos (uses two fingers to refer to top and bottom pairs of*
10. *triangles per square), 2, 4, 6, 8, 10, then 12 (referring to the two triangle sides).*

11. *I: Alright if we skip all the way to stage 10, how might it look like?*
12. *R: 10 squares in the middle. (He starts counting the number of triangles in his head.)*

13. *I: You don't have to find the total number of triangles, just describe it for me. So 10*
14. *squares and in the middle and then what?*

15. *R: And then I put triangles.*

16. *I: How many triangles?*

17. *R: (Uses his fingers and counts by 2 per finger) 22.*

18. *I: And how did you get the 22 triangles?*

19. *R: So I put 2 each and counted with my fingers plus 2 more.*
20. *I: But where do you see the 22 triangles? I see where the 10 squares are.*

21. *R: Ahm 2 (triangles) on the sides and there are 10 triangles on the top and then 10 on*
22. *the bottom.*

23. *I: Alright for stage 25?*

24. *R: (Uses his right hand and his drawn stage 5) 25 squares and ... triangles on the sides.*

25. *Two triangles on the two sides, 25 triangles on the top, and 25 triangles on the*
26. *bottom.*

27. *I: Okay how about stage 100?*

28. *R: (Uses his stage 5 and finger) 100 squares, 2 triangles on the sides, and (with his right*
29. *hand) 100 on the top and 100 on the bottom.*

30. *I: Okay, next question. Is there a mathematical expression for the total number of*
31. *squares and triangles that will allow you to find the total number of squares and*
32. *triangles without having to construct each one of them?*

33.   *(Figure 3.1b shows the series of mathematical expressions that R wrote beginning*
34.   *with $2 \times 2 + 2$ and closing with $2 \times 100 + 102$. Due to space constraint, we are*
35.   *skipping the remaining interview conversation relevant to this emergence.)*

36. *I: [Refers to R's stage 100 formula, $2 \times 100 + 102$] okay so explain those numbers.*

37. *R: Ahm 100 on the top, 100 on the bottom, and 102 squares and triangles in the*
38.   *middle.*

Thirteen-year-old student Ricky joined Rivera's (2010b) 2-year longitudinal study on pattern generalization and algebraic thinking at the elementary level when he was in third grade. In Year 1, the second-grade participants dealt with growth pattern generalization tasks near the end of the school year as an enrichment topic. During the school year, they learned the appropriate grade-level state standards involving whole numbers and operations up to 1,000 consistently from a visually driven structural perspective (see Chaps. 5 and 7). The Year 2 study operated within the same learning trajectory involving numbers and operations, but the numbers they dealt with spanned to 10,000. The above interview with Ricky took place toward the end of the school year. At the time of the interview, he did not know how to process pattern generalization (PPG) tasks. However, his conceptual understanding of multiplication was sufficiently strong, which encouraged Rivera (2010b) to investigate whether he could apply his emerging multiplicative thinking ability on pattern generalization tasks

Fig. 3.1b Ricky's series of mathematical expressions for the Fig. 3.1a pattern

without the benefit of an intervening teaching experiment on the topic. In the above interview he initially generalized by drawing on his empirical experiences with both the given stages and his constructed extensions of the pattern. When his incipient verbal and arithmetical-based expressions worked with several near stages, that enabled him to formulate similar expressions for the far stages. The expressions in Fig. 3.1b capture the manner in which his generalized thinking transitioned from attending to the individual stages to focusing on a stable process that enabled him to obtain the total number of figures for any stage in his pattern. Ricky initially manifested additive thinking in lines 3 and 4 when he saw stage 5 as consisting of five squares and the 12 triangles around the sides of the squares (Fig. 3.1c). He then started to manifest multiplicative thinking in line 9 when he counted in pairs (Fig. 3.1d).

What we found remarkable in the above interview with Ricky was the manner in which he manifested at least two different multiplicative structures that were all equivalent and equally valid. In lines 7 through 20, he saw pairs of triangles around the squares that grew by the stage number (Fig. 3.1d). In lines 21 through 38, he saw two rows of triangles and another row of squares that became the basis of his incipient general statement (Fig. 3.1e). In the absence of formal instruction on pattern generalization, his thinking in the above episode conveyed a complex emergence of algebraically useful structures in which his only context was his strong prior knowledge of addition and multiplication of whole numbers and operations. He eventually managed to verbally construct and justify a mathematical expression in closed form that he thought would apply to any stage in his pattern. Certainly, the joint activity with the interviewer provided an additional context that mediated in his thinking process.

In this chapter, we synthesize at least 20 years of research studies on pattern generalization that have been conducted with younger and older students in different parts of the globe. Figure 3.2 is an organizing framework that takes into account various aspects of pattern generalization that emerged from the interpretive synthesis account. Central to pattern generalization are the inferential processes of abduction, induction, and deduction that we discussed in some detail in the previous chapter, which we now assume in this chapter. What needs to be explained are the other equally important (and overlapping) dimensions of pattern generalization, namely: kinds and sources of generalization; types of structures; ways of attending

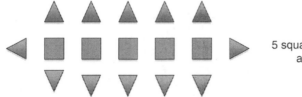

5 squares and 12 triangles
around each side

Fig. 3.1c   Ricky's initial additive thinking on the Fig. 3.1a figural pattern

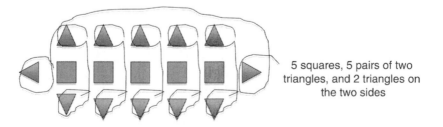

5 squares, 5 pairs of two
triangles, and 2 triangles on
the two sides

Fig. 3.1d   Ricky's beginning multiplicative thinking on the Fig. 3.1a figural stage

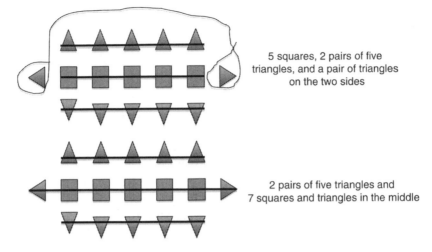

5 squares, 2 pairs of five
triangles, and a pair of triangles
on the two sides

2 pairs of five triangles and
7 squares and triangles in the middle

Fig. 3.1e Ricky's evolving multiplicative thinking on the Fig. 3.1a figural stage

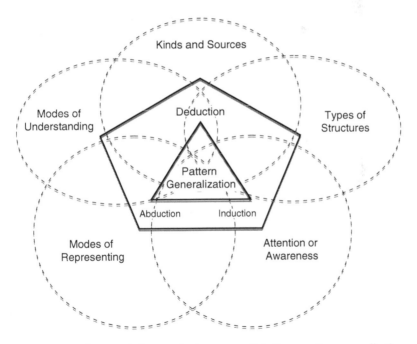

Fig. 3.2 Organizing framework for a synthesis account of studies on pattern generalization

to structures; and modes of representing and understanding generalizations. In this chapter we remain consistent as before in articulating the complexity of pattern generalization due to differences in, and the simultaneous layering of, processes relevant to constructing, expressing, and justifying interpreted structures.

Kinds and Sources of Generalization

Considering the studies we discuss in this section, which appear to share more similarities than differences, the basic concern involves understanding the different kinds and sources of generalization. At the outset, the findings identify two possible sources of generalization whenever individual learners generalize. That is, some of them construct invariant relationships that they infer on the given instances or stages (i.e. objects), while others tend to pay more attention on the generality of the inferred ideas, relationships, methods, or processes than on the objects themselves. Implications of these findings suggest the need for all students to be provided with every opportunity to smoothly transition from working with particular objects to working with general ideas and methods with a clear and sustained attention on justification. In other words, the implications foreground the pedagogical value of having students learn pattern generalization in contexts that enable them to engage in both empirical and theoretical generalization processing.

Harel (2001) distinguishes between process pattern generalization (PPG) and result pattern generalization (RPG), which represent two different ways of student thinking in relation to tasks that involve (mathematical) induction. In PPG students dwell on the relevant processes that support the construction of a generalization. In RPG they focus their attention on the perceived regularities that they initially draw on the available results. An example of a student's RPG is shown in Fig. 3.3a, which stems from the student's empirical-based conviction that his or her generalization about the product rule for logarithms is correct on the basis of several randomly drawn instances that enabled him or her to verify its validity (see also Fig. 2.10b for another example of an RPG based on Pedemonte's (2007) study). In contrast, Fig. 3.3b illustrates a different student's PPG on the same proposition noted in Fig. 3.3a, which reflects an indirect use of mathematical induction (see also Fig. 2.10b for a PPG version of the task shown in Fig. 2.10b).

Harel notes that while a RPG might initially motivate a PPG, the latter has more transformational than empirical content—that is, there is

> (a) [a] consideration of the generality aspects of the conjecture, (b) [an] application of mental operations that are goal oriented and anticipatory—an attempt to predict outcomes on the basis of general principles—and (c) [a sequence of] transformations of images that govern the deduction in the evidencing process (Harel, 2001, p. 191).

In other words, two different levels of evidence apply to generalization with PPG going beyond RPG by focusing on general principles that support the anticipation and prediction of subsequent outcomes in a pattern.

Drawing on Davydov, Dörfler (1991) distinguishes between empirical generalization (EG) and theoretical generalization (TG). Individual learners who perform EG, on the one hand, mentally extract and isolate stable and common features or systems of features from their original contexts through processes of comparing and observing. For example, triangularity is a general property that they can easily infer on all triangles. Individual learners who perform TG, on the other hand, focus on either the relevant actions or systems of actions that accompany the general process, the

$$\log(4 \cdot 3 \cdot 7) = \log 84 = 1.924;$$
$$\log 4 + \log 3 + \log 7 = 1.924.$$
$$\log(4 \cdot 3 \cdot 6) = \log 72 = 1.857;$$
$$\log 4 + \log 3 + \log 6 = 1.857.$$
$$\therefore \log(a_1 \cdot a_2 \cdots a_n) = \log a_1 + \log a_2 + \ldots + \log a_n.$$

Fig. 3.3a An empirical-driven RPG example involving the product rule for logarithms (Harel, 2001, p. 180)

(1) $\log(a_1 a_2) = \log a_1 + \log a_2$ by definition

(2) $\log(a_1 a_2 a_3) = \log a_1 + \log a_2 a_3$. Similar to $\log(ax)$ as in step (1), where this time $ax = a_1 a_2$.

Then $\log(a_1 a_2 a_3) = \log a_1 + \log a_2 + \log a_3$.

(3) We can see from step (2) any $\log(a_1 a_2 a_3 \cdots a_n)$ can be repeatedly broken down to $\log a_1 + \log a_2 + \cdots + \log a_n$.

Fig. 3.3b A transformational-driven PPG example involving the product rule for logarithms (Harel, 2001, p. 180)

outcomes or products of such actions or systems, or the conditions (i.e., relationships and properties) that make the actions or systems feasible (Dörfler, pp. 69–70). (Systems of) Actions recruit either cognitive (e.g. interiorized) or symbolic (e.g., use of variables) tools that support the conceptualization process and oftentimes the initial phase of acting is grounded in the concrete. Meaningful and purposeful actions in the concrete phase transform into invariants or abstract schemes of actions that are then symbolically described and captured via a prototype model. The goal eventually is to deemphasize the concrete objects that provide the initial sources of constructive actions. The symbolic descriptions are expected to evolve over time with more reflective action, from symbols as substitutes for concrete actions to symbols as objects that represent the invariants of the relevant actions and, still further, to symbols as variables with the character of being abstract objects that can be further manipulated and generalized into other domains and range of reference, leading to the generation of new actions or systems of actions.

To illustrate, the student response in Fig. 3.3a represents his or her system of concrete actions that enabled him or her to construct a generalization that matched the product rule for logarithms. The other student's response in Fig. 3.3b indicates a more sustained focus on a general structure for manipulating logarithmic products. Eventually the student should be able to substitute his or her generalization with other mathematical objects (e.g. functions) representing a higher level of generalization. Another example is taken from arithmetic in which the distributive law of multiplication over addition $a(b+c) = ab + ac$ is seen to be a generalization of a system of actions involving arithmetical and later algebraic objects, which can then be further generalized into $a*(b+c) = a*b + a*c$, where a, b, c, and $*$ pertain to other symbols and operations that apply to any object.

Relying on Dörfler's generalization framework, Iwasaki and Yamaguchi (1997) distinguish between generalization of objects (GO) and generalization of method

(GM). A group of Grade 8 Japanese students (mean age of 14 years) participated in the authors' two-hour problem-solving session involving the two tasks shown in Figs. 3.4a and 3.4b. In part 1 of Fig. 3.4a, the students performed calculations on the numbers using trial and error that enabled some of them to abduce the mathematical relation "the sum of three numbers on the vertical direction in the frame is equal to that on the horizontal direction." In part 2 of the same task, they moved the location of the frame several times to other parts on the calendar, which enabled them to further verify the invariance of the abduced relationship. When they repeated the process several times, that supported them in constructing a generalization. For instance, they noted the invariance of adding and subtracting by 1 and 7 to the central number in the frame with the number seen as a variant since the frame was allowed to move freely on the calendar. They also saw the invariance of 1 and 7 in the context of how each triad of numbers in one direction appeared to them as being arranged in a particular way. When they eventually constructed the identity $(n-1)+n+(n+1) = (n-7)+n+(n+7)$ and explained that the sum, $3n$, holds for any pair of vertical and horizontal triads of numbers regardless of their location on the calendar, this phase marked a deeper level of generalization on the task. Furthermore, the transposition to the algebraic form signified a detachment from the actual objects that consequently formalized for them a semantic relationship in syntactical terms using variable expressions. In part 3 of the same task, they further engaged in generalizing when they constructed new mathematical relationships on the basis of changing either the shape of the frame or the arrangement of the numbers (e.g. rotating the frame by 45°).

In Fig. 3.4b, tasks 1-a and 1-b were meant to assist the students distinguish between a pentagon and a pentagram, respectively. In parts (2) and (3) of the task, some students drew several pentagrams and measured all five vertex angles with a protractor in each case. That activity enabled them to infer that the angle sum indeed measured 180° across the constructed instances. Other students "realized the limitations" of the measurement approach, which then encouraged them to prove the statement in part (3) deductively. In that situation, they regarded a single drawn pentagram as a general icon or prototype that enabled them to reason deductively.

Based on their findings relative to the students' work on the two tasks shown in Figs. 3.4a and 3.4b, Iwasaki and Yamaguchi note that

> there are two types of generalization: one is the *generalization of object* in the algebraic situation, the other is *that of method* in the geometrical situation. In other words, in [the Figure 3.3a task], the object of one's thinking such as the concrete number is generalized by the use of letter n. On the other hand, in [the Figure 3.3b task], the way of viewing itself is generalized. It realizes the change of inference form, that is, from inductive to deductive (Iwasaki & Yamaguchi, 1997, pp. 111–112).

Yerushalmy (1993) distinguishes between *generalization of ideas* (GI) and *generalization from examples* (GE). In GI, students construct a more general statement from several specific ideas. In GE, they establish a generalization by drawing on particular cases or examples in a given set. Further, in GI, the most complex type of generalization" (Yerushalmy, 1993, pp. 68–69), it is not crucial to draw on examples

[Numbers on the calendar]

This is a calendar of June in 1995.
Let's consider about it.
(1)We enclose five numbers on this calendar
   with the frame ✛ . What relations can you
   find among these numbers ?
(2)Move this frame freely. How is the relations
   you find in problem (1) ?
(3)Changing the shape or location of the frame,
   find various relations among numbers on a
   calendar.

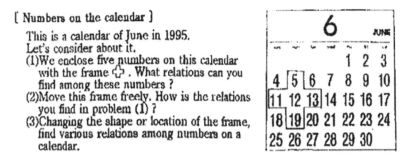

Fig. 3.4a Numbers on the calendar task (Iwasaki & Yamaguchi, 1997, p. 108)

[The Pentagram]
(1) Connect the following five points.
   (1–a) Connect each point with the next one.   (1–b) Connect each point with every other point.

(2) Find the features of the pentagram in the above (1–b) .
(3) Explain the reason why your anticipation is true. [Note; $\angle$ A, $\angle$ B, $\angle$ C, $\angle$ D, $\angle$ E are
   vertical angles of the pentagram in (1–b) respectively.]
$$\angle A + \angle B + \angle C + \angle D + \angle E = 180°$$

Fig. 3.4b The pentagram task (Iwasaki & Yamaguchi, 1997, p. 110)

since what matters significantly are the relevant ideas that can be dropped, ignored, relaxed, and/or combined in order to achieve a greater generality (Holland, Holyoak, Nisbett, & Thagard, 1986; Yevdokimov, 2008). In Yerushalmy and Maman (1988), for example, an experimental group of students was explicitly taught the GI strategy of "what if not" in order to assist them assess how relaxing certain conditions, assumptions, components, or restrictions in a general statement can yield further general understanding. GI strategies can also be used to investigate:

- The possible effects on a general claim when structural changes are imposed on an initial diagram (e.g. changing a parallelogram to a rectangle to a square when investigating a theorem involving diagonals of quadrilaterals)
- The impact of nonstereotypical cases, positions, and examples in a further analysis of a general claim (e.g. changing the position of the vertices in, or shape of, a triangle in examining altitudes and circumcenters)
- A sufficient number of samples of instances ("hypothesis space") in order to test the validity and scope of a general claim, including the need to pay attention to extreme and negative samples

Drawing on their work with younger and older students and teachers, Zazkis, Liljedahl, and Chernoff (2008) note that GE provides students with an opportunity to notice commonalities among examples that then translate into meaningful generalizations. However, GE can constrain, especially in cases when they manifest a limited example space. For example, it is an unavoidable situation that some students will generate invalid "coincidental examples" that show the validity of a narrow or inappropriate generalization. When that happens, they will need to learn the strategy of using big numbers in order to cope with the complex situation and eventually "serve as a stepping stone toward expressing generality with algebraic symbols" (p. 134). Employing big numbers as a GE strategy helps draw students to infer possible underlying structures. Below are a few characteristics of big numbers.

• They cannot be performed with (and by) a calculator.
• They do not encourage computation but instead favor structure spotting.
• They do not belong in the typical or usual repertoire of numbers that can be recalled from memory.
• They operate within a numeric variation logic, where numbers are changed in the context of a problem that has a fixed structure (e.g. the problem, "if the price of a can was \$10 and it increased by 400%, then what is the new price," can be explored by continuously changing the numbers until a structure for solving the problem is established).
• They play the role of being pivot examples in situations that either create or deal with a cognitive conflict resulting in a cognitive accommodation of new knowledge. They are not necessarily counterexamples.
• They function as judicious examples that can refute coincidental examples.

Types of Structures

In this section, we discuss types of structures along two basic categories of patterning problems in the K-12 school mathematics curriculum, namely, repeating (or oscillating) patterns and increasing/decreasing (or growth/decay) patterns. Across the two categories, we can infer the following basic features of structures in patterning contexts: there is a core unit of repeat, which is the basis of extensional generalization; multiplicative thinking is involved in one way or another, which enables the iteration of the explicit core unit of repeat and the eventual construction of an intentional generalization; and the discernment, formation, and construction of structures in exact terms are interpretive actions, which bring forth multiple layers and routes of generalization.

Drawing on both their investigations with 2–7-year-old children involving repeating sequences of objects and the available research evidence in the field, Clements and Sarama (2009) infer the following learning trajectory in young children's developing competence in pattern generalization: pre-explicit patterner; pattern recognizer; pattern fixer; pattern extender; pattern unit recognizer; and numeric patterner (pp. 195–198). In the *pre-explicit patterning phase*, 2-year-old children have an implicit and approximate sense of what constitutes a pattern. In the *pattern recognition phase*, which takes place at around age 3, they begin to recognize a pattern. At age 4, the *pattern fixing phase*, they are able to fill in the unknown object in a repeating pattern in at least three different ways. One way involves constructing their own repeating pattern in another location with a close eye on a given pattern involving two objects (duplicating). A second way involves adding elements at the end of a given row of repeating pattern involving two objects (extending). A third way involves duplicating far more complex repeating patterns beyond two objects. At age 5, the *pattern extending phase*, they extend simple repeating patterns. In the *pattern unit recognition phase*, which occurs around age 6, they begin to interpret, recognize, and construct a core unit of repeat for a given pattern, which also enable them to translate the same pattern in different media and in some cases create patterns of their own choice. At age 7, the *numeric patterning phase*, they are able to describe figural growth patterns numerically and translate between their figural and numerical representations.

Mulligan and her colleagues (e.g.: Mulligan & Mitchelmore, 2009; Mulligan, Prescott, & Mitchelmore, 2004; Papic, Mulligan, & Mitchelmore, 2009, 2011) extrapolate progressions or changes in structure that they inferred on young children who dealt with a mixture of age-appropriate repeating and nonrepeating patterning tasks. The children were exposed to a variety of mathematical tasks that focused on time, measurement, data, and numbers (see Fig. 3.5 for task examples). By structure, they mean the many different ways in which children organize objects or sets of objects according to what they meaningfully interpret to be their nature, shape, or component parts and relationships. Further, the authors assume that there is a continuous relationship between children's internal and external representational systems, and that features relevant to structure discernment and construction appear to be shared across different mathematical content strands.

The empirical studies that Mulligan and her colleagues have conducted with several different cohorts of Australian preschool and Grade 1 children (with ages ranging from 3.75 to 6.7 years) illustrate how young learners' structural representations transition from the *prestructural* stage, followed by *emergent* and then *partial* before finally achieving the *full stage of structural development*. The transition is enabled by appropriate habituation lessons that focus on the notions of a common unit (of repeat) and relevant spatial concepts that all support the development of, and growth in, multiplicative and functional thinking. Students in the *prestructural phase* tend to produce idiosyncratic responses that have little to no semblance of any kind of structure in both aspects of numerical count and spatial arrangement. For example, one student drew a horizontal sequence of 9 circles in response to the Triangular pattern task in Fig. 3.5. Students in the *emergent phase* produce invented or approximate structures in either numerical count or spatial arrangement and are oftentimes influenced by what they find meaningful and relevant. For example, one student drew a Christmas tree that consisted of segments instead of circles when asked to redraw on paper the triangular pattern in Fig. 3.5 from memory. In this case shape and not count appears to be a factor in the child's structural discernment of the given task.

Students in the *partial phase* produce at least one consistent and organized structural feature with some missing or incomplete necessary features. In the case of patterns, either shape or count is correctly accounted for but not both. For example, a student drew a triangle with three segment-sides (and not circles) to convey his or her view that he or she knew that the figure on the flash card looked like a triangle. Shape consistency without numerical consistency might indicate a valid recognition

Triangular pattern: (Show a flash card with a triangular pattern of six dots) Draw from memory exactly what you saw.

Length (ruler): (Show a drawing of a long thin rectangle) Imagine this strip is a ruler. Draw as many things as you can remember about a ruler.

Picture graph: (Show a table of data) There are 7 dogs, 5 cats, and 3 birds. Finish drawing the graph to show the number of animals.

Fig. 3.5 Some structural tasks for Grade 1 children (Mulligan et al., 2004)

of a correct and replicable unit of repeat, which is central to any structural arrangement involving objects and sets of objects.

Finally, students in the *full stage of structural development* exhibit responses that represent an organized, exact (vs. approximate), and integrated interplay of all the relevant structural features (i.e. numerical count and spatial arrangement) that are consistent and valid in their respective contexts. For example, a student drew on paper an exact copy of the triangular pattern with six dots that was initially presented to him or her on a flash card.

In a series of articles that have been drawn from their longitudinal studies with middle school students, Rivera and Becker (2011) document the existence of several different types of *full algebraically useful structures* relative to figural pattern generalization tasks (e.g. Fig. 3.6). Figural patterns involve shapes as the primary objects of generalization. As with all shapes in mathematics, they are analyzed in terms of subconfigurations or parts or components that operate or make sense within some interpreted structures. Hence, the term *full algebraically useful structure* fulfills all the requirement of a full stage of structural development and the additional constraint that an interpreted structure can be captured by a variable-based explicit equation, that is, a formula in function or closed form.

Depending on how individual students perceive a figural pattern, students' algebraically useful structures can either be constructive or deconstructive at least in the initial abductive stage of the structuring process. *Constructive* indicates the abductive action in which they see a particular stage in a pattern as consisting of nonoverlapping parts that form an interpreted stable shape when they are added together. The same action is then applied within and across the stages in the pattern. *Deconstructive* involves seeing overlapping parts that can be decomposed rather conveniently. For example, Ricky relative to the Fig. 3.1a pattern figurally parsed each stage along three disjoint parts that enabled him to express his incipient generalizations in four ways as shown in Figs. 3.1c, 3.1d, and 3.1e. Another example involves Pattern 1 in Fig. 3.6 in which a constructive generalization can mean seeing an initial forward slash diagonal side that then grows by consistently adding a set of two segments per stage number completing a triangle (i.e. stage 1 has 1 segment and 1 set of 2 segments to form the first triangle, stage 2 has 1 segment and 2 sets of 2 segments forming two adjacent triangles, stage 3 has 1 segment and 3 sets of 2 segments to form a chain of three adjacent triangles, and so on), which leads to the direct formula $S = 1 + 2n$, where n refers to any stage number and S pertains to the total number of segments in stage n of the pattern. Also, in Pattern 1 of Fig. 3.6, a deconstructive generalization can involve initially seeing a chain of adjacent triangles that overlap along a shared side beginning with stage 2 of the pattern (i.e. stage 1 consists of 1 triangle with 3 sides, stage 2 consists of 2 adjacent triangles with 1 overlapping side, stage 3 consists of a chain of 3 triangles with 2 overlapping sides, etc.), which leads to the direct formula $S = 3n - (n - 1)$. In both cases of generalizing, it is assumed that the figural pattern grows linearly with a horizontal structure that resembles a bridge.

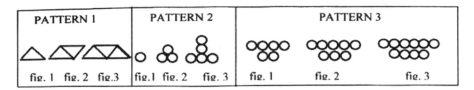

Fig. 3.6 Figural patterns used in Radford's studies on generalization (Radford, 2000, p. 83)

When transformed in algebraic form, constructive and deconstructive generalizations can be expressed in either standard or nonstandard form. *Standard form* means the terms in the corresponding direct expression are already in simplified form, whereas *nonstandard form* means the terms can still be simplified. For example, the formula $S = 1 + 2n$ is a constructive standard generalization, while $S = 3n - (n - 1)$ exemplifies a deconstructive nonstandard generalization. Two more examples are taken from Chua and Hoyles's (2011) empirical study with Singapore secondary school students (mean age of 13 years). Clark's numerical-based method 3 and Dawn's figural-based method 4 in Fig. 3.7 exemplify constructive nonstandard generalizations. Clark transformed the visual task numerically in the form of a structuring table, while Dawn saw each stage in her pattern as consisting of the union of three distinguishable configurations.

In a few reported cases of pattern generalization tasks, some older students have been documented to be engaging in *auxiliary-driven generalizing,* which involves seeing and/or configuring a figural stage in a pattern in the context of a more familiar pattern that has either a simpler or well-known structure. Figure 3.8a shows a US eighth-grade student's auxiliary-based constructive nonstandard generalization of the given pattern and Fig. 3.8b illustrates an auxiliary-driven generalization relative to the classic triangular number pattern. Tamara in Fig. 3.8a initially imagined 4 groups of n stars that emanated from a fixed middle star, which enabled her to construct the expression $4n+1$. She then took away one group of n circles since those circles were not a part of the original stages, which led to establish her nonstandard direct formula, $S=4n+1-n$. In Fig. 3.8b, several students constructed two copies of the same stage to form a rectangle with dimensions n and $(n+1)$, which then enabled them to eventually infer the formula, $S(n)=n\,(n+1)/2$. Ben's method 2 in Fig. 3.7 exemplifies another auxiliary-based generalization in which case he initially saw the stages as representing a growing rectangle with dimensions $3\times(n+3)$, which also meant adding 4 squares to complete each rectangle and then taking them away in the final count since they were not part of the original stages of the pattern.

Drawing on their empirical work with secondary school students and teachers, Chua and Hoyles (2010, 2011) also extrapolate the scheme underlying *transformation-based generalizations*, which involves initially performing actions

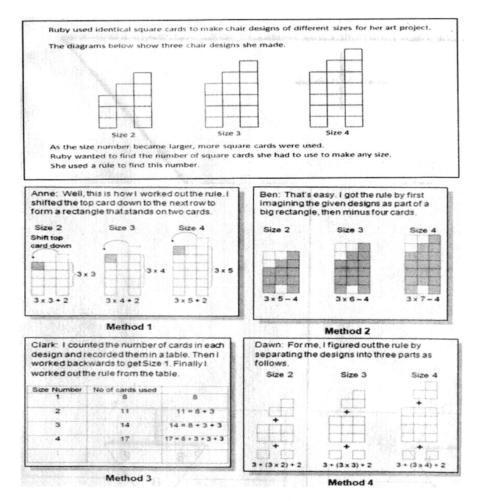

Fig. 3.7 Secondary students' generalizations of the high chair patterning task (Chua & Hoyles, 2011)

of moving, reorganizing, and transforming parts or subconfigurations in a figural stage of a pattern into some recognizable figure that has a more familiar or well-known structure. Anne's method 1 in Fig. 3.7 illustrates a transformation-based generalization in which case she interpreted each stage in the pattern in terms of a growing $3 \times (n+1)$ squares and 2 square legs, where n refers to size number.

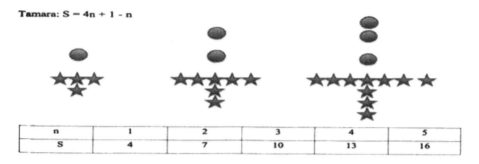

Tamara: $S = 4n + 1 - n$

n	1	2	3	4	5
S	4	7	10	13	16

Fig. 3.8a Eighth grader Tamara's auxiliary-driven generalization of the star pattern (Rivera & Becker, 2011, p. 359)

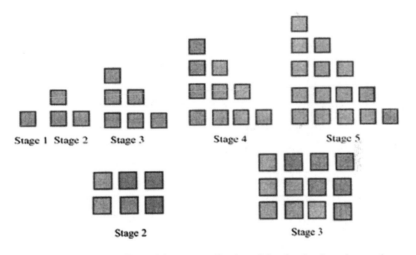

Fig. 3.8b Eighth graders' auxiliary-driven generalization of the classic triangular number pattern (Rivera, 2010a, pp. 316–317)

Attending to, or Being Aware of, Structure

The studies we discuss in this section address the fundamental epistemological issue of structure formation in patterning contexts. In particular, we are concerned about the context of its emergence. That is, should a structure be imposed first on the basis of a single generic case or should it be allowed to emerge over a larger domain? Küchemann (2010) captures this dilemma in terms of the generic versus sequential approach to patterning activity.

While Mulligan and her colleagues are able to categorize students' structures by type, Mason and colleagues (Mason, Stephens, & Watson, 2009; Watson, 2009) articulate a theoretical framework that focuses on different awareness levels or attentional states relative to structural discernment, appreciation, and formation. By a (mathematical) structure, they refer to general properties that are "instantiated in specific situations as relationships between elements" (Mason et al, 2009, p. 10), and elements encompass different types of mathematical objects from numbers and geometric figures to sets, relations on sets, and relations between relations. Structures are like general axioms that enable individual learners to deduce more specific properties. Hence, structural thinking is not a mere act of recognizing relationships and properties as it is more about employing it in their own thinking relative to (sets of) mathematical objects (e.g. figural and numerical patterns, functions, sets).

There are at least five attentional states that support the development of structural thinking, as follows:

1. Holding wholes (gazing);
2. Discerning details (making distinctions);
3. Recognizing relationships (among specific discerned elements);
4. Perceiving properties (as generalities which maybe instantiated in specific situations);
5. Reasoning on the basis of identified properties.

(Mason et al, 2009, p. 11)

Holding wholes involves a certain way of gazing that produces images that will undergo further analysis. need to be analyzed in more detail. In this awareness state, students basically "foreground and background structures inherent in [an] object of attention" (Watson, 2009, p. 219). Graphs of functions, for example, can be noticed primarily at the level of their notational forms and overall shape and direction.

Discerning details shifts the students' attention toward further analysis and deep description. Parts begin to be constructed and described in detail based on what they find meaningful to investigate. The content can focus on parts that either change or remain the same. Referring to the graphs of functions, they may investigate them for symmetry, number and nature of the calculated intercepts, changes in the graphs when coefficients are modified by domain, and so on and so forth.

Recognizing relationships happen when changing and invariant relationships are clearly delineated and analyzed more critically than before. Further, constructed (conceptual) relationships may be covarying, correlational, and/or causal along some dimensions. For example, graphs of linear functions can be categorized by the nature of their slopes, graphs of polynomial functions can be explained in terms of the parity nature of their corresponding degrees, and behaviors of algebraic and transcendental functions can be assessed for similarities and differences by investigating their symbolic and graphical representations.

Perceiving properties marks the transition toward explicating generalities (i.e. stable properties) that characterize the objects undergoing analysis and their implications to other kinds of objects. Having established the properties, this state enables a further categorization of different objects and "general classes of related objects" (Watson, 2009, p. 220).

Reasoning on the basis of the identified properties is the important phase in which inductive and abductive reasoning about specific objects and related objects transition into deductive reasoning by investigating what other instances may or may not belong to the perceived structure. Following a deductive model, structural understanding proceeds from the experiential to the formal, from generalizing within classes to abstracting that will include the most number of classes, and from the available objects to the generation and construction of "new objects and relations that might never be perceived except in the imagination" (Watson, p. 220).

For Noss, Healy, and Hoyles (1997), and, more recently, Küchemann (2010), structural awareness may need to occur first in situations or "environments in which the only way to manipulate and reconstruct [the relevant] objects is to express explicitly the relationships between them" (Noss et al., 1997, p. 207). In Mason et al.'s (2009) current terminologies, the starting point is *not* empirical counting but structural generalization. Küchemann (2010), especially, recommends the use of pattern generalization tasks that are *not always* presented "in the form of sequential elements" (see, for e.g., Fig. 3.5) because they are likely to engender empirical generalizations that may be "divorced" from structures that produce them in the first place. Ainley, Wilson, and Bills (2003) also point out that "term-by-term" patterns may "obscure the need for algebraic generalization" (p. 15). Küchemann (2010), thus, proposes the need for pattern generalization tasks that "can be tackled generically," say, by "inspecting a single generic case," where the primary focus of students' attention is "directly on the search for structure" (p. 242; see, for e.g., Figs. 3.9a and 3.9b) or equivalent structures that emerge due to the "semantically ambiguous nature" of the relevant symbolic expressions of generality (Samson, 2011; Samson & Schäfer, 2011). Noss et al (1997) are also critical of the empirical practice (i.e. *pattern spotting*) in which "playing with matches and thinking about the visual pattern will lead to algebra" (p. 206). For them, concrete actions on sticks and circles as an initial way of dealing with, say, the sequential stages of the patterns in Fig. 3.6 do not necessarily "push toward generality" and encourage the "need for mathematical expression" (p. 206).

Drawing on their case studies with two 12–13-year-old students in the UK who generalized in the context of a computer microworld, Noss et al. (1997) express the view in which "language as the mechanism for controlling objects" (in the dynamic microworld) can, in fact, "make the algebra of relationships between things semiformal, concrete, [and] meaningful" (p. 207). Hence, instead of presenting each pattern in Fig. 3.6 stage by stage, individual students can be presented first with a generic case, say, the fifth or a particular term(s) in a sequence (e.g. Figs. 3.9a and 3.9b). Such format can then motivate them to abduce a plausible general structure or "write a general procedure (i.e. a program)" (p. 211) that can "draw any term in the sequence …, [determine] how many matches would be needed …, [and] predict the number of matches for any terms of the sequence" (p. 214). The two students did not focus on the relevant numerical data. Instead, the "microworld's activity structure supported—perhaps even encouraged—a theoretical rather than a pragmatic approach, in which an elaboration of structure was a means to an (empirical) end, rather than an end in itself" (p. 230).

Steele and Johanning's (2004) work with eight US Grade 7 students around pattern generalization tasks that are similar to the ones that Küchemann (2010) recommends and those that Noss et al. (1997) used in their study is worth noting in this regard. Figures 3.9a and 3.9b show two of several tasks in Steele and Johanning's study. In Fig. 3.9a, the students in their study were provided only with a 3×3 grid

In the diagram a 3 x 3 grid of squares is colored so that only outside squares are shaded. This leaves one square on the inside that is not shaded and 8 squares that are shaded. If you had a 25 x 25 grid of squares and only the outside edge of squares are shaded, how many squares would be shaded? If n represents the number of squares on a side and you have all the outside squares of a n x n grid shaded, write an expression representing the total number of shaded squares in the figure.

Fig. 3.9a $N \times N$ square grid patterning task (Steele & Johanning, 2004, p. 74)

In the diagram below is a 5-dot triangle. It is a triangle made by using 5 dots on each side. The 5-dot triangle is made using a total of 12 dots. How many dots will be used to make a 13-dot triangle? If *n* represents the number of dots on each side of a *n*-dot triangle, write an expression to represent how many total dots are in the triangle?

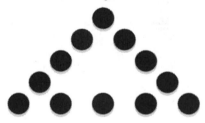

Fig. 3.9b N-dot triangle patterning task (Steele & Johanning, 2004, p. 75)

of squares in which case they needed to obtain a generalization for the total number of shaded outside squares in an $n \times n$ grid. In Fig. 3.9b, a 5-dot triangle was given with the same objective of developing a generalization for the total number of dots in the case of an n-dot triangle. While the subjects in Steele and Johanning's study performed the tasks in a paper-and-pencil environment, the authors underscore the need for students to build structural schemes in problem-solving situations that might be useful later in other situations of transfer. For example, seventh grader Cathy initially developed a deconstructive generalizing scheme in establishing her formula, $(N\cdot4) - 4 = \#$ of squares, for the pattern in Fig. 3.9a. Starting with the 3×3 grid, she counted 8 shaded outside squares. Next she drew a 4×4 grid, a 5×5 grid, followed by a 6×6 grid, and counted the totals in each case. She then made the following claims below based on the diagrams she drew.

> In a 25×25 grid, 96 squares would be shaded. I got this because there are 25 squares to a side. But 4 squares, the corner ones, are shared so you don't count them twice. I will use a smaller example to tell what I mean.
>
> If you count the corners twice, you get 12. If you don't, you get 8. …. So knowing this information, the formula is $(N \cdot 4) - 4 = \#$ of squares. You times n by 4 because a square has 4 sides that are all equal. You subtract 4 because the corners are shared (Steele & Johanning, 2004, p. 74)

When Cathy was later presented with the pattern in Fig. 3.9b, she drew on her initial experience with the pattern in Fig. 3.9a and applied the same deconstructive generalizing scheme in the case of the pattern in Fig. 3.9b, as follows:

> I looked at this problem and realized it was exactly like the problem I did last time only with a triangle instead of a square. The reason there are only 12 dots in the triangle … and 5 dots to a side is because you don't count the corners twice. You multiply the number of dots on a side times 3 because there are 3 sides in a triangle, and you subtract 3 because there are 3 corners in a triangle and they are shared. So for a 13-dot triangle there will be 36 dots $(13 \cdot 3) - 3 = 36$. So the formula is $(N \cdot 3) - 3 = \#$ of dots (Steele & Johanning, 2004, p. 75).

We should note, however, that studies conducted with some elementary school children indicate a predilection toward either "impos[ing] a pattern by modifying or ignoring some elements in a given configuration" (Lee & Freiman, 2004, p. 249) or engaging in narrow and, thus, invalid, specializing on a single case as a generic example. Among the 35 kindergarten Canadian children (ages 5–6 years) that Lee and Freiman (2004) interviewed, for example, 9 to12 of them interpreted the two patterns in Fig. 3.10 as repeating sequences with cycles 3 (i.e., the first three given stages) and 2 (i.e. alternating square and circle), respectively. Also, in the case of the pattern on the left, five of them used the successor property for whole numbers by drawing 6, 7, and 8 squares, while two others corrected the given pattern by filling in the missing terms (2 and 4 squares) and then continuing the stages by constantly adding 1 square for each new stage. Rivera (2010b) investigated 21 US second-grade students' patterning ability involving the two related open-ended patterning tasks shown in Figs. 3.11a and 3.11b. The students' extensions in the case of the Fig. 3.10 task specialized on the second step as the generic case without needing to establish a connection with the first step, which led them to their answers 4, 5, and 6 squares for steps 3, 4, and 5 in their emerging pattern that had no structure to start with other than the fact that the answers employed the successor property ("after 3 squares comes 4, then 5, and then 6"). Realizing that the Fig. 3.11a task might have been too difficult for them, the task was then modified so that instead of two steps they were given three steps in a growing L-shaped pattern as shown in Fig. 3.11b. The results show that most of them consistently ignored the first two steps and narrowly specialized on the third step with only 2 out of 21 students producing a reasonable structure for their emerging pattern. Dexter interpreted the task in terms of a growing L-shaped pattern beginning with step 1. When asked to determine step 10, he saw that "there are 10 across and 10 up." For Gerry, the initial three steps gave him the impression that 1 and 2 squares could be concatenated in an alternate manner to each column of squares that grew by the step number. He described his figural pattern in the following manner: "1, 2+1, 3+2, 4+1, 5+2, 6+1, 7+2, [and] 8+1."

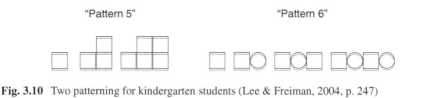

Fig. 3.10 Two patterning for kindergarten students (Lee & Freiman, 2004, p. 247)

Let us begin with a square and call it step 1.

Now suppose step 2 looks like as shown. How many squares do you see?

A. How might step 3 appear to you? Show me with the blocks.
B. Show me steps 4 and 5. How many squares do you see?
C. Pretend we don't have any more blocks and suppose we skip steps. If someone asks you how step 8 looks like, how might you respond? Can you describe or draw for me?
D. If someone asks you how step 10 looks like, how might you respond? Can you describe or draw for me?

Fig. 3.11a Open-ended patterning task for second-grade students (Rivera, 2010b, p. 84)

Let us begin with a square and call it step 1.

Now suppose steps 2 and 3 looks like as shown. How many squares do you see?

Step 2   Step 3

A. How might step 4 appear to you? Show me with the blocks.
B. Show me step 5. How many squares do you see?
C. If someone asks you how step 10 looks like, how might you respond? Can you describe or draw for me?

Fig. 3.11b Modified Fig. 3.11a patterning task for second-grade students (Rivera, 2010b, p. 84)

Modes of Representing Generalizations

The preceding three sections focused on issues surrounding structures in pattern generalization situations. In this and the next section we deal with matters that pertain to representing and expressing generalizations, in particular, algebraically useful generalizations. Among elementary school students, representing generalizations takes several different forms. Many of their generalizations occur in contexts that involve various aspects of the number sense strand of the elementary mathematics curriculum (Britt & Irwin, 2011; Carpenter, Franke, & Levi, 2003; Cooper & Warren, 2011; Empson & Levi, 2011; Kaput, Carraher, & Blanton, 2008; Norton & Hackenberg, 2010; Schliemann, Carraher, & Brizuela, 2007; van den Heuvel-Panhuizen, 2008). Bastable and Schifter (2008), for example, share a finding drawn from a US third-grade class in which the students established equivalent multiplication expressions for the number 36. Beginning with the arithmetical problem, "Kevin has three pencils in his desk with 12 pencils in each case. How many pencils does Kevin have?," the students' responses evolved from $3 \times 12 = 36$ to 6×6, 12×3, 3×12, 4×9, and 9×4. Suffice it to say, the arithmetical problem in the initial phase transitioned into a number patterning activity among the children. Further, a few students became interested in understanding the general significance of the commutative property for multiplication that motivated them to investigate and establish concretely with the use of unifix cubes following an array model of multiplication. In the same article, the authors note other episodes in which second- and third-grade students tried to make sense of the inverse relationship between addition and subtraction and the commutative property of addition by drawing on relevant "relationships that a set of number facts might exemplify" (p. 171).

Among elementary school children, Bastable and Schifter point out that they "use English, a natural language, to describe relationships that are more frequently expressed with algebraic formalisms" (p. 175). For example, a fourth-grade US student with some assistance articulated the following verbal observation regarding square numbers: "If you take two consecutive numbers, add the lower number and its square to the higher number, you get the higher number's square" (p. 173). While the fourth-grade class inductively verified the student's claim on two near cases (2 and 3; 7 and 8), they expressed their abductive proposition verbally. Bastable and Schifter (2008) also note a finding drawn from a US second-grade class in which the students conveyed their general understanding of square numbers in a verbal format. When they were asked to pay particular attention on their construction process, they expressed their written conclusions verbally (e.g.: "square numbers go odd, even, odd, even"; "if you times a square number by a square number, you get a square number"; "when you add a row at the bottom and a row to the side and make a corner, you get another square number").

Stacey and MacGregor (2001) articulate the importance and necessity of the "verbal description phase" in the "process of recognizing a function and expressing it algebraically" (p. 150). Based on their findings, they underscore students'

difficulties in "transitioning from a verbal expression to an algebraic rule," especially those "students with poor English skills" who are either unable to "construct
a coherent verbal description" or produce "verbal description[s that] cannot be [con-
veniently and logically] translated directly to algebra" (MacGregor & Stacey, 1992,
pp. 369–370). Bastable and Schifter note as well that the "ambiguities of natural
language may, at times, cause concern" (p. 175). For example, the following written
verbal generalization of a US second-grade student regarding square numbers, "take
any square number, add two zeros to it, and you will get another square number,"
uses the word "add" to convey a sense of "concatenating" rather than adding in an
operational sense (p. 175).

Recent research studies by Cooper and Warren (2011) and Britt and Irwin
(2011), however, highlight the significance of having students engage in *quasi-
generalization* processing or the use of *quasi-variables*, which basically involves
expressing generalizations "in terms of specific numbers and even to an example
of 'any number' before they can provide a generalization in language or symbols"
(Cooper & Warren, 2011, p. 193) or "thinking of numbers themselves as variables"
(Britt & Irwin, 2011, p. 152), respectively. For example, Cooper and Warren's
work with Australian Years 2–6 students (ages 6–10 years) on figural growth patterns indicates students' success in establishing quasi-generalizations from tables.
They also note that figural-driven quasi-generalizations produced "more equivalent solutions" and "better process generalizations [following Harel (2001)]"
(p. 197) than quasi-generalizations that relied on data tables alone (p. 198). In
Britt and Irwin's (2011) study, they found that a significant number of New
Zealand Year 8 prealgebra students (mean age of 12 years) that participated in a
numeracy project that emphasized algebraic-driven operational strategies were far
more successful than those who did not participate in the project when tested on
basic arithmetical tasks that had them transferring relevant knowledge in a variety
of situations and examples. The numeracy project primarily focused on "the
development of awareness of generality" (Britt & Irwin, p. 147) by emphasizing
both the construction of arithmetical relationships and the use of quasi-variables.
For example, project participants initially used a ten-frame to work out an answer
to, say, 9 + 3, that helped them produce an equivalent expression, say, 10 + 4. The
ten-frame with the 9 + 3 was also used to generate other equivalent expressions.
When instruction purposefully shifted to a discussion of the many different ways
in which arithmetical problems such as finding the sums of $29+3$, $37+8$, $146+9$,
and $4899+5$ could be processed, the students reflectively drew on their concrete
experiences with the ten-frame. Consequently, the reflective experience enabled
them to develop an underlying structure or generalization such as the additive
compensation strategy $a+b=(a+c)+(b-c)$ on the basis of how they manipulated
quasi-variables. In the reported empirical studies of Cooper and Warren (2011)
and Britt and Irwin (2011), the representational path toward the construction
of generalizations proceeds from using concrete models, then numbers as
quasi-variables, followed by words, and finally using literal symbols and variables
in algebra. That path seems to resemble a movement from the enactive and iconic
to the symbolic.

Concrete modeling in patterning activity prior to using quasi-variables is another way of representing a generalization. Figure 3.12 provides examples of concrete (geometric) models that illustrate several well-known mathematical generalizations. Katz (2007) especially notes the underscores the initial conceptual significance of geometry in the history of algebra, that is, "in the geometric stage, most of the concepts of algebra [were] geometric" (p. 186). Mesopotamian or Babylonian mathematicians some 4,000 years ago employed cut-and-paste geometry as their way of solving arithmetical problems that were algebraic in nature, which engendered Katz to ask:

> Should one begin the study of algebraic reasoning by using geometric figures? These are more concrete objects than the x's one usually uses. Squares could be exactly that. Products of numbers can be represented as rectangles. The distributive law is simply a statement about two different ways to represent a given rectangle. And so forth (Katz, 2007, p. 197).

There is an extensive body of research evidence that shows the important meditational role of various dynamic and interactive software in reifying generalizations (e.g.: Heid & Blume, 2008; Pedemonte, 2007; Rivera, 2007; Tabach, Arcavi, & Hershkowitz, 2008; Wilson, Ainley, & Bills, 2005; Yerushalmy, 1993). We note a few examples. Rivera (2007) documents ways in which a group of US precalculus secondary students used a TI-89 to develop generalizations regarding the behaviors of odd- and even-powered polynomial functions. Pedemonte (2007) illustrates a cognitive unity thesis by drawing on the thinking of Grades 12 and 13 students in France and Italy who used their experiences with the dragging function of Cabri Geometry to establish a continuous relationship between conjecturing and proving. Tabach et al's (2008) 2-year study with two cohorts of Grade 7 students in Israel demonstrates the emergence of and growth in students' generalizations in a computer-intensive environment that used spreadsheets from representations that relied on computer-based strategies to nonnumerical recursive and explicit symbolic generalizations.

While Radford's categories of factual and contextual generalizations in the next section underscore the significance of context-bound representations in the case of older children's pattern generalizations involving figural sequences of objects, Bastable and Schifter (2008) articulate their concern regarding contextual generalizations and the relevant domains that younger children develop and produce in activities that initially draw on their everyday experiences. For example, a US first-grade class was asked to develop conjectures in relation to the "Snow Ball" parity task in which snowmen could only come with a partner. Some of the responses were as follows: "Each time you add one number to a group that can go, you get a group that can't"; "If you add two to a number that could go, you got another even number"; "if you added two groups that couldn't go, you would get a group that could." Bastable and Schifter (2008) note that with such responses, it would not be easy to "determine whether their reasoning is limited to the given context or if they are thinking in more general terms about odd and even numbers" (p. 177). The domain could also be a potential problem since generalizations involving, say, zero and rational number operations oftentimes require "the need to develop new tools, models, and criteria of justification" (p. 181). The issue of domain came about in several

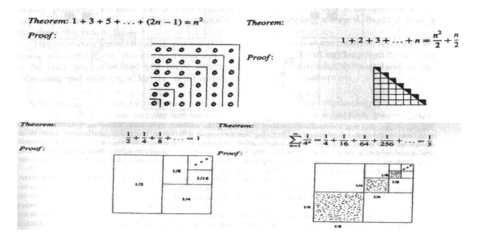

Fig. 3.12 Concrete (geometric) models involving well-known mathematical generalizations (Brown, 1997)

elementary classes in which different groups of students found themselves asking whether 0 was a square number (in a fifth-grade class), whether 0 was even or odd (in a third-grade class), and whether a unit fraction of some whole number necessitated the use of the operation of multiplication and why (in a sixth-grade class).

Ainley et al (2003) investigated the significance of context and calculations in the representations of pattern generalizations among two high school groups of UK students (ages 11–12 years) that participated in clinical interviews conducted near the end of their first year of schooling. Figure 3.13a shows the patterning task that the authors analyzed in some detail in their reported study. Unlike the patterning tasks shown in Figs. 3.1a and 3.6, Fig. 3.13a involves a context, that is, chairs and tables that have been arranged in a particular way in a school dining room. Further, Fig. 13.3a contains only a single image instead of the usual presentation of sequences of consecutive stages such as the ones shown in Figs. 3.1a and 3.6. Ainley et al. (2003) found that the students' generalizations in the case of Fig. 3.13a fell under two different categories. One set of verbal statements provided general descriptions of an inferred context (e.g. "two on each table except for the ends, which is three," "for every table there's two chairs plus the other two that are on the end"). The other set of verbal statements utilized arithmetical calculations in order to obtain the total number of chairs that were needed for any number of tables (e.g. "just how many tables double that, and then, plus two for the ends," "you take the tables and you times it by two and then plus two"). The authors note that some students who generalized on context alone experienced difficulty in obtaining total counts because the complexity of their verbal descriptions did not easily translate into algebraically useful expressions. In such cases, their context-based responses were narrowly confined to their favored ways of seeing in which case they also found other possibilities to be confusing and distracting. However, those students who generalized by drawing on both context and calculations were easily able to articulate justifiable direct expressions. Thus, Ainley et al. (2003) write, "generaliz[ing a] context is not sufficient to enable students to express relationships [symbolically] in algebra-like notation(s), and that generaliz[ing] the calculations that are required is a significant bridge that [can] support [them] in constructing meaning for a symbolic expression of the [inferred] relationships" (p. 13). Further, the transition in generalizing from context to calculation can be done by, say, "adding an element to the task which signals clearly the need to describe a calculation (such as 'Could you tell the caretaker how to work out how many chairs should get out of the storeroom?')" (p. 15).

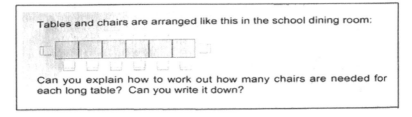

Fig. 3.13a The tables and chairs patterning task (Ainley et al., 2003, p. 11)

Ellis (2007) also addressed the issues of context and domain in generalizing in her work with 7 US Grade 7 prealgebra students. They initially explored linear relationships in two everyday situations involving speed and gear ratios. They used physical gears in performing the ratios activity and the SimCalc Mathworlds program in making sense of speed. Based on the students' responses and the teacher's prompts in various aspects of the two activities, their pattern generalizations underwent a conceptual evolution from thinking about them as number patterns (in discrete terms) to situating them in the context of quantitative relationships (in continuous terms), which eventually supported and "encouraged the development of more powerful general principles related to linearity" (Ellis, p. 223). For Ellis, asking students to prove, appropriate to their level of proficiency, could be "a way to help [them] generalize more effectively, rather than as an act that necessarily follows generalization" (Ellis, 2007, p. 224). Further, Ellis underscored the importance of problem-solving situations that "focus on relationships between quantities instead of number patterns or procedures alone" since the former are more likely than the later to support powerful and productive pattern generalizations.

Beyond concrete and verbal forms of representations, another documented way of generalizing at both the elementary and secondary levels involves the use of tables, which has emerged to be a controversial issue especially when discussed in the context of figural pattern generalization (e.g.: Cooper & Warren, 2011; Küchemann, 2010; Rivera, 2011; Swafford & Langrall, 2000). Carraher, Martinez, and Schliemann (2008), for example, initially asked a group of US Grade 3 students (ages 8–9 years) to use the data table of values shown in Fig. 3.13b in order to help them make sense of the Separated Dinner Tables patterning task and eventually obtain a direct expression for the pattern. The students' constructed generalizations ranged from additive-arithmetical to multiplicative-arithmetical generalizations (e.g. repeatedly adding 4 or multiplying the number of dinner tables by 4 to obtain the total count of people). Vale and Pimentel (2010) also used tables in assisting their Grade 3 participants from Portugal to obtain a generalization for the Lace patterning task shown in Fig. 3.14a. However, they thought that tables from patterns that only show totals tend to encourage students to recursively discover outputs by a process of differencing. Unfortunately, such processes "do not allow an understanding of the structure of the patterns" (p. 245). In lieu of differencing, they proposed a multi-representational approach that uses words, mathematical language, and a structural generalizing table of values, which enable students to focus on relationships that could be translated in variable form as direct expressions. Figure 3.14b shows the structuring table and the concrete model that the students eventually produced when they reappropriated the Fig. 3.14a task in contexts that were more meaningful to them (see Clark's method 3 in Fig. 3.7 for another example of a structural generalizing table).

Swafford and Langrall's (2000) study with a group of US Grade 6 students on pattern-related algebraic tasks also addressed the issue of student-generated tables and presented tables. They note that presented tables appear to "be more of a

Handout: Detached Tables

Name: _____

In your restaurant, a maximum of four people can sit at each <u>dinner table</u>.

Fill in the following <u>data table</u>.

If you know the number of tables, figure out the <u>maximum number of people</u> you can seat.

If you already know the number of people, figure out the <u>minimum number of tables</u> you need.

Number of Dinner Tables	Show How	Number of People
1	1 × 4 ⟶	
2	2 × 4 ⟶	
3	⟶	
4	⟶	
	⟵	24
	⟵	20
	⟵	11

How many people can you seat at **t** tables? [hint: More than **t** people? Less than **t** people? Exactly **t** people?]

How many tables do you need to seat **n people**? [hint: More than **n** tables? Less than **n** tables? Exactly **n** tables?]

Fig. 3.13b   Separated dinner tables patterning task (Carraher et al., 2008, p. 9)

distraction than an aid [and] divert students' focus from the context of the problem to a string of numbers" (p. 107). Tanish's (2011) study with four Grade 5 students (mean age of 11 years) in Turkey focused on the content and quality of their linear functional thinking on 16 decontextualized numerical patterning tasks that were all presented in data tables such as the one shown in Fig. 3.14a. Clinical interviews were conducted after a teaching experiment on the topic. In lieu of variables and verbal descriptions, the two columns of values in each data table were assigned the triangle and square symbols that conveyed input and output, respectively. In the first part of the interview, Tanish found that even if the students could efficiently use (a vertical) differencing strategy to establish a linear pattern, they were unable to

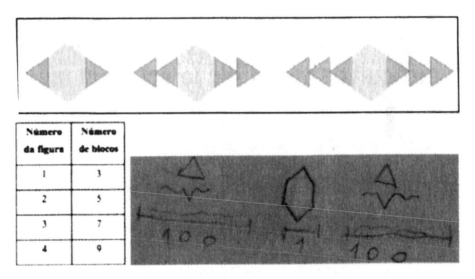

Número da figura	Número de blocos
1	3
2	5
3	7
4	9

Fig. 3.14a Lace patterning task and the initial table of values (Vale & Pimentel, 2010, p. 245)

Número da figura	Número de blocos
1	$1+1+1=1+2\times1$
2	$1+2+2=1+2\times2$
3	$1+3+3=1+2\times3$
4	$1+4+4=1+2\times4$
...	...
100	$1+100+100=1+2\times100$

Fig. 3.14b Reappropriated lace patterning task and structuring table (Vale & Pimentel, 2010, p. 245)

"produce a formula expressing the functional relation" (Tanish, p. 212). Also, even with a second numerical generalizing strategy—that is, a two-step process that first uses a within-row (horizontal) differencing strategy between independent and dependent values and then adds or subtracts a number (corresponding to the independent value) that matches all the dependent values—they were still unable to establish a functional rule. In the second part of the interview, however, with more indirect questioning from the interviewer, the students' thinking transitioned from the recursive to a variety of functional modes. Tanish's study further illustrates complex numerical methods that students tend to exhibit when they try to establish generalizations from data tables that merely indicate linear functions and nothing else by way of meaningful contexts.

Patterning contexts vary, of course, and in this particular case we discuss linear functions as instances of numerical patterns that can be naturally described and expressed in several different representational formats (symbolic, graphical, verbal, tabular, etc.). Nathan and Kim (2007) investigated US sixth-, seventh-, and eighth-grade students' performance on discrete and continuous linear function models that have been conveyed in graphical and verbal forms. Discrete linear function tasks pertain to problem situations in which individual given instances are explicitly stated and assumed to be related in some way, while continuous linear functions convey problem situations that have a continuous relationship among the relevant quantities. Figure 3.15a is an example of a discrete linear function task, where the top box lists the individual cases in words and the bottom box represents its corresponding graphical representation. Figure 3.15b is an example of a continuous linear function task, where the top box contains the verbal rule that describes the associated graphical representation in the bottom box. Each function task is also accompanied by three subtasks, namely: determine a near prediction output (i.e., a near generalization patterning task); calculate the value of a far prediction output (i.e. a far generalization patterning task); and establish a closed formula for the function.

Results of Nathan and Kim's (2007) empirical study show that the sixth-grade group was adept at far prediction, the seventh-grade group dealt with both far prediction and formula construction on similar levels of proficiency, and the eighth-grade group produced more correct formulas than far predictions. The authors also note that while both the sixth- and seventh-grade groups employed similar generalizing processes in dealing with both far prediction and formula construction tasks, the eighth-grade group found the formula construction tasks easier than calculating far prediction tasks in both discrete and continuous contexts. Further, they point out that across grade level the students were more successful in situations when the function tasks appeared to them in continuous form (i.e., as verbal rules and line graphs) than in situations when similar tasks were presented in discrete form (i.e. in the form of a list of cases and point-wise graphs). Finally, the authors underscore the fact that those students who were provided with both verbal and graphical forms for representing linear functions outperformed those students who were exposed to either representation alone.

One important strand of research findings involving figural patterning activity addresses the symbolic and numeric modes of representing the interpreted generalizations. For example, Clark in Fig. 3.7 re-represented the figural task numerically, while Anne, Ben, and Dawn in Fig. 3.7 consistently employed a figural abductive strategy. Research results from around the globe, as a matter of fact, echo the consistent finding that some students have a tendency to construct numerical-based generalizations for figural patterns such as those shown in Figs. 3.1a and 3.6 with varying levels of success in the aspects of justification and transfer (Bishop, 2000; Cañadas & Castro, 2007; Garcia, Benitez, & Ruiz, 2010; Garcia-Cruz & Martinón, 1998; Küchemann, 2010; Lin, Yang, & Chen, 2004; MacGregor & Stacey, 1992; Samson & Schäfer, 2009; Stacey, 1989; Stacey & MacGregor, 2001; Tanisli & Özdas, 2009). Rivera and Becker's (2011) 3-year study with a US middle school cohort (from grades 6 through 8, ages 11–14 years) documents the negative effects of differencing

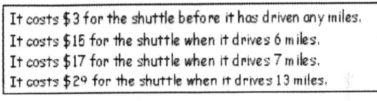

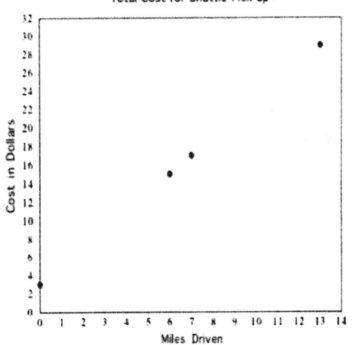

Fig. 3.15a Discrete linear patterning task in words and in graphical form (Nathan & Kim, 2007, p. 201)

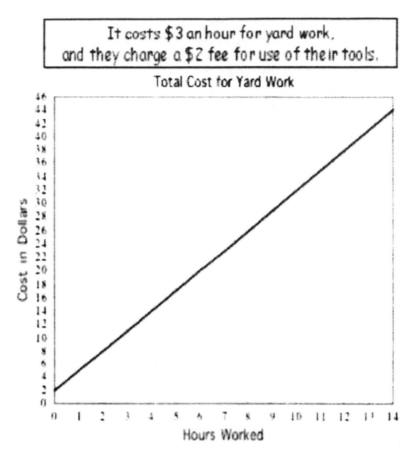

Fig. 3.15b Continuous linear patterning task in words and in graphical form (Nathan & Kim, 2007, p. 201)

on the participants' ability to justify algebraically useful generalizations involving linear figural patterns. *Differencing* is a numerical strategy that involves initially establishing a common difference between pairs of consecutive outputs, which then becomes the basis for constructing a direct formula. For example, in Fig. 3.14a, the data table could be used to establish a linear pattern with common difference of 2 that would then encourage students to construct the formula $T = 2n + 1$, where T refers to the total number of objects and n stands for the figure number. In many cases, however, the nature of justification also shifts from the figural to the numerical. That is, instead of using the stages to explain the validity of a constructed direct formula, they are likely to employ *formula appearance match*, a numeric-based empirical verification strategy that involves merely fitting the formula onto the corresponding generated data table without regard to how it might explain the structure of the stages in the first place. Rivera and Becker (2011) also document how differencing as a numerical generalizing strategy does not easily transfer to other patterning contexts such as those that involve negative common differences (e.g. decreasing linear patterns) and nonlinear order differences (e.g. quadratic patterns exemplify second-order differences).

Levels of Understanding Structure-Driven Algebraically Useful Generalizations

In this section, we focus on algebraically useful generalizing that involves the construction and justification of direct expressions, closed formulas, or explicit equations (between two variables of interest that co-vary in some way) in some interpreted structural context. While Lee (1996) has certainly popularized the felicitous phrase, *algebraically useful*, we also point out a historical dimension regarding the significance of function-based representations. There has been a sustained interest in expressing solutions of equations and descriptions of motions in explicit form in various conceptual stages of the subject in the history of algebra (Katz, 2007). In the culminating stage, especially, which Katz has referred to as the structural phase, objects and their relationships were defined and manipulated in the context of an axiomatic system. Hence in alignment with this particular conceptual legacy algebraically useful generalizations in patterning activity and the relevant notations emerge in interpreted and valid structures that shape their meanings and usage.

In a series of papers, Radford (1999, 2000, 2001a, 2001b, 2003, 2006) empirically demonstrates the semiotic emergence of direct or closed expressions in the context of culturally mediated activity. Semiotic emergence refers to ways in which expressions of generalizations come about "in processes of sign use" (Radford, 1999, p. 90) at least initially with others (teachers, students) in joint activity using readily available tools and processes (e.g. shared language, notations, and practices). Results of his longitudinal study with a cohort of 120 Grade 8 students and their 6 teachers in Canada over the course of 3 years of classroom research indicate the existence of the following three types of direct expressions in the context of figural pattern generalization tasks: *factual*; *contextual*; and *symbolic*. The patterns in Fig. 3.6 were three of several figural pattern generalization tasks that Radford used in his studies with the students, and his protocol had them constructing near generalizations (i.e., stages 9 and below) and far generalizations (i.e., stages 10 and up) prior to conveying a generalization for any stage or figure number in the pattern.

Like Mason et al (2009) in the preceding section, Radford distinguishes between arithmetical generalization (empirical counting) and algebraic generalization (structural generalization). For example, one way of obtaining the total number of toothpicks that would form stage 25 of Pattern 1 in Fig. 3.6 involves the painstaking recursive process of counting toothpicks figure after figure up to stage 25, which exemplifies an arithmetical counting strategy. However, algebraic strategies are likely to encourage more efficient nonrecursive modes of counting because the primary source is rooted in an interpreted multiplicative structure of a pattern and its parts (i.e. parts are themselves seen as multiplicative units in an emerging structure of the pattern). Having such a structure, Mason et al. (2009) point out, yields the same effect as initially drawing on axioms in order to make sense of resulting propositions relevant to some (sets of) objects and their relationships.

In the context of figural pattern generalization, Radford's initial layer of structural generalization is *factual*, that is, it is "a generalization of numerical actions in the form of an operational scheme (in a neo-Piagetian sense) that remains bound to the numerical level, nevertheless allowing the students to virtually tackle any particular case successfully" (Radford, 2001b, pp. 82–83). So, for example, one group of Grade 8 students in his study noticed that since the first two stages in Pattern 1 of Fig. 3.6 seem to follow the sense "it's always the next … $1+2$, $2+3$," they then imposed the factual structure of "25 plus 26" in the case of stage 25 of the pattern. The next structural layer called contextual generalization involves replacing any reference to particular stages, including rhythm and pointing, with "linguistic-objectifying" actions. Here the multiplicative dimension pertains to the two growing composite parts corresponding to the top and bottom rows of circles (vs. the additive strategy of a count all in which case circles are counted one by one and from stage to stage). Ricky's incipient generalizations in Fig. 3.1b also exemplify factual generalizations. Such generalizations are oftentimes accompanied by the use of adverbs such as "the next" or "always," including the effects of rhythm of an utterance and movement (e.g. a pointing gesture). While perhaps necessary in the beginning stage of generalizing, unfortunately, factual generalizations remain context bound and numerical and oftentimes draw on shared "implicit agreements and mutual comprehension" (ibid, p. 83) among those who construct them in social activity.

The next structural layer called contextual generalization involves replacing any reference to particular stages, including rhythm and pointing, with "linguistic-objectifying" actions that are performed not on a concrete stage but at the abstract level. For example, the terms "add," "the figure," and "the next figure" in reference to the stages in Pattern 1 of Fig. 3.6 replace factual actions that depend heavily on context. In contextual generalizations, "the abstract object appears as being objectified through a refined term pointing to a non-materially present concrete object through a discursive move that makes the structure of relevant events visible" (Radford, 2001b, p. 84). However, such abstract objects remain context-based on the particularities of the relevant concrete objects, hence the use of the category "abstract deictic objects." That is, while the operational schemes have undergone objectification and the objects have transitioned into their abstract form, however, they are still connected to both the positional features and the individual(s) that made them possible in the first place.

The third, and final, structural phase of *symbolic generalization* exemplifies what Radford classifies as an algebraic generalization. *Contra* contextual generalizations, symbolic or algebraic generalizations have overcome their spatial-temporal character; that is, they are "unsituated and temporal" and disembodied or desubjectified objects (Radford, 2001b, p. 86). The use of letters marks an entry into algebraic generalization. For example, in Pattern 1 of Fig. 3.6, a student eventually suggested and justified the formula $(n+n)+1$, where the variable n is viewed in the context of an impersonal voice that has overcome the spatial, temporal, and positional constraint in a contextual generalization. Further, desubjectification or disembodiment marks a further stage in algebraic generalization, where symbolic expressions $(n+n)+1$ and $(n+1)+n$ in the context of Pattern 1 in Fig. 3.6 are not seen as different but equivalent actions. The full stage necessitates a total decentration of such actions, where the dual relation between subject and object is "shattered" and the variables seen as "objects in a different way" and bearing "a different kind of existence" that is not "haunted" by the "phantom of the students' actions" (ibid, p. 87).

Radford notes that the entry to variable-based generaliing does not necessarily convey meaningful algebraic generalizations. This claim underscores his much larger view in which the presence and use of letters do not necessarily "amount to doing algebra," that "just as not all symbolization is algebraic, not all patterning activity leads to algebraic thinking" (Radford, 2006, p. 3). There are students, for example, who produce symbolic generalizations on the basis of some "procedural mechanism" following a "trial-and-error" heuristic that they are sometimes unable to explain beyond the response "Uh .... because it works!" on the basis of a number of additional extensional generalizations (Radford, 2000, p. 82; Radford (2006) categorizes this process as *naïve induction*). Also, there are those who produce recursively additive formulas (in the form Next=Current+Common Difference, which Radford (2006) classifies as *arithmetical generalizations*), however, they are unable to use them correctly when confronted with a far generalization task. Even in situations when some students are able to verbalize regularities and talk about the general through the particular in some cases their underlying understanding of the pattern under investigation appears to remain at either the iconical or indexical level in which case they are oftentimes unable to establish equivalent structures. Suffice it to say, pattern generalizations that yield variable-based generalizations depend significantly on the context in which individual learners understand variables and, more generally, sign use.

From a psychological context, one's embodied apprehension of such objects can either hinder or support understanding (Samson & Schäfer, 2011). Samson (2011) and Rivera and Becker (2011) note the "inherent [and subtle] ambiguities in [the structure of] symbolic expressions of generality" (Samson, 2011, p. 28). For example, in year 2 of Rivera and Becker's (2011) 3-year study with middle school students involving linear patterns, a number of US Grade 7 students (mean age of 12 years) who learned more about the commutative property for multiplication interpreted the expressions $a \times b$ and $b \times a$ as referring to the same grouping of objects, which confused some of them who generalized numerically from a data table and tried to justify their structures relative to the patterns. Also, drawing on their study with a group of Grade 9 students in South Africa, Samson and Schäfer (2011) pointed out that the variable expression $2(n+1)$ in reference to the pattern in Fig. 3.16 could in fact be interpreted either as 2 groups of $(n+1)$ segments or as $(n+1)$ copies of 2 segments. The recommendation, of course, is not to prevent such situations from occurring but to encourage classroom discourse in ways that enable learners to "validate multiple visually mediated interpretations" of such patterns resulting from the "always-already" embodied nature of generalizing. Hence, perception should be seen in a central role in any account of structural generalization—that is, in Samson and Schäfer's (2011) words, while perception is "critically related to the manner of one's interaction with perceptual objects, it also remains sensitive to both the phenomenological and semiotic aspects of the generalization process" (p. 42).

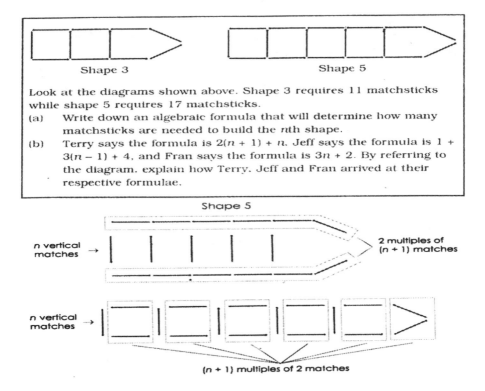

Look at the diagrams shown above. Shape 3 requires 11 matchsticks while shape 5 requires 17 matchsticks.

(a)   Write down an algebraic formula that will determine how many matchsticks are needed to build the nth shape.

(b)   Terry says the formula is $2(n + 1) + n$. Jeff says the formula is $1 + 3(n - 1) + 4$, and Fran says the formula is $3n + 2$. By referring to the diagram. explain how Terry. Jeff and Fran arrived at their respective formulae.

Fig. 3.16 A patterning task for Grade 9 students (Samson, 2011)

Toward a Theory of Graded Pattern Generalization

Performing pattern generalization is a complex act due to individual learner differences in, and the simultaneous layering of, processes that pertain to constructing, expressing, and justifying interpreted structures. Each time learners such as Ricky in the introduction confront a pattern generalization task, they will always need to navigate through the different regions shown in Fig. 3.2, and any path is never smoothly linear but graded due to learning (i.e. more training) and experience. If, for instance, Ricky did not acquire an appropriate understanding of multiplication, his incipient generalization might have been limited to either mere additive thinking or the use of a simple arithmetical counting strategy involving recursion ("keep adding x," a rather inefficient multiplicative strategy).

Attending to structures occur at different levels and develop in different ways with and without formal pedagogical intervention. If there is one convergent observation that can be inferred on the studies we have discussed and highlighted in this chapter, it may very well be the case that the difference between an easy or familiar pattern and a nonroutine or unfamiliar pattern is fundamentally a matter of graded paths of connectedness that individual learners develop over time. Further, the frequently noted pedagogical reflection regarding multiple entry points in pattern generalization significantly and ultimately depends on individual learners' (semiotic) contexts and the inputs they recruit to help them build structures that they consider meaningful and appropriate. Certainly, the hidden layer (p. 20), which is not directly influenced by either the relation or input layer, mediates in the generalizing process. Instruction, however, is a type of cultural mediation that makes the generalizing process more equitable for all learners.

The difficult reality, of course, is that pattern generalization performance will always manifest different and, in most cases, parallel and dynamical forms of cognitive processing based on a complex of known and unanticipated factors. That is, the comportment of any interpreted structure is basically a function of its emergence in an individual learner's complex system, from his or her apprehensions to meanings that he or she infers on the limited external representations that so often characterize pattern generalization activity. Hence, the primary issue in pattern generalization is not about whether students can generalize but how teachers can design and sustain learning experiences that will enable them to have the ability to choose necessarily and sufficiently optimal connections between inputs, relations, and representations on the one hand, and outputs, on the other hand.

Figure 1.10 (p. 20) shows an example of a parallel network model involving a performance on a pattern generalization task. The network consists of at least three major independent layers, where each layer is assigned a particular function or role in the pattern generalization process. While the process begins with a paired set of input and relation units, within-layer units acquire changing probable values based on learning. Consequently, ongoing changes in the values enable the construction of multiple, dynamic, and parallel pathways or connections. Thus, it is normal for individual learners to construct several generalizations on a single pattern before they finally choose the most reasonable one for them. The flexibility of the network relations, more generally, allows the possibility of several different manifestations of pattern generalization processing, which initially relies on a given input/relation pair. So, for example, a student can exhibit PPG and RPG simultaneously at first that might then evolve into either type with more learning. Also, frequent exposure on familiar patterning tasks is likely to strengthen and stabilize desired connections among the units. However, a single unfamiliar or nonroutine patterning task can also engender different or new connections.

While the preceding sections in this chapter might have given the impression that structures and their representations in the context of pattern generalization activity evolve and progress in a fixed stage-like manner, that is not necessarily the case. What we do know for sure is that most, if not all, the studies took place in the context of some habituation activity (e.g. intervening teaching experiment, exposure to sample items in an interview, joint activity between teacher and student), which means that ideal closures emerged in purposeful activity. For example, while transitions in direct formula construction from the factual, then to the contextual, and finally to the algebraic may have taken place among students in pattern generalization activity, it remains unclear whether students are able to retain their algebraic ability through several different kinds of patterning tasks.

Many of the claims and recommendations drawn from existing patterning studies are worth assessing in more detail through further research. For example, it has been recommended that classroom tasks avoid sequential forms of patterning tasks in favor of a generic approach involving one, or at most two, instances or stages. However, there is no sufficient empirical evidence that the approach will guarantee that the patterning process will always yield algebraically useful structural generalizations. Besides some patterning tasks are better stated with sequential stages than otherwise. Another recommendation involves minimizing the use of data tables and graphs with discrete data points in favor of more structuring tables and continuous graphs. However, all forms can support high-level pattern generalization provided they are accompanied by a sufficiently rich context, mathematical and otherwise (e.g. having a strong conceptual understanding of mathematical relationships, equal emphasis on both construction and justification aspects, purposeful cooperative activity in a Vygotskian sense). A third recommendation that encourages the practice of exposing students to all forms of representations at the same time deserves further research and investigation.

One of our many interests in this book involves examining the nature of the patterning tasks that students have to deal with, which justifies the proposed theory of graded representations that we explore in greater detail in the next chapter. Well-defined patterning tasks enable students to construct and justify valid mathematical relationships from them in a systematic manner. However, all patterns are inherently ambiguous due to incomplete data, which means that individual learners have to make them well defined first, say, by imposing a structure on them in order for meaningful generalization to occur. But we should note that a graded representational view of pattern generalization such as the one shown in Fig. 1.10 (p. 20) situates the emergence of an interpreted structure—or multiple structures for that matter—in terms of "cooperative and competitive" (Plaut, McClelland, Seindenberg, & Patterson, 1996, p. 56) interactions within a network that draws on a large number of units within and across layers. Since the network learns over time, interactions change and evolve with more training, which in computational terms means that "weights on connection between units" adjust based on "the statistical structure of the environment [that] influences the behavior of the network" (Plaut et al, 1996, p. 56). Further, Plaut et al (1996) note that

> there is no sharp dichotomy between the items that obey the rules and the items that don't. Rather, all items coexists within a single system whose representations and processing reflect the relative degree of *consistency* in the mappings for different items (Plaut et al., 1996, p. 56).

Hence, consistency rather than progression is a central feature in pattern generalization performance, and the cognitive phenomenon of progression is fundamentally dependent on input/relation pairs and their representations that feedforward to the hidden layer, which influences the choices that are selected in the output layer. In other words, patterns that seem to be endowed with the character of being well defined may depend on individual learners' frequent and consistent exposure and familiarity on similar tasks, which may likely, but not necessarily strongly, contribute to the stability and regularity of the exhibited generalizing process.

Chapter 4 tackles these views in greater detail. At this stage it suffices to say that the nature of a well-defined pattern is always an emergent phenomenon that is sensitive to a complex of factors. Chapter 4 is organized in four sections. We first clarify the meaning of an emergent structure from a parallel distributed processing (PDP) point of view. We then provide other well-known points of view in cognitive science regarding the nature of structures such as symbol structures, theory–theory structures, and probabilistic structures. We then discuss the theory of PDP in semantic cognition and close the chapter with a discussion of its implications in pattern generalization processes that bear on mathematical learning.

Chapter 4
A Theory of Graded Representations in Pattern Generalization

Cross Pattern Task. Below are three stages in a growing pattern of squares.

Fig. 4.1a Cross pattern

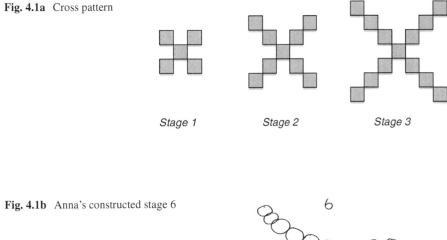

Stage 1   Stage 2   Stage 3

Fig. 4.1b Anna's constructed stage 6

1. *Interviewer (I): Show me stage 4. If it's easier for you, you could draw circles.*

2. *(Anna ("A," Grade 3, age 8) drew stage 4 and then stage 5 using circles. Figure 4.1b*
3. *shows her extended stage 6.)*
4. *I: So in words what do you think is the rule?*

5. *A: Add 3? Oh, add 4.*

F. Rivera, *Teaching and Learning Patterns in School Mathematics:*
Psychological and Pedagogical Considerations, DOI 10.1007/978-94-007-2712-0_4,
© Springer Science+Business Media Dordrecht 2013

6. *I: Where do you add 4?*

7. *A: Coz right here (stage 1) it's 5, then here (stage 2) it's 9. It's 5 + 4. So add 4 (to stage*
8. *3), add 4 (to stage 4), add 4 (to stages 5 and 6, supported by gesturing in circles).*
9. *I: Okay, so can you describe stage 10? If you don't draw, how do you describe stage*
10. *10?*
11. *(A uses a count-all strategy to obtain the total number of circles for stage 6. Then she*
12. *keeps adding 4 with her fingers until she arrives at stage 10.)*
13. *A: I'm adding and adding 4. So if you add 4 more, so right here it has 21 (stage 5), right*
14. *here (stage 6) 22, 23, 24, 25. Then 26, 27, 28, 29 for stage number 7. Then 30, 31,*
15. *32, 33. 34, 35, 36, 37. So there's 37 for number 9. Then 38, 39, 40, and 41 for stage*
16. *10.*
17. *I: So if I ask you for stage 15, how would you solve that? How would you describe it for*
18. *me?*
19. *A: Keep counting until you get to 15?*
20. *I: Okay, I see. In terms of multiplication, like stage 2. I want you to give me a*
21. *multiplication expression that describes stage 2. Remember from our warm up*
22. *when I asked you to write multiplication expressions?*
23. *(A nods in agreement. She then writes $4 \times 2 + 1$.)*
24. *I: How did you get that expression?*
25. *A: Coz ahm there's 4 groups (referring to the 4 legs in stage 2), then there's 2 in each*
26. *group. And then you add 1 more for the middle square.*
27. *I: Okay, I see. So for stage 3, what would your expression be?*
28. *(A writes $4 \times 3 + 1$.)*
29. *A: There's 4 more groups and there's 3 in each one. And then you add 1 more (the*
30. *middle square).*
31. *I: Okay so let's see for stage 10. What would your expression be? No more drawing*
32. *but an expression to describe stage 10.*
33. *(A starts counting by 4 from stage 3 with her fingers. Sensing A's additive action,*
34. *I intervene.)*
35. *I: What about for stage 5?*
36. *(A writes $4 \times 5 + 1$.)*
37. *A: There's 5 circles in here. And then 4 groups of 5 and then I add 1 more.*
38. *I: Now for stage 10?*
39. *(A writes $10 \times 4 + 1$.)*
40. *I: Okay, how did you get those numbers?*
41. *A: Coz ahm there's gonna be 10 circles and then there's 4 groups of it. And then you*
42. *add 1 more.*
43. *I: Okay so let's see for stage 15.*
44. *(A writes $15 \times 4 + 1$.)*
45. *I: Okay so how about for stage 25?*
46. *(A writes $25 \times 4 + 1$.)*
47. *I: Okay so how about for stage 100?*
48. *(A writes $100 \times 4 + 1$.)*
49. *I: Okay so how did you get these numbers?*
50. *A: For stage 25, there's 25 circles in each group of 4 and add 1 more. For stage*
51. *100, there's 100 circles in each group of 4 and you add the middle.*

Third-grade student Anna (age 8 years) learned the concept of multiplication involving two single-digit whole numbers by drawing on both equal group and array models. She also understood quite well the commutative property for multiplication. In her third grade class, they discussed the significance of the two factors a and b in $a \times b$ in which case they learned to refer to *a* as the number of (equal) groups and b the number of elements in each group. Further, they learned that while the commutative property preserved the result of multiplication, they also needed to pay careful attention to the grouping of objects. This background information provides the context for understanding the interviewer's remarks in lines 20–22. At this stage in the interview, Anna and the interviewer began the task of finding an alternative structure for the visual stages by initially establishing a multiplicative expression that would capture a stable relationship among the three stages in her emerging pattern. While the multiplication probe was meant to basically assess Anna's understanding of the equal groups concept, the more interesting concern was to know whether she could transfer such knowledge in a pattern generalization context without any formal intervention. Fortunately, Anna managed to do so, which she expressed in lines 23, 28, 36, 39, 44, 46, 48, and 50–51.

Anna's pattern generalization route in relation to the Cross Pattern in Fig. 4.1a involves cycles of additive and multiplicative thinking about the pattern. In lines 5 through 19, her beginning structure conveyed a recursively additive arithmetical generalization. In lines 20 through 32, the interviewer encouraged her to express her inferred mathematical relationship about the pattern multiplicatively, which she did in cases involving stages 2 and 3. However, in lines 31 through 34, she reverted to a recursively additive strategy. Sensing that far stage 10 was a big jump for Anna, the interviewer made a quick decision and modified the task by switching to near stage 5 (line 35). She then produced a multiplicative expression (line 36), which she confirmed on her drawn pattern. We should note that while her direct expression in lines 44, 46, and 48 differed from those shown in lines 23, 28, and 36, she clearly knew what the numbers meant, which reflected her fundamental grasp of the concept of multiplication and its properties.

Anna's thinking in the above interview is typical of recent findings drawn from younger and older children who tend to exhibit different kinds of structural generalizations for the same pattern (Rivera & Becker, 2008). In her case, in particular, her abduced structures shifted from seeing four circles that were consistently being added one on each leg at every stage in the pattern to seeing a fixed middle circle and four legs that were growing at a constant rate. She then employed the same abduction in dealing with the far generalization tasks. When she was presented with a different pattern generalization task, she exhibited the same thinking process that shifted back and forth between two different generalization l strategies.

The main point that we explore and argue in some detail in this chapter involves the view that the emergence and complexity of the pattern generalization process cannot be reduced to a simple narrative of permanent cognitive shifts from the arithmetic to the algebraic, from the recursive to the multiplicative, from discerning details to perceiving properties, and so on and so forth. Depending on how a pattern generalization task appeals to an individual learner, it is not possible to either anticipate or predict an optimal or best route. Why and how this happens might be explained sufficiently in terms of what we refer to as a *parallel distributed processing phenomenon* that also enables us to explore the implications of a *graded view of pattern generalization*, which takes a more realistic analysis of emergence across tasks.

This chapter is organized into four sections. We initially clarify what we mean by an emergent structure from a parallel distributed processing (PDP) point of view. Then we contrast an emergent structure from other well-known points of view of structures in cognitive science, in particular, symbol structures, theory–theory structures, and probabilistic structures. Next, we expound on the theory of PDP in semantic cognition in some detail and close the chapter with a discussion of the implications of the PDP theory on pattern generalization processes that matter to mathematical learning. In the closing discussion we also address the need to modify some of the elements in the original PDP model based on cognitive factors that bear on pattern generalization processing involving school mathematical patterns. Here we demonstrate the usefulness of a PDP network structure primarily as a thinking model that enables us to describe the complexity of students' pattern generalization processes not in terms of fixed or permanent transitions from, say, arithmetical to algebraic generalizations but as parallel and graded, adaptive, and fundamentally distributed among, and dependent on, a variety of cognitive and extracognitive sources.

The Emergence of Structure

Pattern generalization processing is an emergent phenomenon—that is, borrowing from McClelland, (2010), is "context-sensitive, flexible, graded, and adaptive" (p. 752). Referring to Fig. 1.10 (p. 20), it recruits cognitive factors that complexly cooperate with each other in a neuron-like manner, which leads to varying and in many cases simultaneously parallel kinds of pattern generalizations. While familiarity with patterning tasks may contribute to regular and predictable paths of cooperation involving the relevant factors, which may yield algebraically useful structures, it certainly need not be the case. In other words, individual learners can hold both algebraically useful and recursive structures at the same time. The units that comprise the *hidden* layer, which are drawn from combinations of units under the *relation* and *representational* layers in Fig. 1.10, are an inherent property of the emergent network, including the connections and interactions between and within units that depict and model graded effects of certain combinations and "collaborative engagements" (McClelland, p. 760) of units. Emergence, in other words, is a feature of "the system as a whole" (ibid, p. 752).

An emergent structure is not necessarily reduced to a mere combinatorial process because there are a number of possible choices to begin with; it can also be grounded in several sources. McClelland writes:

> [A]ll of these [creative intellectual] products of the mind are essentially emergents. I do not think that anyone who emphasizes the importance of emergent processes would deny that planful, explicitly goal-directed thought plays a role in the greatest human intellectual achievements. However, such modes of thought themselves might be viewed as *emergent consequences of a lifetime of thought-structuring practice supported by culture and education*. Furthermore … key flashes of insight and intuition may not have arisen from

planful, explicit goal-directed thought alone, but instead might reflect *a massive subsymbolic constraint-satisfaction process [e.g., intuition in discovery] taking place outside of awareness.*... This sequence in discovery may be the rule even in formal domains such as mathematics and physics, where the intuition may come first, followed only later by formal specification and rigorous proof (McClelland, 2010, p. 753; italics added for emphasis).

Further, constructed physical and conceptual objects involving everyday phenomena (e.g. ant colonies, cities, solar systems, physical laws) can be interpreted as "consequences of particular configurations" whenever several factors combine and interact with one another, illustrating the view that "there are many structures in nature that are not produced by design, but that emerge as a result of simple forces operation on the individual objects [themselves]" (McClelland, 2010, p. 754). Suffice it to say, every individual's emergent structure

is different, and that the forces that shape each one are highly nonlinear and context dependent, to the extent that a full understanding of how it [comes] out the way it [does] may not be possible. .... (W)e may never understand how we came to be as we are, nor should we be deluded into thinking that we are truly optimal in any of our properties (McClelland, 2010, pp. 754–755).

An emergent view of choice and decision-making is worth noting at this time in light of the fact that pattern generalization activity in the K-12 school mathematics curriculum is premised on the construction and justification of particular forms of algebraic expressions and equations (i.e. direct expressions and functions). For example, Anna in the introduction initially abduced a recursive rule for the Fig. 4.1a pattern. Her inferred rule then transitioned to a direct formula that enabled her to easily predict the total number of squares in any stage in her pattern. From an emergent perspective, her decisions can be seen in dynamical terms as being about making choices from pools of units and activated response possibilities that "creat[e] a decision-like state in which the population of units associated with one outcome reaches a sustained activity state while the activation of units in populations associated with alternative outcomes are relatively suppressed" (McClelland, 2010, p. 760). In other words, her choice of pattern generalization is a matter of activating a response that wins out over, and suppresses, other possible responses.

An emergent view of the development of cognitive ability also has implications in the way we perceive so-called transitions in structural thinking. There is now solid evidence that refutes the very popular Piagetian hypothesis in which development is seen as a continuous phenomenon in stages. An emergent approach interprets the stability of stages in development in terms of consequences of learning, where some relevant network models accelerations and decelerations that produce appearances of transitions or stage-like effects. However, such transitions are not necessarily "completely abrupt" but around them "performance is graded and only approximately characterizable as characteristic of the stages others have seen" (McClelland, 2010, p. 762). "(S)tage theorists now," McClelland (2010) points out, "speak in terms of 'overlapping waves' instead of discrete transitions between stages" (p. 762).

Alternative Theories to Emergence

Several perspectives have also been proposed that contrast with the above emergent view on cognitive ability and (semantic) knowledge. The *physical symbol systems view* assumes that formal systems have both "the necessary and sufficient means for generating intelligent action" (Newell & Simon, 1976, p. 116). Thinking is, thus, about manipulating symbols and formal rules that operate within some kind of a computational model.[1] However, as Dreyfus (1979) points out, such symbol systems do not explain well the roles of, say, instinct and intuitions in problem-solving that cannot be simply subsumed within artificial models of formal symbolic manipulation. They also become problematic in cases when rules fail to fit and cannot be used correctly for that matter (Bereiter, 1991). Further, manifestations of expert action oftentimes exceed the mere application and execution of rules (e.g. a chef's actual performance is only a crude version of the recipes he or she follows and uses; Bereiter, 1991; Dreyfus, 1988). Against the positing of such rules, the emergent component in PDP foregrounds ways in which cognitive systems are able to acquire knowledge by making small adjustments in the connections between the units shown in Fig. 1.10. In Bereiter's (1991) terms, if we think of the units as frisbees and the connections as rubber bands, weakening and strengthening the rubber bands between frisbees continuously will in the long term "home in on [a] desired pattern" (p. 12).

In the *theory–theory view*, causes of explanations are fundamentally grounded in implicit beliefs and personal, naïve, or informal theories, which justify why observable relations appeal the way they are to knowers (Carey, 1985; Gopnik & Wellman, 1994; Murphy & Medin, 1985). Our knowledge of concepts reflects innate causal relations that we consider to be true and is likely to change over time and development. Having such relations operate in much the same way as the theories that scientists and mathematicians develop scientists and mathematicians whenever they perceive and construct conceptual relationships about certain objects and events (McClelland & Rogers, 2003). Certainly, there is no argument concerning the view that conceptual development and reorganization occur as a result of adaptive changes in individual learners' (initial and ongoing) domain structures. Unfortunately, as Rogers and McClelland (2008) note, theory–theory does not explicitly identify the relevant cognitive mechanisms that might explain semantic processing, representing, and reorganizing beyond the ingenious experiments that characterize work in

---

[1] Glenberg, de Vega, and Graesser (2008) and Steels (2008) note that the meaning of symbols in cognitive science differs from, say, a Peircean view of symbols that grounds ideas from objects. Grounding refers to those processes that we and other computer-driven systems use to link mental structures onto external objects (p. 3). For Peirce, symbols as a type of signs mediate between an object and an interpretant (i.e. how the object appeals to individual learners). Cognitive science in general, however, has a more theoretical conception of symbols beyond grounding—that is, symbols convey "an arbitrary relation between symbol and referent" (ibid p. 2). Hence, they can be "arbitrarily related to objects, abstract, or amodal (i.e. they are nonperceptual or not tied to particular sensory modes)" (ibid). For example, the word "chair" as an amodal symbol does not in any direct way resemble an actual chair with four legs.

this area. Also, causal information that explains the properties of many objects and events can, in fact, be learned through more experiences without having to presume initial knowledge structures. For instance, it has been shown that children and adults possess good or central concepts in the sense that they are natural and easier to learn or acquire than others. However, the presence of observable causal structures in real time also allows them to construct concepts with a coherently covarying property. This property assumes that some things tend to naturally fit or occur together in a stable and regular manner that consequently shape and influence the weighted and distributed connections among them over time with increased experiences and more learning. For Rogers and McClelland (2004), "it is not the identity of the properties themselves, but their patterns of covariation that is essential to the [cognitive] model's behavior" (p. 117).

The *probabilistic view of cognition* situates the emergent framework in a bottom-up perspective. In lieu of initial neural or psychological (hardware) mechanisms or first explanations, which influence emergent behavior, probabilistic models favor a top-down or function-first perspective via "abstract principles [i.e. computational principles] that allow agents to solve problems posed by the world—the functions that minds perform—and then attempting to reduce these principles to psychological and neural processes" (Griffiths, Chater, Kemp, Perfors, & Tenenbaum, 2010, p. 357). One advantage of probabilistic models is the built-in computational capacity in dealing with noisy or partial data and complexes of assumptions, biases, and representations that are involved in, say, dealing with a generalization issue. So, instead of assuming graded representations and gradual error-correcting learning schemes, which are central principles in the emergent model, probabilistic inferences are made on the relevant neural functions that matter relative to an object or event being acquired. Such inferences involve identifying hypotheses and relationships between hypotheses and the observable data being analyzed. Hypotheses encompass both weights in a neural network and symbol systems, including the distributions that characterize the inductive biases of hypotheses. However, a fundamental dilemma with probabilistic models, McClelland et al. (2010) point out, is that if the probabilistic inferences are not correct, then the generated results are more likely to mislead than support cognition and knowledge construction. Further, while probabilistic models can generate high levels of probabilistic descriptions, they also might fail when the underlying contexts or factors that shape their explanations are ignored. For example, when individuals make a correct prediction about an object or an event, it depends on how much time is given to them to process the relevant object or event. The emergent model does not dispute the significance of probability in cognitive action. The dilemma stems from the view that depicts cognitive goal and outcome as being only about choosing between several different structured statistical models. For McClelland et al (2010), "the hypotheses, hypothesis spaces and data structures of the structured probabilistic approach are not the building blocks of an explanatory theory. Rather they are sometimes helpful but often misleading approximate characterizations of the emergent consequences of the real underlying processes" (p. 350).

A Parallel Distributed Processing View of (Semantic) Cognition

A PDP view of cognition is concerned with fundamental mechanisms that enable individuals to perform inferences, construct conceptual schemes, and make judgments about objects and events in real time and in some environment that consists of an input space and some relational context(s). Such context(s) can be about a behavior, a part, a name or category, or a property or attribute of some object or event. A PDP mechanism operates within connectionist principles, similarity, and spreading activation frameworks. That is, knowledge emerges and gets stored in connections among neuron-like processing units with experiences and learning altering, strengthening, and continuously making adjustments in connections among the units.[2] *Contra* its classical associationist legacy, the connectionist component in PDP evolves and learns using general learning mechanisms without predetermined rules and "without initial knowledge or domain-specific constraints" (Rogers & McClelland, 2008, p. 690). Knowledge happens via similarity mechanisms that enable individuals to infer shared features between information that is stored and observable information that is drawn from an object or situation under investigation. Knowledge is also distributed across the network of units through patterns of activation that emerge and produce constraints from one unit to the next. While similarity mechanisms enable categorization, it is the gradedness of categories that is worth noting in similarity and this is captured through the different spreading activation routes that take place among the units. Frequency, typicality, and expertise all bear on the spreading action and similarity formation.

A PDP framework addresses six issues on (semantic) cognitive ability (see Table 4.1). We note the following explicit concerns that a PDP framework seeks to resolve: (1) How do individuals progressively differentiate between concepts? (2) When is it reasonable to use one kind of grouping over another and how does it emerge in a semantic system? (3) Related to item (2), how does the system know that some features are more central than others in a given object or situation, which explains domain-specific attribute weighing? (4) How do illusory correlations between actual experience and some hypothesized conceptual claim come about? (5) How do changes in abductive–inductive schemes occur over some period of development? (6) What factors predispose individuals to be sensitive to causal features in objects and situations?

Figure 4.2 is a distributed connectionist model that illustrates a PDP. Figure 1.10 has been drawn from the basic network structure of Fig. 4.2, which we further explore in some detail in the concluding section. In this section, however, we focus on the Fig. 4.2 model and discuss relevant terminologies and properties that comprise the

---

[2] As Bereiter (1991) notes, older connectionist views put premium on connections and associations between individual units, say, word to word. The newer version, such as PDP, the units, "like the neurons they are modeled after—do not individually signify anything. Instead, as Rumelhart (1989), puts it, 'all the knowledge is in the connections'" (p. 11).

Table 4.1 Six issues and questions regarding the nature of cognitive ability

Issues	Scope
Progressive differentiation of concepts	Fine-grade (or analytic and local) knowledge emerges from course (or general and approximate) beginnings
Category coherence	Some grouping of objects and situations tend to fit well together than other kinds of grouping
Domain-specific attribute weighing	Some features tend to be more important than others relative to an object or situation
Illusory correlations	Individuals sometimes make claims or assumptions about objects and situations that evidently contradict their actual empirical experiences
Conceptual reorganization	Changing abductive and inductive schemes over time
The importance of causal knowledge	Greater sensitivity to causally central features over others (which maybe salient but noncausal)

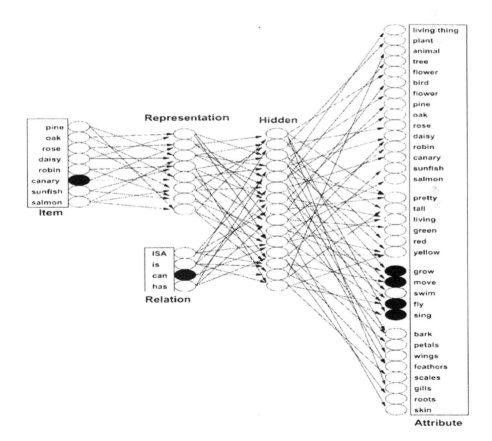

Fig. 4.2 Typical network model of PDP (Rogers & McClelland, 2008, p. 692; reprinted with the permission of Cambridge University Press)

network model. The model basically consists of three major processing layers, namely: *item*, which refers to the things that are being analyzed; *hidden*, which is further subdivided into *representation* and *relation* layers; and *attribute*, which consists of outputs and characteristics that completely describe an activated item. The *relation* layer has four contexts that target any of the following aspects: constructing a name; establishing a behavior; naming a part; or producing a property. Each relation unit constrains the manner in which some information is retrieved, including the similarity relations that are constructed. The *representation* layer consists of cues that capture features of an item, which could be perceptual, linguistic, or visual in form. The context-driven nature of the hidden layer enables the network model to produce different conceptual relationships since the relation contexts determine how objects and events are encountered and experienced by an individual. Over time the system learns to differentiate between and among (similarity) relationships and features with the representation units undergoing continuous and dynamic reorganization depending on the available inputs that are drawn from the environment.

The network begins when an *input pair*, which consists of units from the item and relation layers and some of the units in the representation layer, is activated and then turns on the relevant attribute units in the output layer, thus, producing complete propositions about the item in the process. For example, when the units *canary* and *can* are turned on as an input pair, the network learns to activate the output units *grow*, *move*, *fly*, and *sing* yielding complete propositions about canaries. The processing layers are nonlinear and operate in a feedforward manner—that is, units under the *item* layer and units under the *relation* layer are first activated, which then spread forward throughout the network but are constrained by the current connection weights.[3] Once outputs are obtained, they are then compared with some desired value with the difference converted to a measure of error. Each weight has a corresponding measure of error that causes the network to recalculate following a backward pass and make adjustments on the weights as a way of minimizing discrepancies. We should note that while every input pair is independent from each other, they still project to all the units under the *representation* layer. This means that any activation in the input produces a distributed pattern of activity across the units with the weights expected to change and evolve due to ongoing training. "Since the values of these connection weights change with experience," Rogers and McClelland (2008) write, "the model's generalization behavior strongly depends on the extent and nature of its prior experience with the items in its environment" (p. 693). Further, while the input pairs can be either perceptual, visual, or linguistic, the propositional generalizations that are eventually produced need not be directly evident in the environment. Also, the choice of activating a representation depends on the item units and the relational context(s) that the individual finds relevant. Consequently, different item and relation pairs together will likely activate different patterns of connection across

---

[3] Readers who are interested in details involving the mathematical calculations that are needed to determine the weights are referred to Rogers and McClelland (2008, pp. 692–693).

the representation units that then moves forward until the desired outputs are identified in which case features are successfully constructed and encoded.

A PDP network is an ongoing learning system. Changes in both its internal representations and the values of the connection weights among the relevant units occur naturally as a consequence of (prior and current) experiences and the surrounding environment. Also, units that comprise the layers do not possess semantic content, which means to say that meaning can be inferred only when certain inputs and activations of outputs are probed together and analyzed. Despite this fact, however, there is sufficient evidence to indicate that they "capture the semantic similarity relations that exist among the items in the network's training environment, and so provide a basis for semantic generalization" (Rogers & McClelland, 2008, p. 693). Rogers and McClelland (2008) offer the example of a young child who observes a robin flying away once it detects an approaching cat to show how interactions between an object and a situation give rise to observations, anticipations, and implicit predictions that are either met or violated with discrepancies between expected and observed outcomes (i.e., experiences) becoming the basis for making adjustments in the connection weights.

A PDP view of semantic cognition shares the developmental finding that inferred conceptual relationships concerning objects and situations tend to evolve from broad (or general or course) to finer-grade descriptions. However, the nature of progression is that it is not a linear phenomenon from beginning to end but instead is a clustered phenomenon—that is, conceptual descriptions tend to cluster around some properties that Rogers and McClelland (2008) characterize to be *coherently covarying* in some way. A coherently covarying group of objects or events indicates that such a set appears to join well together in a natural and reliable manner, which then makes the task of performing inferences easy to accomplish. Based on their PDP experiments, Rogers and McClelland (2008) note that "properties that covary coherently across items tend to move connections coherently in the same direction, while idiosyncratic variation of properties tend to move weights in opposite directions that cancel each other out" (Rogers & McClelland, p. 695). These movements imply that different patterns of activation do not linearly move from one endpoint to the other endpoint but instead tend to lump or cluster together in teams around the same pattern(s).

The central principle of coherent covariation in PDP also addresses the difficult concern that certain groupings of objects and situations are not intuitive and, thus, will likely constrain generalization. It is them reasonable to ask how such a semantic system is able to determine which grouping will lead to meaningful, useful, and productive generalizations, including those that do not. At the very least, performing (surface) similarity by way of identifying the possible maximum number of common properties is not a sufficient condition. It is also necessary to assess the importance of a property relative to an object's or a event's representation. Possible sources of importance can be attributed to beliefs and personal causal theories that influence the way objects or situations are grouped or held together. As Keil (1991) notes, "(a)t the psychological level, we may be especially sensitive to picking up many of these sorts of homeostatic causal clusters such that beliefs about those causal relations provide an especially powerful cognitive 'glue,' making features cohere and be easier to remember and induce later on" (p. 243; quoted in Rogers & McClelland, 2008, p. 699). Based on Rogers and McClelland's (2008) PDP experiments, however, they note that despite the fact that the items and their properties are always available in equal frequencies, coherent covariation tends to occur more frequently than idiosyncratic distributions with certain properties "pushing" themselves coherently in the same direction. That is, "attributes that vary coherently together [tend to] exert a greater degree of constraint on the model's internal representations" (p. 700). This means to say that coherently covarying properties are much easier to acquire and learn in a shorter period of time than properties that are not coherently covarying. The authors acknowledge, nonetheless, the presence of illusory correlations, which could be interpreted as by-products of such correlational learning systems that are "sensitive to coherent covariation among object properties—the higher-order patterns of covariation may overwhelm learning of weaker pairwise object-property correspondences that violate the higher-order regularities" (Rogers & McClelland, p. 702).

Aside from having the property of coherent covariation, a PDP network can also be taught be learn "in domain-specific ways about attribute importance" (Rogers & McClelland, 2008, p. 702) using a backpropagation-to-activation technique. Initially, all attribute units relative to an object or a situation are acquired and activated by the network following a feedforward strategy. Then a backpropagation-to-activation strategy (i.e. from the attribute units to the representation units) is used to further classify novel objects or events within the network assuming a very limited number of known attributes. This means that no prior knowledge concerning attributes that are important is needed since "such constraints can be learned, and there is no chicken-and-egg problem—category-specific attribute weighting can be explained by the sensitivity of a domain-general learning mechanism of high-order covariation among stimulus properties" (Rogers & McClelland, p. 703).

The *hidden* layer plays an important role in accounting for an individual's conceptual reorganization. While developmental research has extensively investigated children's changing generalization profiles over time (e.g. a 10-year-old child generalizes differently than a 3-year-old child, say, in matters involving living things), which explains the changes in which they organize and construct their concepts, a PDP network accounts for conceptual changes in terms of the activation of units under the *hidden* layer. A hidden unit turns on different combinations of units from the representation and item-relation layers that then activates units in the attribute layer, the outputs. In Fig. 4.2, for example, the relation units consist of four contexts that address different features of an object or event (i.e. "isa" pertains to a name, "is" pertains to a property, "can" refers to behavior, and "has" refers to parts). Over development, changes occur with more experiences with each of the different representation and relation units. What in principle takes place involves a process called *coalescing*—that is, earlier or initial generalizations might be drawn to superficial representations reflective of the coherently covarying properties that are visually evident on the objects or events, which then undergo conceptual restructuring as a consequence of increased exposure on, and familiarity with, other relation units. "Gradually," McClelland and Rogers (2003) point out, "as [the network] acquires more information about the other three types of relation, the[ir] coherent covariation information comes to dominate learning, and the internal representations reorganize to capture the underlying taxonomic organization rather than the appearance information" (p. 320).

Finally, a PDP network can be trained via coherent covariation to be sensitive to causal information or causal and explanatory properties that can also emerge from and within the same basic cognitive processes of making inferences and establishing generalizations involving features of objects and events. Without a doubt, knowing the relevant causes provides a deeper understanding of an object or event beyond knowing their relevant properties or features. In a PDP network, this higher-order semantic processing can be accomplished by using the same learning mechanisms that are employed in establishing properties of objects and events. What needs to be done involves training the network so that both causal information and the relevant properties are allowed to coherently covary. In this case, the order in which objects and events are known by their properties (i.e. "event and object sequences") is an important consideration as the network model is being trained to construct causal knowledge or causal mechanisms underlying some target properties. Such training experiences can take place in the context of a recurrent model, where repetitive experiences with the properties of some object or event are meant to foreground and emphasize the underlying causal knowledge or mechanism. Also, some objects and events appear to possess causal potency that enables individuals to easily predict and establish causal properties and consequences beyond their shapes and appearances. Further, Rogers and McClelland (2008) write, "the words we use to refer to such objects covary more consistently with their causal properties than with surface attributes such as shape and size, with the consequence that these causal properties become more important in determining how such object's names will generalize" (p. 710).

Implications of Parallel Distributed Processing on Pattern Generalization Processing

Individual learners who perform pattern generalization on mathematical objects draw on a complex of factors. Some of the factors may be external to them such as pictures of geometric figures in a pattern that may possess sufficient causal potency and enable them to make interesting abductions about the pattern and its possible extensions. Other factors may be hidden and, thus, cannot be directly manipulated externally. In cases of familiar patterns, coherent covariation may suffice in generating a generalization, arithmetic or algebraic. In unfamiliar or nonroutine types of patterns, however, the hidden factors, which target both aspects of the representation and relation units, may need to undergo (re)training and feedback.

Any semblance of stability or coalescence in a PDP network gives the appearance of emergent constructed knowledge. However, progressive emergence necessitates the continuous introduction of (higher order) novel tasks that, thus, involves an increasingly complex PDP network system. In this complex system what matters are not the transitions in but the graded quality of connections among the relevant unit pairs, where quality is interpreted in terms of the weight (i.e. strength) of the connections. For example, typical empirical microgenetic accounts of transitions or stages in pattern generalization (e.g.: Moss & London McNab, 2011; Radford, 2001b; Rivera, 2011) offer powerful and insightful understanding of conceptual changes that occur. However, a PDP account takes an even more fundamental epistemological position than establishing shifts that have taken place, that is, (1) it is multiple-routed and, hence, chaotic, nonlinear, and parallel; (2) it is context-sensitive and, hence, emergent; and (3) all the factors (e.g. cognitive and environmental) that bear on pattern generalization ability continuously and fluidly cooperate in a purposeful manner. That gradedness is more typical than transitions or stages, which are temporal and episodic to some extent. Also familiar and unfamiliar patterns whose structures are common and novel, respectively, may or may not appear to be the case with an individual learner. Hence, a concern for the teacher involves how to effectively orchestrate and scaffold meaningful instruction in pattern generalization activity so that individual PDP mechanisms are both respected and allowed to learn, evolve, and achieve stability over time.

Certainly in both classroom and outside contexts, teachers are fully aware that the development of individual pattern generalization skill is not a simple matter of instruction, direct or otherwise, where instruction is viewed in terms of purposeful interaction between them and their students. At the very least, it is just not possible to provide instruction that will anticipate all cases of pattern generalization tasks. It is also very difficult to state in sufficient terms all the relevant sociomathematical norms, rules, and mechanisms that can support the transition from arithmetical to algebraic generalization within and across task. A consequent dilemma is that oftentimes the norms, rules, and mechanisms tend to privilege some (adult) perspective, which may or may not be compatible with individual learners' ways of thinking about the same objects.

Another issue that is worth noting is that there is more to pattern generalization processing than following rules or instructions. Instructional cues, say, the use of guided questions to help students transition from recursively additive to either additively or multiplicatively functional generalizations appear easy to accomplish mainly by asking students to to follow rules and directions. However, they tend to construct and process information that they find meaningful to manipulate, which recent research on pattern generalization among younger and older children has shown to be true and consistent across cases (Rivera & Becker, 2008). Hence, while instruction can provide support and closure that aid individual learners in seeing and experiencing the whole pattern generalization process, the reality is that they do not progress at the same time. More frequently than otherwise, they use their own practical actions as a guide that may or may not map well to instruction, which reflects intentional knowledge and formal mathematical practices.

The preceding two paragraphs do not convey that instructional interventions in PDP processing are useless. All students, especially young learners such as 8-year-old Anna in the beginning section of this chapter, stand to benefit from knowing the intentional concepts and formal mathematical practices that comprise effective pattern generalization processing. One of these practices involves justification. In the preceding three chapters, we have frequently pointed out that pattern generalization in school mathematics addresses conceptual aspects relevant to the construction and justification of a direct expression or a formula. In the above interview with Anna, the interviewer implicitly conveyed to her the need to construct a pattern generalization that also had explanatory or justificatory goodness. When Anna initially stated a recursively additive generalization that enabled her to extend her pattern stages one at a time, she saw that it was not sufficient in explaining any far generalization stage in her constructed pattern unless she constructed the preceding stages one by one. She then understood the interviewer's prodding as an indication that she needed to choose and construct a better expression, which eventually led her to produce a multiplicative-driven structural generalization. Suffice it to say, instruction is still necessary so that students are able to see the significance of providing relevant and mathematically appropriate explanatory good generalizations based on intentional practices.

A PDP approach takes a more realistic view of the complex emergence of causal information or explanatory goodness that actually depends on choice and the strengths of the connections between the relevant unit pairs in the network. In the above interview with Anna, the interviewer effectively intervened when Anna was in the process of choosing between an additive and a multiplicative formula. What was evident in her generalization network were the parallel conceptions of formulas that she thought applied to her pattern, but purposeful intervention became necessary when she was trying to figure out which one offered the best justifiably good explanation. Pattern generalizations that have explanatory or justificatory goodness are (1) able to explain all the hypothesized far generalization stages in a pattern, (2) simple and parsimonious with very minimal assumptions, (3) able to justify an interpreted structure of the pattern, and (4) competitive, which means they are able to rule out other alternative generalizations (e.g. preference for multiplicative-based structural generalizations over mostly additively recursive arithmetical generalizations; Read & Marcus-Newhall, 1993; Thagard, 1989). Instruction is, thus, clearly a significant factor in shaping this particular aspect of the PDP generalization process.

A PDP view of pattern generalization captures the progressive and dynamic emergence of algebraic generalizations relative to collections of mathematical objects whose arrangements are always interpretive in context. It does not offer a linear and an unchanging teleological account of conceptual progress from beginning to end across individual learners. While the end goal of a PDP is clearly knowledge construction, it is at the same time concerned with the diversity and distributed nature of cognitive actions, including the many different ways in which connections are established toward achieving some goal. Hence, while combinations of input and output units produce complete propositions at the global level, a PDP view also underscores the local distributed complexity that is involved when units are being recruited for a purpose. It, thus, seems to makes sense that claims reflective of transitions in pattern generalization from, say, naively recursive to functional, need not be grounded in sources such as effect of instruction or innate ability because a PDP view draws on a complexity of factors that cooperate in some way with the construction of patterns of covariation a primary interest. The issue then becomes a matter of how factors cooperate and distribute themselves in a network that brings about the skill.

In the quote below, Thelen and Smith's (1994) view of behavior and development from a dynamical systems perspective poignantly expresses the overall sense in which we conceptualize pattern generalization processing in a PDP perspective.

> Although behavior and development appear structured, there are no structures. Although behavior and development appear rule-driven, there are no rules. There is complexity. There is a multiple, parallel, and continuously dynamic interplay of perception and action, and a system that, by its thermodynamic nature, seeks certain stable solutions. These solutions emerge from relations, not from design. When the elements of such complex systems cooperate, they give rise to behavior with a unitary character, and thus to the illusion of structure. But the order is always executory, rather than rule-driven, allowing for the enormous sensitivity and flexibility of behavior to organize and regroup around task and context (Thelen & Smith, 1994, p. xix).

Empirical evidence in the succeeding chapters will show the extent to which complexes of factors—shape students' thinking, especially why they deal quite well with some patterns and fail in other kinds of patterns. This is what is meant by "relations [and] not design," where design conveys a superset of fixed and permanent rules for obtaining, say, an algebraically useful structure for a pattern. Instead, depending on individual interactions within a relevant system of network factors, pattern generalization skills emerge depending on such factors.

Further, following Bereiter (1991), acquiring desirable rule-driven actions (e.g. direct formula construction as a gold standard in pattern generalization) is still a significant aspect in a PDP process. However, what a PDP view conveys is not the classical perspective in which the end goal of mathematical learning and understanding is mainly about the acquisition of a repertoire of rules, where rules are seen as practical algorithms that enable computations for all kinds of problems. Instead, rules emerge as a result of satisfying or stabilizing constraints in a mathematical problem situation. Hence, rules are not the end product of ossified stages in transition accounts but emerge "as a way of representing and talking about mathematics" in a particular way (Bereiter, 1991, p. 15), which means to say that they are always emergent and changing depending on context. Unfamiliar patterns or familiar patterns with added constraints may likely cause individual learners to produce additively recursive generalizations despite the prolonged manifestations of expertise in direct formula generalization. In PDP, any rule-like behavior, or knowledge for that matter, is a function of the connections in the network system.

As an aside, the above quote by Thelen and Smith (1994) has been drawn from "a decade's research that we could not interpret using available models. The data were intriguing and perplexing, but we clearly needed new ways to make sense of them. We each soon realized that the puzzles in our own data sets were not unique, but mirrored the larger issues for developmental study as a whole" (p. xxi). Current research knowledge on pattern generalization studies involving school mathematical objects appears to be in the same situation. That is, the transferability of qualitative findings drawn from intensive clinical interviews with students and groups of students in several different interaction formats (e.g.: students and teachers; within groups of students; classrooms in design research environments) seems to be more contextual than universal. Consequently, the findings should encourage us to be more cautious than dogmatic. Some transition accounts in several microgenetic studies on pattern generalization now appear to be understood or translated in terms of rules, stages, or schemes. However, we also learn from other studies about their limited applicability, especially in situations when the same kinds of patterns are (slightly) modified by either reducing a condition or adding more conditions. Following Norman (1986), perhaps it might be more apt to think in terms of states rather than stages and to use metaphors such as "'stability,' 'harmony,' 'local,' and 'global minima'" (p. 533). Generalization schemes are, thus, not interpreted as fixed patterns of actions but are "interpretive states" and "flexible configurations" that draw on input from both old and current information.

In this chapter, we endeavored to explain how pattern generalization processing is a PDP type of cognitive system that requires "continual adjustment and learning" (ibid, p. 533) and adaptation. Borrowing from Norman, the processing "develops neither rules nor generalizations" but

> *acts* as if it had these rules. Thus, the system really mirrors experience; the regularities of its operation result partially from the regularities of the world, partially from the interpretations of the beholder. It is a system that exhibits intelligence and logic, yet that nowhere has explicit rules of intelligence or logic (Norman, 1986, p. 536).

Figure 1.10 (p. 22) is a PDP network involving a pattern generalization task. It demonstrates a student's network processing of a pattern beginning with five pattern stages as the input units. The student then sees and manipulates the stages in both pictorial and numerical form. The parallel processing of two representations captures a frequent learning or clinical interview event in which students oftentimes do not dissociate between pictorial and numerical representations. Further, the student interprets the pattern stages as possessing certain properties (with the activation of the "have" relation unit). Following a PDP mechanism, input–relation unit pairs together with the activated representation units feedforward to several output units in parallel sequences of actions enabling the student to produce at least one generalization about the pattern. When certain repeated pairings are done, that further strengthen the connections in some unit pairs causing the student to choose the most appropriate generalization. Justification or explanatory goodness occurs through backpropagation (from the output units to the relevant input–relation pairs).

One cognitive factor that is missing and needs to be clarified and inserted in the Fig. 1.10 model involves the central role of the inferential trivium of abduction, induction, and deduction when choices are made and connections are developed. Implicit in the input–relation pair is the utilization of abductive strategies, which also depend on the representation units that are manipulated. For example, young children with very minimal expertise in the use of exact language and cardinality are more likely to convey abduced pictorial and gestural relationships than older children who have significant competence in those two aspects. Induction can assist in strengthening certain unit pairs due to the frequency of testing that is done before a general proposition is constructed. Deduction is then manifested when PDP processing begins to explore causal or explanatory information relevant to the pattern. Readers are referred to Fig. 2.11 (p. 48), which demonstrates the complex relationships that occur between abduction and induction and the input and hidden layers of the PDP.

Another issue that also needs to be taken into account in the Fig. 1.10 model is the potential influence of personal and sociocultural factors in the construction of the input–relation pairs. As we have noted in Chap. 2, drawing on the work of Luria and the reflections of Vinner, a learner's level of curiosity, needs, desires, and impulses, and shared experiences and expectations can significantly shape the manner in which he or she perceives the input units and his or her choice of relation units.

In the following two chapters, we illustrate graded pattern processing involving different groups of learners. In Chap. 5, in particular, we focus on pattern generalization findings drawn from elementary school children from Grades 1 through 5 (ages 6 through 10 years) in different contexts. We note that a huge chunk of data that is reported and discussed in this chapter has been drawn from the author's longitudinal studies with intact classes of Grades 2 and 3 students in the USA. Our basic aim is to highlight the graded nature of young children's pattern generalization states on the basis of their constructed structures and incipient generalizations, which involve the use of various representational forms such as gestures, words, and arithmetical symbols that convey their expressions of generality.

Chapter 5
Graded Pattern Generalization Processing of Elementary Students (Ages 6 Through 10 Years)

Building Houses Pattern: These are how our stages in a pattern look like.

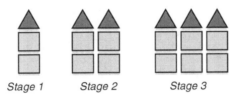

Fig. 5.1a Building houses pattern

1. *Interviewer (I): David ("D," Grade 2, age 7), will you show me what comes next? How*
2. *does stage 4 look like with the blocks?*
3. *D: There's one of them (pointing to the whole figure in stage 1, refer to Fig. 5.1b).*
4. *There's two of them (pointing to the two full figures in stage 2). Now there's three of*
5. *them (pointing to the three full figures in stage 3).*

Fig. 5.1b David's initial abductive inference on the Fig. 5.1a pattern

6. *I: OK, great. Can you show me what would come in stage 4? (D builds stage 4, as shown*

7.   *in Fig. 5.1c.) What would come next? Stage 5, build that here (see Fig. 5.1c).*

Fig. 5.1c David's constructed stages 4 and 5 of the Fig. 5.1a pattern

8. *I: So what if we skip what comes next in stages 5, 6, 7, 8, and 9. We want to know what*
9.   *would come next in stage 10. Can you draw with little squares and triangles what*
10.   *stage 10 would look like? (D draws on paper stage 10, as shown in Fig. 5.1d.)*

Fig. 5.1d David's constructed stage 10 of the Fig. 5.1a pattern

11. *I: Very nice.*

Triangular Pond Pattern: Below are the stages in our pattern.

| Stage 1 | Stage 2 | Stage 3 |

Fig. 5.2a Triangular pond pattern

12. *I: Will you show me what comes next? How does stage 4 look like with the blocks?*
13. *(D gathers several pieces of stage 4, as shown in*
14. *Fig. 5.2b below.)*

Fig. 5.2b David's constructed stages 4 and 5 of the Fig. 5.2a pattern

15. *I: Okay. Can you show me what's next? (D's stage 5 is shown in Fig. 5.2b above.)*
16. *I: Now suppose we skip steps and build stage 10. How would it look like to you?*
17. *(D draws his stage 10 on paper, as shown in Fig. 5.2c).*

Fig. 5.2c David's constructed stage 10 of the Fig. 5.2a pattern

18. *I: Okay can you explain to me how you knew what to do?*
19. *D: Because I kinda copy these (points to stage 3) because the triangles were like kinda*
20. *surrounding these little squares so that I have these (referring to his stage 10).*
21. *I: How'd you know how many squares to put there?*
22. *D: Because I wanted them to fit in.*
23. *I: Okay, great.*

The two patterns shown in Figs. 5.1a and 5.2a were given to second-grade student David (age 7 years) in the same clinical interview session that occurred four months before a teaching experiment on pattern generalization. In first grade, David learned to sort objects, extend repeating patterns, and skip count by 2, 5, and 10. He also became familiar with context-based finding of rules in a function table (e.g. determining the total number of ears for *n* dogs, where *n* is a whole number). These topics formed part of the statistics and data analysis strand of the state-mandated mathematics curriculum for Grade 1 students. The above clinical interview took place after the students have been in school about 4½ months since the start of classes. During this period, no patterning activity was done because the district pacing guide stipulated the learning of other more essential state objectives in the second-grade mathematics curriculum.

David's processing of the above two tasks in the same session exemplifies *graded pattern generalizing*, which happened because a complexity of factors influenced his actions on the patterns. The Triangular Pond Pattern task in Fig. 5.1a appeared to him as being more complex than the Building Houses Pattern task. "The main difference between complex and simple sets," Stavy and Babai (2008) point out, "is the amount of information [that] one has to process when comparing," which is further magnified in situations when "two stimuli are incongruent" (p. 175). Where David seemed to be consistent in his generalizing approach across the two tasks was the manner in which he perceived the stages in each pattern, that is, he saw them as whole objects that were similar in shape. In the Fig. 5.1a pattern, for example, he abduced a whole unit (stage 1 in Fig. 5.1b) that grew by the stage number that enabled him to correctly apply an incipient generalization on a far task (Fig. 5.1d) after successfully inducing stages 4 and 5 (Fig. 5.1c) of his emerging pattern. In the Fig. 5.2a pattern, however, he began to experience difficulty coping with the exact nature of, and relationships between, the triangles and squares in stage 4 (Fig. 5.2b). When he constructed stages 4 and 5 with the blocks, in fact, he first built triangle borders and then added the squares that filled the interior of the borders (lines 19–20). But an effect of David's shape abduction relative to the Fig. 5.2a pattern produced inconsistent inductions, which consequently led to an incorrect generalization. Suffice it to say, the Fig. 5.2a pattern had at least one interpretive dimension that interfered with David's generalizing actions.

David's work on the Fig. 5.2a pattern had a happy ending, of course. An additional 4 months later and an intervening teaching experiment on patterns provided him with enough time and practice to further hone his generalizing skills. Consistent with PDP principles, too, certain connections within units and between unit pairs in David's graded pattern processing over the course of the teaching experiment on patterns strengthened and stabilized. This change enabled him to make harmonious choices and state incipient generalizations that convey exact and consistent relationships. In his final clinical interview, David once again dealt with the same two pattern generalization tasks shown in Figs. 5.1a and 5.2a. With respect to the Fig. 5.2a pattern, he initially employed gestures (Fig. 5.3) when he pointed out what he interpreted to be three invariant parts that comprised every stage in his pattern (lines 25 through 28 in the interview below). He applied the same set of gestures repeatedly over several more stages, which enabled him to produce a consistent pattern generalization for far stages 10, 25, and 100 that he conveyed rhythmically in verbal form without having had to draw each one (lines 33 through 40).

24. *I: Okay how did you know what to draw?*

25. *D: Because here [stage 4], this one has 4 [squares], and 4 triangles [on top], and*
26. *2 [triangles] on the sides, and 4 figures [bottom triangles]. And this one [stage*
27. *5], it's supposed to have 5 triangles [top row], 2 [triangles] on the sides, and 5*
28. *[triangles] right here [bottom row] (see Fig. 5.3 for the gestures).*

Fig. 5.3 David's gesture-driven description of his stage 5 relative to the Fig. 5.2a pattern

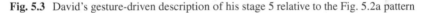

29. *I: And what did you put in the middle?*

30. *D: These are ducks.*

31. *I: Oh, so are these squares?*

32. *D: Yeah.*

33. *I: Okay, so what about stage 10. Can you explain what it would have?*

34. *D: It would have 10 triangles on the top and on the bottom, 2 triangles on the*
35. *   sides, and 10 squares in the middle.*

36. *I: Okay, and what about stage 25?*

37. *D: 25 triangles on the top, 25 triangles on the bottom, 2 triangles on the sides,*
38. *   and 25 squares in the middle.*

38. *I: What about stage 100?*

39. *D: 100 triangles on the top, 100 triangles on the bottom, 2 triangles on the*
40. *sides, and 100 squares in the middle.*

Consistent with PDP principles, David's graded pattern generalization processing underwent retraining when he had to deal with novel tasks. However, we note the significant positive influence of prior knowledge in the ongoing construction of connections between and among input, relation, and representation layers in David's graded pattern generalization processing. For example, his extensions of the ambiguous pattern in Fig. 5.4a were premised on his interpreted structure of stage 3, which he interpreted to be consisting of two overlapping diagonal sets of three circles and an interior circle. David then pointed out that

41. *for stage 4, there's 4 circles here and 4 circles here plus a middle circle. For stage 5,*
42. *there's 5 circles here and 5 circles here plus a middle circle. For stage 10, there's 10*
43. *circles here and 10 circles here plus a middle circle.*

Growing Pattern of Circles Pattern: Below are stages in a growing pattern of circles.

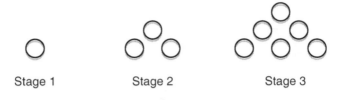

Fig. 5.4a   Growing pattern of circles pattern: an ambiguous patterning task

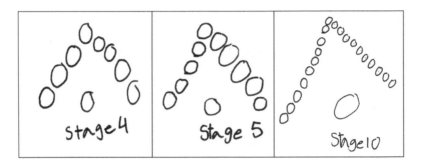

Fig. 5.4b   David's extensions of the Fig. 5.4a pattern

   In the above situation, David was evidently drawing on his prior learning experiences with familiar patterns. He was aware that he needed to find a way of counting the parts in his pattern by initially establishing a relationship with the corresponding stage number. Lines 41 through 43 conveyed how he applied this requirement. However, he lacked additional information such as how to deal with cases that involve overlapping parts and the need to establish consistent pattern generalizations that take into account both the known and the extended stages in a pattern. When the interviewer asked him to explain how he saw stage 3 in the Fig. 5.4a pattern, his reply reflected seeing overlapping diagonal parts: "There's 3 circles here [along one diagonal] and 3 circles here [along another diagonal] and a middle circle here." When the interviewer further prodded him to analyze stage 2, he saw two overlapping diagonal parts but no middle circle. Finally, when the interviewer asked him whether his pattern consisting of stages 1 through 10 made sense to him, he said yes but did not explain how so.

   In this chapter, we focus on pattern generalization studies that have been conducted with elementary school children from Grades 1 through 5 (ages 6 through 10 years) in different contexts. We note at the outset that a huge chunk of data that is reported and discussed in this chapter is drawn from the author's longitudinal studies with intact classes of Grades 2 and 3 students in the US. Our contribution to the current research base on elementary students' understanding of patterns involves extrapolating the graded nature of their pattern generalization processing states on the basis of their constructed structures, incipient generalizations, and use of various "semiotic means of objectification" (Radford, 2003) such as gestures, words, and arithmetical symbols that convey their expressions of generality. The graded condition foregrounds the dynamic emergence of parallel types of pattern generalization processing that is sensitive to a complex of factors (cognitive, sociocultural, neural, constraints in curriculum content, nature and type of tasks, etc.), where progression is seen not in linear terms but as states and waves that continually evolve based on more learning. In a graded pattern generalization processing view, there are no prescribed stages or fixed rules but only states of conceptual coalescences and coherent covariations that change with more experiences.

The four sections in this chapter address different aspects of pattern generalization processing that matter to elementary school children. In the first section, we characterize approximate and exact pattern generalizations along three dimensions, namely: whole number knowledge, shape sensitivity, and figural competence. In the second section, we focus on the representational modes that elementary students oftentimes use to capture their emergent structures and incipient generalizations. These modes include gestural, pictorial, verbal, and numerical. In the third section, we address grade-level appropriate use and understanding of variables via the notions of intuited and tacit variables. We close the chapter with an analysis of the relationship between elementary children's structural incipient generalizations and the natural emergence of their understanding of functions.

Distinguishing Between Approximate and Exact Generalization: Changing Competencies in Number, Shape, and Figural Processing

David's work on stage 10 in Figs. 5.1d, 5.2c, and 5.4b exemplify responses that exhibit both approximate and exact generalizations. In Fig. 5.2c, an approximate incipient generalization, he constructed and established stage 10 by inferring a global shape similarity. He abduced what he interpreted to be the pertinent figural characteristics across the given stages in order to carry out his global inductions for stages 4, 5, and 10. Consequently he became inconsistent in counting the number of squares and triangles from stages 4 to 100. His constructed stages in Fig. 5.4b also reflect the use of global similarity. He interpreted the structure of stages 2 and 3 along the same shape of a growing angle with an interior point. However, it did not matter to him that he was counting the vertex of the angle twice. In fact, that was how he interpreted the given pictorial representations for stages 2 and 3 of the pattern. *Approximate generalizations (AG) are fuzzy generalities of an emergent structure.* Especially among elementary students, approximate generalizing on a task fails to sufficiently coordinate the three aspects of number, shape, and figural properties in a harmonious and stable manner. But interestingly enough, David exhibited exact generalization in

Fig. 5.1d. For far stage 10 of his emergent pattern, he abduced that it would have ten sets of the same figural unit consisting of a triangle and two squares. Also consistent with the three given stages in the pattern, he inferred growth along the same horizontal direction. *Exact generalizations (EG) are conceptually consistent generalities of an emergent structure. Contra* approximate generalizing, exact generalizing on a task involves sufficiently coordinating the three aspects of number, shape, and figural properties in a harmonious and stable manner.

Among elementary students, graded pattern generalization processing yields at least three cognitive consequences, as follows:

- (Implicitly) Choosing between AG or EG is a task-dependent phenomenon. It can be task-based, which depends on how an individual learner perceives, interprets, and constructs the structural complexity of a given patterning task. It can also be task-induced, which is driven by the causal potency of the given stages.
- Both AG and EG routes are inherent choices in every individual learner's network system. While a stable system reflects strong connections around EG, a host of relevant factors such as novelty of task, weak prior knowledge, and student disposition during processing can potentially produce AG.
- Different levels of AG exist, which can be distinguished according to conceptual competencies in the three aspects of number, shape, and figural property discernment.

Number

There is no argument concerning the view that elementary students have number sense.[1] In fact, the most significant finding in neuroscientific research involving children's natural numeric competence is the approximate nature in which they exhibit number sense early in their experiences (Dehaene, 1997) that under stable circumstances should transition to (adult) exact understanding with more social and cultural learning. There is no permanent shift, of course, as adults in neuroimaging experiments appear to activate regions in their parietal lobe associated with approximate number processing when they perform mental calculations (Pinel, Dehaene, Riviere, & Le Bihan, 2001). Changes in numeric processing from approximate to exact counting are primarily mediated by language, and developmental research has consistently documented young children's initial difficulties in learning their correct meanings following adult practices (Condry & Spelke, 2008; Le Corre & Carey, 2007; Lipton & Spelke, 2005). For example, some children do not map the correct number word for a set of concrete objects, while other children can recite number words rather proficiently but fail to grasp the correct meanings.

---

[1] We exclude younger children who have neurological impairments in approximate numerical processing (Ansari, 2010; Dehaene & Cohen, 1997).

Considering the implications of the above findings on elementary children's developing skills in exact numerical processing, Rivera (2010b) assessed the nature of second-grade students' preinstructional competence on the two numerical pattern generalization tasks shown in Fig. 5.5a, b. Twenty-one US Grade 2 students (ages 7–8 years; 7 girls and 14 boys; 20 Hispanic-Americans; and 1 African-American) each participated in two clinical interview sessions in which they dealt with the Fig. 5.5a, b tasks two times. Each numerical patterning task involves five to six near generalization items (i.e. stages 1 through 6), one to two far generalization items (i.e., stages 10 and 20), and an inversion problem (i.e. determine the stage number or input for a given total or output). The first clinical interviews took place 6 weeks after the start of classes, and the second interviews occurred 6 weeks after the first interviews. During the first interview, the students were provided with a construction pad and a number line of whole numbers from 0 to 100. Since the author anticipated that some students would exhibit conceptual difficulties with exact counting as noted in the above paragraph, the number line offered them additional support in case they needed to use it to count. During the second interview, both construction pad and number line were provided. Further, due to the students' difficulties with the inversion problems during the first interview, sheets containing pictures of dog eyes and zebra legs were made available for them to use as well.

Table 5.1a, 5.1b provide summaries of the results drawn from the first clinical interviews with respect to the two numerical pattern generalization tasks shown in Fig. 5.5a, b. More than half of the students initially engaged in perceptual subitizing (two to four objects) in dealing with stage 1. Then a conceptual shift toward the use of counting all strategy took place when the students obtained the total number of the objects in stage 2 for each pattern. Further, the same counting all strategy was more frequently used than the other arithmetical strategies when it came time to processing the remaining near generalization tasks (stages 3 through 6). As shown in the two tables, the other arithmetical strategies used were counting on, skip counting by 2 and 4, and knowledge of the doubles facts (e.g. "$2+2=4$, so 2 dogs have 4 eyes"). Also, less than half of the students found the number line on the table useful despite the consistent reminder from the interviewer that it could be used at all times. When the students dealt with the far generalization tasks (stages 10 and 20), at least two-thirds of them shifted to approximate processing, which explains the very low percentage of correct responses on the two tasks (about 22% for the dog eyes pattern and about 10% in the case of the zebra legs pattern). Examples of students' approximate values for stages 10 and 20 for the Fig. 5.5a pattern are 24 and 32, respectively. For the Fig. 5.5b pattern, approximate values for stages 10 and 20 are 30 and 42, respectively. Almost all of the students who suggested incorrect approximate values for the far stages offered numbers that they thought were reasonable. One student, for example, suggested 42 legs for far stage 20 of the zebra legs pattern and said, "I just know in my head that it is a lot." There were also a handful of other incorrect responses that involved adding the sum of the last known total count on a near generalization task (stage 5 or 6) and the targeted far generalization stage number. For example, one student argued that since "there are 12 eyes that I counted for stage 6 [in Fig. 5.5a]," then "stage 10 has 22 eyes [since

Number of Dog Eyes: Here is 1 dog puppet on the table. How many eyes does one dog have? Here are 2 dog puppets. How many eyes do 2 dogs have? How do you know? Can you explain it to me? Here are 3 dog puppets. How many eyes do 3 dogs have? How do you know? Can you explain it to me? We only have three dog puppets on the table. So you need to imagine more dogs in your head.

A. How many eyes do 4 dogs have? How do you know for sure? Can you tell me how you were thinking about it?

B. How many eyes do 5 dogs have? Can you tell me how you were thinking about it?

C. How many eyes do 10 dogs have? Can you tell me or show me on paper how you were thinking about it?

D. How many eyes do 20 dogs have? Can you tell me or show me on paper how you were thinking about it?

E. A normal dog has two eyes. How many dogs are there with a total of 17 eyes? Can you tell me or show me on paper how you were thinking about it?

Fig. 5.5a   Number of dog ears pattern generalization task for Grade 2 students

Number of Zebra Legs) Here is 1 zebra toy. How many legs does one zebra have? Here are 2 zebra toys. How many legs do 2 zebras have? Can you show me how you know so? Here are 3 zebra toys. How many legs do 3 zebras have? How do you know? We only have three zebra toys on the table. So you need to imagine more zebras in your head.

A. How many legs do 4 zebras have? How do you know for sure? Can you tell me how you were thinking about it?

B. How many legs do 5 zebras have? How do you know for sure? Can you tell me or show me on paper how you were thinking about it?

C. How many legs do 10 zebras have? How do you know for sure? Can you tell me or show me on paper how you were thinking about it?

D. How many legs do 20 zebras have? How do you know for sure? Can you tell me or show me on paper how you were thinking about it?

E. A normal zebra has four legs. How many zebras are there with a total of 21 legs? Can you tell me or show me on paper how you were thinking about it?

Fig. 5.5b   Number of zebra legs pattern generalization task for Grade 2 students

$12 + 10 = 22$]." Finally, the students found the inverse tasks very difficult to process. In fact, only one student on each task was able to explicitly articulate a reasonable answer ("there are 8 and a half dogs," "there are 5 zebras and another one with just one leg"). The primary source of difficulty was language with a majority of them confusing input numbers and output values. Also, about one third of them who initially drew the required number of objects corresponding to the output value used sticks and circles. However, they did not know how to proceed further (e.g. grouping the drawn figures by two or by four) and eventually gave up.

Table 5.2a, b provide summaries of the results drawn from the second clinical interviews with respect to the two numerical pattern generalization tasks shown in Fig. 5.5a, b. None of the students used the number line on the table to help them

Table 5.1a Grade 2 students' first round interview results on the dog eyes patterning task ($n=21$)

Subtasks	Perceptual subitizing	Counting all without number line	Counting all with number line	Counting on without number line	Counting on with number line	Skip counting by 2 without number line	Skip counting by 2 with number line	Using doubles facts	Could not do	Initial struggle stage
NG stage 1	20	1								
NG stage 2	2	12						7		
NG stage 3		14		1		4		2		
NG stage 4		7	5	2		2		2	3	2
NG stage 5		1	10	1		2	2	1	4	6
NG stage 6		3	1	1	5	3			8	2
FG stage 10				1		3	2	1	14	4
FG stage 20						1	1	1	18	1
Inverse						1[a]			20	

[a]Drew 19 circles first

Table 5.1b Grade 2 students' first round interview results on the zebra legs patterning task ($n=21$)

Subtasks	Perceptual subitizing	Counting all without number line	Counting on without number line	Counting on with number line	Skip counting by 2 without number line	Combined counting all and counting on with number line	Drew sticks and grouped by 4	Could not do	Initial struggle stage
NG stage 1	12	8	1						
NG stage 2		15	4		1			1	1
NG stage 3		13	5					3	
NG stage 4		11	6	1				3	2
NG stage 5		8	4	1				8	5
NG stage 6									
FG stage 10						2		19	2
FG stage 20								21	
Inverse							1	20	

Table 5.2a Grade 2 students' second round interview results on the dog eyes patterning task (n = 19)

Subtasks	Perceptual subitizing	Counting all without number line	Counting on without number line	Skip counting by 2 without number line	Using doubles facts	Skip counting by 10	Grouped by 2	Could not do	Initial struggle stage
NG stage 1	17								
NG stage 2	2	7	2	7	1				
NG stage 3		7	2	9	1				
NG stage 4		7	3	6	1			2	3
NG stage 5		9	3	6	1				1
NG stage 6									
FG stage 10		1	2	8		1		7	6
FG stage 20				1	1			17	
Inverse							6	13	

Table 5.2b Grade 2 students' second round interview results on the zebra legs patterning task (n = 19)

Subtasks	Perceptual subitizing	Counting all without number line	Counting on without number line	Skip counting by 4 without number line	Using doubles facts	Skip counting by 2	Grouped by 4	Could not do	Initial struggle stage
NG stage 1	14	5							
NG stage 2	2	6	7	2	2				
NG stage 3		11	7	1					
NG stage 4		9	8	1					
NG stage 5		8	8	1				2	2
NG stage 6									
FG stage 10		1	3	1		1	1	14	1
FG stage 20								14	
Inverse							5	14	

count. Perceptual subitizing was evident when the students initially attended to stage 1 in both patterns. In dealing with the near generalization tasks beyond stage 2, there was a noticeable use of other arithmetical strategies beyond counting all. Further, about one-third of the students successfully dealt with all far generalization tasks. Sources of support on these tasks were the intensive classroom learning and instruction in exact number sense and student-generated diagrams (i.e. sticks and circles) during the interview session that enabled them to count correctly and obtain the correct values. Figure 5.6 shows two instances in which the students drew diagrams in order to help them monitor their counting processes and remember the numbers that they already counted. Nikki on the left drew 10 pairs of circles corresponding to stage 10 of the Fig. 5.5a pattern that enabled her to count to 20. Skype on the right obtained the same final value as Nikki but in his case he drew 10 circles and filled them one by one with numbers that corresponded to consecutive multiples of 2. Finally, while the inverse tasks continued to be difficult for most students despite the availability of drawn pictures of dog eyes and zebra legs, those who successfully processed them grouped each picture set either by 2 or by 4. Figure 5.7 shows two examples of student work on the inverse task involving the Fig. 5.5b pattern. David on the left circled sets of 4 legs that enabled him to conclude that 7 zebras had 28 legs in all. Manny on the right initially labeled all the square pictures with consecutive numbers from 1 to 4. He then noted that since there were 7 groups of consecutive numbers from 1 to 4, there were 7 zebras with 28 legs altogether.

Fig. 5.6 Second-grade student-generated diagrams in dealing with far generalization tasks

The development of different arithmetical strategies plays a significant role in graded pattern generalization processing, especially at the upper elementary levels when numbers taken as input units in patterning activity need to be interpreted in the context of a mathematical relationship. For example, the prevalent use of a counting all arithmetical strategy on both tasks in Fig. 5.5a, b prevented a majority of the second-grade students from establishing other meaningful invariant structural

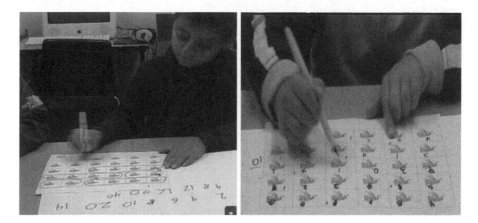

Fig. 5.7 Second-grade student-generated methods in dealing with an inverse task

relationships. Further, we also note that even with a noticeable shift toward the use of counting on, double facts, and skip counting strategies during the second interview, the students still needed additional training in interpreting them as instantiating particular structural relationships within and across the given input units. For example, when Lina was asked to explain her doubles fact $3+3=6$, which led her to conclude that 3 normal dogs had 6 eyes altogether, she said, "I first counted 3 [eyes] here [pointing to the three left eyes] and then I counted 3 more [eyes] here [pointing to the right eyes]." In dealing with 4, 5, and 10 dogs, however, she changed her arithmetical strategy and employed combinations of counting all and counting on strategies that enabled her to obtain the correct output values without needing to pay attention to possible mathematical relationships that she could have abduced from the strategies. None of the students employed the same arithmetical strategy consistently within and across the input units of the two patterns, which partly explains why they experienced considerable difficulties in dealing with the far generalization tasks. While they clearly exhibited parallel distributed processing on each pattern generalization task, the presence of several different choices (and connections) and the lack of metacognitive strategies such as perceptual agility and the need to stay consistent from one subtask to another in arithmetical processing prevented them from establishing meaningful incipient generalizations that would have worked for all far generalization tasks. Perceptual agility in pattern generalization involves "see[ing] several patterns and [a] willing[ness] to abandon those that do not prove useful [i.e., those that do not lead to a direct formula]" (Lee, 1996, p. 95).

Several recent research investigations that have been conducted with other groups of elementary (and middle) school students on number patterns have also articulated similar issues. Carpenter and Levi's (2000) studies with small groups of first- and second-grade students on true-false number sentences and open number sentences assessed their ability to think about properties of number operations, including the evidence and rules they employed to justify their generalizations. They note how many of the students "experienced difficulty" in developing explanations "that went beyond examples, although a number of students did recognize the necessity of more generalizable justifications" (p. 16). Central to the noted difficulty was the lack of a more sophisticated understanding of the equal symbol (i.e., the relation/ product issue) and appropriate notational systems for conveying, and rules for justifying, general explanations. Carraher, Schliemann, Brizuela, and Earnest's (2006) work with third-grade students in relation to the additive comparison task shown in Fig. 5.8a highlights the students' conceptual difficulties with mathematical language. Several students, for example, confused between the terms "taller" and "tall" and "shorter" and "short." It was only when the students reenacted the problem with three volunteers that they came to understand the relational terms. Also, even when they managed to generate correct values for the problem and illustrate their relationships with a diagram, there were still a few students who "remained hesitant about what region of their diagram corresponded to the values [4 inches and 6 inches]" (Carraher, Brizuela, & Schliemann, 1999, p. 2). Figure 5.8b illustrates samples of students' work on the Fig. 5.8a problem. Continuous engagement with particular instances (i.e. story situations) enabled them to engage in abduction and induction that eventually enabled them to establish a structural argument in the form of variable expressions (i.e. T, $T-4$, and $T+2$).

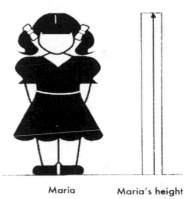

Tom is 4 inches taller than Maria.
Maria is 6 inches shorter than Leslie.
Draw Tom's height, Maria's height, and Leslie's height.
Show what the numbers 4 and 6 refer to.

Maria   Maria's height

Fig. 5.8a Additive comparison task (Carraher, Schliemann, Brizuela, & Earnest, 2007, p. 72)

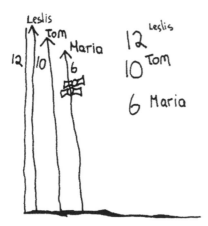

Tom is 4 inches taller than Maria.
Maria is 6 inches shorter than Leslie.

Fill out the table for Story 1.
Imagine Tom is 34 inches tall. How tall will Maria and Leslie be?

What if...	Tom	Maria	Leslie
Story 1	34 in.	30 in.	36 in.
Story 2	37 in.	33 in.	39 in.
Story 3	41 in.	37 in.	43 in.
Story 4	35 in.	31 in.	37 in.
Story 5	T	T−4	T+2

Then work out the answers for Stories 2, 3, and 4.

Fig. 5.8b Samples of student work on the Fig. 5.8a problem (Carraher et al., 2007, pp. 74 and 76)

Schliemann, Carraher, and Brizuela's (2007) work with third-grade students on function tables involving number relationships articulates the necessity of building meanings drawn from everyday contexts: "(W)hat makes everyday contexts powerful is not the concreteness of the objects or the realism of the situations dealt with in everyday life, but the meaning attached to the problems under consideration" (p. 103). For example, the authors used multiplication tables to introduce functional understanding involving inputs and outputs. The students learned to fill function tables such as the one shown in Fig. 5.9a involving a cookie seller who relied on the incomplete table for the prices. Over the course of the classroom teaching experiment involving function tables, the students obtained different rules that related the output values with the input terms. Interestingly enough, the conversations shifted from the use of additive strategies (e.g. "add 6 to 2," "add 2, plus 2, plus 2" in the case of the table in Fig. 5.9a) to multiplicative-based generalizations that conveyed direct proportional relationships (e.g. $3n$ or $n \times 3$ in relation to the Fig. 5.9a table) to expressions that reflected the structure of a general linear function (e.g. $n \times 2 + 1$ in the case of the table in Fig. 5.9b).

a

Boxes of Cookies	Price
1	
2	$6.00
3	$9.00
4	$12.00
	$15.00
	$18.00
7	$21.00
8	
9	$27.00
10	$30.00
N	

b

X	Y
1	
2	
3	
4	
5	
7	
8	
9	
10	
20	
30	
100	
N	

Fig. 5.9a, b Function tables (Schliemann et al., 2007)

Carpenter, Franke, and Levi's (2003) work with elementary school children on numeric-based pattern generalization and arithmetical thinking underscore the significance of relational thinking beyond calculating outcomes or results. For example, a second-grade student named Emma in their study initially thought about adding 28 and 32 by counting on from 27 in order to solve the number sentence $28 + 32 = 27 +$___, which was consistent with her early experiences involving smaller numbers (e.g. $7+6=$___$+5$). However, her thinking transitioned relationally when she established a relationship between the two expressions, as follows: "I think maybe 33 [is the answer] ... because 27 is one less than 28 and then 33 is one more than 32."

Numeric-based pattern generalizing that fosters relational thinking in Carpenter, Franke, and Levi's sense further supports growth in structural thinking and justification. For example, when the second-grade students in Carpenter et al.'s study dealt with the Mouse-Cage Patterning Task shown in Fig. 5.10a, they initially solved them in a disorganized manner, naming pairs of numbers that summed to 7 without searching for patterns both at the level of answers and organization. While the students managed to calculate possible pairs of answers, unfortunately, they felt unsure about whether they had generated all the possible answers. They eventually settled the issue when Marsha suggested the organized list shown in Fig. 5.10b. Over the course of several sessions, they solved similar problems involving different numbers (e.g. 52 mice and 147 mice). When they revisited the problem, "the students remember(ed) the problem, easily generate(d) the possibilities, and predict(ed) how many possibilities there would be for any given number of mice" (p. 69). Schweitzer's (2006) account of her longitudinal research in her combined first- and second-grade class also highlights the significance of relational thinking in her students' developing understanding of numbers and operations. Throughout the two years of working with the same group of children, she emphasized a patterns approach to, or a structural way of, thinking about the commutative property of addition, addition and subtraction facts, and fundamental numerical propositions such as $a+b=c$ implies $a+(b+1)=c+1$ (e.g. if $6+6=12$, then what is $6+7=?$) and $a+b=(a-x)+(b+x)$ (e.g. $39+14=(39+10)+(14-10)=49+4=53$), which made the resulting expressions easier and more reasonable to calculate than the original expressions. She also noted that models such as cubes and coupons (in the case of money) became tools her students used to explain their reasoning and understanding.

Ricardo has 7 pet mice. He keeps them in two cages that are connected so that the mice can go back and forth between the cages. One of the cages is big and other one is small. Show all the ways that 7 mice can be in two cages.

Fig. 5.10a Mouse-cage patterning task (Carpenter et al., 2003)

Big Cage	Small Cage
1	6
2	5
3	4
4	3
5	2
6	1
7	0
0	7

Fig. 5.10b Second-grade Marsha's list for the Fig. 5.9a pattern (Carpenter et al., 2003)

Moss & London McNab's (2011) study with 42 Grade 2 students in the USA and Canada investigated the many different ways they generalized rules for constructed (and not presented) function tables that had nonsequential pairs of inputs and outputs. In these cases, the students learned to focus on "the 'across' or function rule, rather than on the 'down' pattern or 'what comes next' strategy' strategy identified as interfering with functional generalizations" (p. 282). Consequently the form of their generalizations became more explicit than recursive and co-variational (i.e. expressing a consistent relationship between input and output).

Shape

Shape is not an inherent but an abstract property of a mathematical or physical object (Pizlo, Sawada, Li, Kropatsch, & Steinman, 2010), which implies that recognizing it involves conceptually constructing its characteristics via processes of abduction and induction in a dynamic manner. Here we foreground the perceptually relative nature of construction in a phenomenological sense, that is, one that draws primarily on individual learners' personal experiences with an object (cf. Hill & Bennett, 2008). The emergence of shape, in other words, is relational and viewpoint dependent (ibid). However, we also note that their (neural and psychological) perception of shapes of objects can change and be modified with (ongoing) experiences and support from the environment (Triadafillidis, 1995; Wallis & Bülthoff, 1999).

In figural pattern generalization, issues involving shape basically deal with the concept of similarity and, especially, the fixed and steady role of similarity in an emerging shape organization relative to a pattern (Gal & Linchevski, 2010). Sequences of figural objects such as the growing squares pattern in Fig. 5.11a are similar because they appear to have the same shape but not the same size.[2] Further, depending on the nature of the sequence or pattern conveyed through the stages, similarity means the relevant corresponding angles across the stages have the same measures and the corresponding parts are proportional according to some (constant) rule.

Sequences of figural objects that all have the same size and shape are congruent. The unit squares pattern in Fig. 5.11b, which is a typical pattern in many lower elementary mathematics textbooks, consists of congruent unit squares with the stage number determining the number of congruent unit squares that are constructed. In this case, the uniform shape conveys that other attributes of the pattern are more relevant to pattern generalization than the figures themselves. When patterns with uniform shapes are given to first-grade students, especially, they often provide

---

[2] Mathematically, the pattern stages in Fig. 5.11a represent dilations (i.e. there is a fixed central point of projection). There is no research that deals with pattern stages that appear as a sequence of similitudes (i.e. similar figures that involve both isometry and dilation). The squares in Fig. 5.11b represent congruent figures that by definition can be established by applying at least one isometric action (Kay, 2001).

useful contexts that engage them in, say, skip counting activity and learn beginning notions of functions. In this section, we dwell on issues surrounding more complex figural patterning tasks such as the one shown in Fig. 5.11a.

Consider the growing pattern of squares below. How might stage 8 look? What is its area and perimeter?

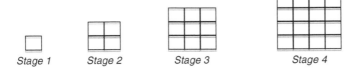

Stage 1   Stage 2   Stage 3   Stage 4

Fig. 5.11a Growing squares pattern

Consider the pattern of unit squares below. How does stage 8 of the pattern appear to you? How many edges are there in all?

Stage 1   Stage 2   Stage 3   Stage 4

Fig. 5.11b Separate unit squares pattern

Basic object or shape recognition is a skill that is central to figural pattern generalization. What is oftentimes assessed in pattern generalization activity is the consistency in which individual learners are able to conserve the same steady shape across the stages in a pattern. For example, the pattern stages in Fig. 5.11a together convey the same shape of squares having different dimensions. David's work in Figs. 5.1c, d, and 5.2b, c preserved the same shapes that he initially abduced on the basis of the given initial stages. Among lower elementary school children, in fact, their initial introduction to figural pattern generalizing involves having them copy the same shape(s) over several cycles (i.e. repeating patterns). Such activities basically target object or shape recognition and the construction of similarity relationships.

But how well do elementary students in the lower grades copy shapes of (complex) figural objects? A recent interesting study by Mulligan, Prescott, and Mitchelmore (2003) conducted with 109 Year 1 Australian children (ages 5–7 years) assessed their ability to copy a given geometric shape. The children were briefly shown a triangle consisting of six circles, as shown in Fig. 5.12a. They were asked to draw what they saw on a separate sheet of paper. The results indicate that only about 20% of them produced the same triangle. Figure 5.12b shows several different responses that the authors categorized according to type of structure, that is, from having no structure to fully structural.

Certainly, Mulligan et al's (2003) findings can be interpreted in several different ways. To begin with, copying a figural object requires the use of working memory. Just like the situation involving simple counting among young students, producing an exact copy of a figure means that they need to remember which aspect(s) of the figure have already been drawn. Feigenson (2011) notes that existing research findings claim that working memory is constrained by the "amount of information it can maintain at any given time"—that is, "observers of all ages appear able to concurrently represent three or four visual items in working memory but no more" (pp. 13–14; cf. Alvarez & Cavanagh, 2004; Feigenson & Carey, 2003; Luck & Vogel, 1997). Of course, the stipulated limit of three to four items can refer to three to four individual objects, sets of objects, and ensembles of objects. Cavanagh and He's (2011) work on spatial attentional mechanisms involving explicit counting of objects in static pictures and dynamic displays might also explain the different constructed figures shown in Fig. 5.12b. The remaining 80% of the students in Mulligan, Prescott, and Mitchelmore's study overcounted with a significant fraction unable to preserve the shape of the triangle. For Cavanagh and He (2011), explicit counting in both static and dynamic displays necessitates the performance of at least four tasks,

Fig. 5.12a   Triangle task (Mulligan et al., 2003, p. 24)

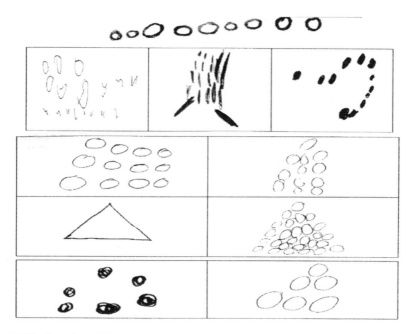

Fig. 5.12b   Samples of Year 1 students' work on the triangle task (Mulligan et al., 2003, pp. 25–26)

as follows: "select[ing] an uncounted item; increment[ing] the count; mark[ing] the just counted item; and stop[ping] when there are no more uncounted items" (pp. 23–24). In cases of static pictures involving figural objects such as the triangle shown in Fig. 5.12a, we should add the task of reconstructing the objects in a particular manner. Cavanagh and He (2011) also underscore the significance of an "attentional indexing mechanism" in which an "attentional system is capable of indexing individual objects in visual space" (p. 30). However, they note that items arranged "in a way that minimizes overcrowding" enables attentional indexing with a larger number of items possible. Hence, among elementary students, psychological issues such as constraints in working memory and their developing spatial and attentional indexing mechanisms can influence the manner in which they deal with complex figural object representing and pattern generalizing such as the ones shown in Figs. 5.11a and 5.12a.

In light of the preceding discussion on possible psychological constraints in recognizing shapes, including the representational modes that are used to describe parts or configurations of shapes (e.g. qualitative verbal descriptions or quantitative count of objects; continuous and approximate or discrete and exact diagrams), Rivera (2010b) assessed a group of US second-grade students' preformal competence in extending several different kinds of increasing patterns. We note that the students involved in this particular study were the same ones that we talked about in the preceding section on numbers. In this particular aspect of the study, they each participated in a series of three clinical interviews. In the first interview, they dealt with the two-stage semi-free (ambiguous) patterning task shown in Fig. 5.13. In the second interview, a slight modification of the same ambiguous figural task was presented with three instead of two initial pattern stages. In the third interview, they dealt with the three figural patterns shown in Figs. 5.14–5.16. In this section, our discussion focuses on the shapes of their extensional (or far) generalizations, which we basically categorize by type of similarity alone. That is, similarity performance in figural pattern generalization ranges in competence from having no similarity across the pattern stages to manifestations of partial similarity and then to evidence of full similarity. A figural pattern that is *fully similar* to a learner means that there is an interpreted consistent (thus, steady) shape that is conserved and shared across the given stages and the constructed extensions of the pattern. A figural pattern that is *partially similar* means that there is at least one notable local inconsistency in any of the constructed shapes despite the manifestation of a common or shared shape across the stages of the pattern. Sources of inconsistency pertain to factors that distort the abduced similarity relationships (e.g. careless attention paid to the relevant angles, drawn stages that have disproportionate features of the same shape). A figural pattern that has *no similarity* implies that there is no steady shape that binds and organizes the pattern stages together in some way. In developing these caegories, we acknowledge the possible interactions of other factors such as the continuous and approximate vs. discrete and exact senses in which young learners perceive objects and their shapes. Such interactions have been carefully monitored in both the collection and analysis aspects of the study.

Table 5.3 provides summaries of the students' responses in relation to the semi-free task shown in Fig. 5.13. About 80% of the students did not construct any steady similarity relationship across the given stages of the pattern. When the given stages were increased from two to three, that also did not help. Consequently, none of them successfully established any kind of incipient generalization. Figure 5.17 shows two common extensions provided by students who exhibited no similarity in their constructed extensions. Many of them simply added one circle to three circles with no further explanation. A few students like Skype in Fig. 5.17 narrowly focused on

2-Stage Ambiguous Task: Let us begin with a square and call it step 1. Now suppose step 2 looks like as shown. How many squares do you see?

Step 1   Step 2

A. How might step 3 appear to you? Show me with the blocks.

B. Show me steps 4 and 5. How many squares do you see?

C. Pretend we do not have any more blocks and suppose we skip steps. If someone asks you how step 10 looks like, how might you respond? Can you describe or draw it for me?

(In the second interview, we added step 3 as shown on the right. Students then constructed steps 4, 5, 8, and 10.)

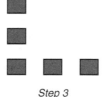

Step 3

Fig. 5.13 A semi-free (ambiguous) pattern

House Pattern: These are how our stages in a pattern look like.

Stage 1   Stage 2   Stage 3

A. Can you show with the blocks what comes next? How might stage 4 might look like to you? How about stage 5?

B. Let us skip stages. Can you draw or describe in words how stage 10 might look like? How do you know for sure?

Fig. 5.14 House pattern task

Flower Pattern: Below are the stages in our pattern.

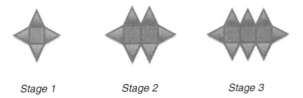

Stage 1   Stage 2   Stage 3

A. Can you show with the blocks what comes next? How stage4 might look like to you? How about stage 5?

B. Let us skip stages. Can you draw or describe in words how stage 10 might look like? How do you know for sure?

Fig. 5.15 Flower pattern task

Triangle Pattern: Let us form a pattern from circles. Stage 1 has one circle. Let me build stage 2. How many circles are there? Let me build stage 3. How many circles are there this time?

Stage 1   Stage 2   Stage 3

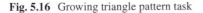

A. Can you show with the circle chips how stage 4 might look like to you? How about stage 5?

B. Let us skip stages. Can you draw or describe in words how stage 10 might look like? How do you know for sure?

Fig. 5.16 Growing triangle pattern task

stage 3. They counted five circles and began constructing extensions that had two circles more than the stipulated stage number, which became the rule for their emerging pattern. A few other students like Katya in Fig. 5.17 initially recognized the sequence 1, 3, and 5, saw that the values increased by 2, and then simply used the blocks on the table to help them obtain the succeeding values without paying any attention to shape at all.

Figure 5.18 shows two students' work that exhibited partial similarity. Lina abduced the same L-shaped figure across her pattern but was inconsistent in terms of the dimensions of the two legs. Gemiliano also abduced the same L-shaped figure but produced the following sequence: $\{1, 2+1, 3+2, 4+1, 5+2, 6+1, 7+2, 8+1\}$. Each stage in his pattern consisted of two columns of circles with the first column of circles corresponding to stage number and the second column oscillating between one and two circles. Unfortunately, he was unable to deal with stage 10 correctly. He also could not explain the role of stage 1 in his pattern.

Table 5.4 provides summaries of the students' responses for the figural patterns shown in Figs. 5.14–5.16. The Flower Pattern task in Fig. 5.15 produced more fully

Jana, Second Interview　　　　　　　　Selma, Second Interview

Skype, Second Interview　　　　　　　Katya, Scond Interview

Fig. 5.17 Examples of no similarity extensions of the Fig. 5.13 semi-free pattern

Lina, Second Grade　　　　　　　　Gemiliano, Second Grade

Fig. 5.18 Examples of partial similarity extensions of the Fig. 5.13 semi-free pattern

similar figures than the House Pattern task in Fig. 5.14, while the Triangle Pattern task in Fig. 5.16 produced fewer fully and partially similar figures than either the Flower Pattern or the House Pattern task. Except for one student who consistently produced fully similar figures in all three tasks, the remaining students' overall performance during the interview sessions exemplified graded pattern generalizing behavior. That is, their similarity performances were influenced by how they perceived the complexity of the tasks. Figures 5.19 and 5.20 show samples of underdeveloped or unsteady similar figures on the Flower Pattern and the House Pattern tasks. Among the partially similar responses such as the ones shown in Fig. 5.19, the

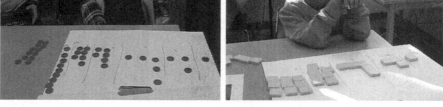

Table 5.3 Grade 2 students' pattern generalization involving the semi-free task shown in Fig. 5.13

Figure 5.13 first interview results ($n=21$)

Given:

	NS	PS	FS
Near stage 3	18	2	1
Near stage 4	18	2	1
Near stage 5	16	2	1
Far stage 10	2	0	0

Figure 5.13 second interview results ($n=19$)

Given:

	NS	PS	FS
Near stage 4	16	2	0
Near stage 5	16	2	0
Near stage 8	14	2	0
Far stage 10	2	0	0

students found it difficult to account for the correct number of triangles surrounding the middle squares. Some of them either overcounted (Eddie and Jana) or undercounted (Jake). In Juan's case, when asked if he saw anything that was interesting within and across the given stages, he claimed that he saw triangles and squares and nothing else. In the case of the House Pattern, Jana in Fig. 5.20 also expressed the same view as Juan in Fig. 5.19. Also, those students who produced partially similar figures once again either overcounted (Lina in Fig. 5.20) or undercounted (Gemiliano in Fig. 5.20) the number of squares under each triangle.

The Triangle Pattern in Fig. 5.16 was a very difficult task for most of the students. While the intent of the task was not to suggest or impose a growing triangle, about 60% of the students produced different figures from stage to stage (Cesar, Lina, and Eddie in Fig. 5.21), which indicate no similarity in their perceptions of the pattern stages. In fact only one student, Joko, inferred a steady growing triangle. Among the no similar responses, a few of them justified their figures by appealing to the successor property of whole numbers (Cesar: "stage 3 has 6 circles, so stage 4 has 7 circles, stage 8 has 8 circles"). A few others abduced that the number of circles at any given stage would be twice the stipulated stage number (Lina: "stage 3 has 6 circles, so stage 4 has 8 circles, and stage 5 has 10 circles"). There were students like Eddie who simply added circles from stage to stage to indicate that they were seeing an increasing pattern and nothing else. Those who produced partially similar figures overcounted (David), narrowly focused on one aspect of their figures (Alain), and narrowly specialized on a given stage (Drake).

Juan, Second Grade   Eddie, Second Grade

Jana, Second Grade   Jake, Second Grade

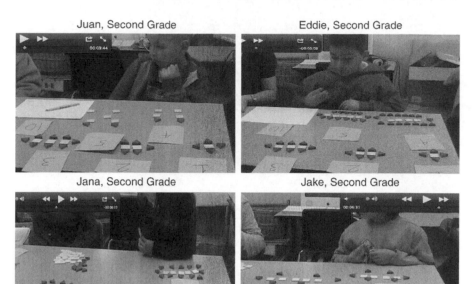

Fig. 5.19 Samples of underdeveloped similar figures for the flower pattern in Fig. 5.15

Lina, Second Grade   Gemiliano, Second Grade   Jana, Second Grade

Fig. 5.20 Partially similar responses on the house pattern in Fig. 5.14

Figural Properties

Establishing stable (i.e. common and repetitive) properties of shapes across the given and extended stages in a pattern is also a graded constructive phenomenon. In this section, we further discuss figural property discernment, which basically employs operative apprehension (Duval, 1999). An operative apprehension of an object involves interpretively generating and constructing stable properties (i.e. units, parts, features, components, configurations, etc.) that characterize and organize an emerging structure relative to the perceived object. Studies with infants and

Joko, Second Grade   Cesar, Second Grade

Lina, Second Grade   Eddie, Second Grade

David, Second Grade   Alain, Second Grade

Drake, Second Grade

Fig. 5.21 Student responses on the triangle pattern in Fig. 5.14

young children indicate a natural (and approximate) ability to recognize, categorize, and organize objects (Bhatt & Quinn, 2011; Goldstone, Son, & Byrge, 2011; Schyns, Goldstone, & Thibaut, 1998). However, in (exact) patterning activity, the primary issue involves understanding the extent to which learners are capable of discerning properties that produce structures of a particular kind (i.e. algebraically useful generalizations).

Elementary school children with no formal experiences in patterning are likely to establish properties that rely on similarity obtained through (surface) appearances. With more formal training, they will learn to perceive such properties in terms of

Table 5.4 Summary of Grade 2 students' responses for the figural patterns 5.14, 5.15, and 5.16 ($n = 20$)

Figure 5.14 house pattern data

	NS	PS	FS
Near stage 4	3	5	12
Near stage 5	3	5	12
Far stage 10	3	5	12

Figure 5.15 flower pattern data

	NS	PS	FS
Near stage 4	1	6	18
Near stage 5	1	6	18
Far stage 10	1	6	18

Figure 5.16 triangle pattern data

	NS	PS	FS
Near stage 4	12	7	1
Near stage 5	12	7	1
Far stage 10	12	7	1

(function) rules that emerge as a result of coordinating their inferential processes of abduction, induction, and deduction. For example, David in Fig. 5.1b initially abduced houses consisting of triangles and squares that increased by the stage number. He then tested his structure on the fourth and fifth steps. His drawn stage 10 in Fig. 5.1d could be interpreted as a consequence of implementing a deductive argument, which involves using both his abduction (general rule) and the available instances on the table (the stages) as his hypotheses, thus, enabling him to necessarily conclude that stage 10 would have the same structure consisting of a definite number of triangles and squares arranged in a particular way. Hence, a mathematically valid figural property discernment in pattern generalization activity involves the construction (abduction and induction) and justification (deduction) of rules that apply within and across the pattern stages. In Duval's (1998) terms, the construction phase recruits both perceptual and operative apprehension mechanisms, while the justification phase employs discursive apprehension in which case the necessary figural properties that apply to the stages in a pattern are causally explained relative to an interpreted structure that produced them in the first place. Discursive reasoning from near to far generalization consequently shifts in context from the particularity of a few instances to the necessary steps (i.e. properties) in constructing the known stages in the pattern independent of the initial operative action, that is, a structure is necessarily imposed discursively (i.e. structurally argued) on the projected far stages of the pattern.

However, the emergence of such rules among elementary school children is fraught with a few conceptual difficulties. Especially in the case of growing patterns, first-grade students' initial patterning experiences oftentimes involve establishing recursively additive generalizations (Blanton & Kaput, 2004; Taylor-Cox, 2003). For example, a rule for the pattern in Fig. 5.11b would have them constructing the rule "add 4," which is not an algebraically useful generalization. In graded pattern generalizing, such prior knowledge is expected to manifest itself in their emerging generalizations. The dilemma, of course, is that discerning the property of adding four each time to generate a new square from one stage to the next does not appear to be as essential as perceiving the pattern in terms of sides that increase by multiples of 4, which is an algebraically useful generalization. When emergent generalizations have the property of algebraic usefulness, any far task can be induced without having to construct the preceding stages, a rather inefficient strategy that is performed in any case of recursively additive generalizations. Figure 5.22 shows a US third-grade student's painstaking additively recursive of generating the total number of squares for stage 10 relative to the given pattern. Nikki initially saw the pattern to be increasing by two squares at every stage. She then constructed stages 4 and 5 with circle counters following her recursive rule. In dealing with stage 10, she transitioned numerically from the figural cues and patiently added two until she obtained 21 squares in all. Tanisli and Özdas (2009) also report similar findings concerning the prevalent use of additively recursive formulas among Grade 5 students (mean age of 10 years) in Turkey when they established generalizations for linear and quadratic figural patterns.

Hence, in this section, figural property discernment involves the construction and justification of algebraically useful configurations. Following Duval (1999), such discernment fundamentally involves cognitive actions of *processing* and *conversion* beyond mere visual perception,[3] where processing involves implementing figural

---

[3] For Duval (1999), visualization is an "intrinsically semiotic" (i.e. neither mental nor physical) cognitive activity. He distinguishes between visual perception (vision), which is primitive, and visualization, which has both epistemological and synoptic functions. Vision primarily engenders direct access and intuition of objects, while visualization involves the construction of a (semiotic) representation (epistemological function). In any semiotic representation, "relations or, better, organization of relations between representational units" are noted, including and especially those that are not at "all that accessible to vision" (Duval, p. 13). Also, while vision initially apprehends objects and their totality, it is never a "complete apprehension" (ibid) unlike visualization that engenders discourse and deductive actions (synoptic function).

operations such as making figural transformations or reconfigurations on the pattern stages in order to see an emerging structure better and conversion involves translating one representational context into another (e.g. Nikki's combined verbal and pictorial description that transitioned to numerical sentences in Fig. 5.22). Figure 5.23 exemplifies three figural processing strategies on a pattern that have been drawn from the work of three Australian Year 5 students (ages 9–10 years) in Cooper and Warren's (2011) study who processed the stages in three different but equivalent ways. Their converted representations reflect the figural processing they imposed on the stages. All three of them operatively apprehended growing twin towers of blocks. Ron saw one tower with height $(n+1)$ and another tower with height n. For Sue, the tower consisted of two equal columns of blocks with an extra block on the top left column. Jane initially imagined a full two-column tower of blocks that enabled her to calculate its height, $2\times(n+1)$. She then subtracted 1 from the total height in order to convey that she was taking away the unnecessary block that was initially added.

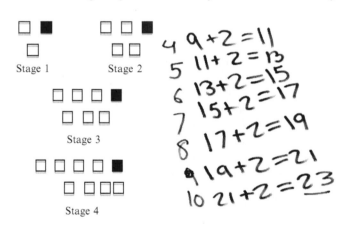

Fig. 5.22 US third-grade student's pattern generalization of the two-row patterning task

What is apparently complex among learners when both cognitive actions of processing and conversion are performed deals with issues that pertain to their coordination, especially "between registers of representation" (Duval, 1999, p. 11). One specific issue relevant to the figural processing of patterns involves perceptual agility, an acquired ability of "seeing several patterns and a willingness to abandon those that do not prove algebraically useful" (Lee, 1996, p. 95). If a certain figural processing strategy will not yield an algebraically useful conversion, the task of changing registers from, say, the verbal to the algebraic will be difficult and almost impossible. Nikki in Fig. 5.22 figurally processed a non- algebraically useful recursive structure that she verbally described in clear terms. However, she was unable to apply it when she had to deal with stage 100 of the pattern. According to Duval (1999), learners need to know how to select relevant configurations that "could cause the anticipation of the kind of" (p. 17) meaningful conversions that are congruent, an "essential condition" that brings forth a sufficient "transparency" and enables an "easy translation" from the "starting register to the target register" (ibid, p. 10).

The task is especially daunting for elementary students since figural patterns, like geometrical objects, "have not one but many possible configurations or subconfigurations" (ibid, p. 17).

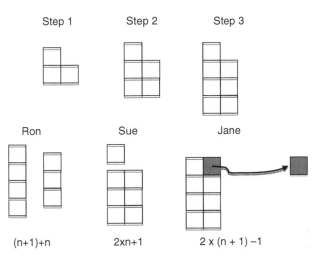

Fig. 5.23 Year 5 students' algebraically useful structures for the tower pattern (Cooper & Warren, 2011, p. 198)

Since figural processing that yields algebraically useful structures appears to be necessary, its emergence and development can effectively take place in socially objectifying situations and activities. The term *socially objectifying* is used in Radford's (2010) sense in which students in joint activity with one another "become acquainted with the historically constituted cultural meanings and forms of reasoning and action" (p. 3). Classroom mathematical activities are seen as the site of relational-driven communal zones of proximal development, where "instruction leads the course of development and that such a course depends on the kind of relationship that is created between [a] student and her context" (ibid). Radford illustrates a socially objectifying figural processing in the context of his work with a class of Grade 2 Canadian students (ages 7–8 years). When the students began to investigate the pattern in Fig. 5.22, one group of students initially abduced the common difference of two squares between two consecutive dependent terms and appeared oblivious to possible spatial configurations. Realizing this, the teacher (Natasha) stepped in and collaborated with them in constructing an algebraically useful structure that consists of a bottom row with n squares and a top row with $(n+1)$ squares. In the joint activity phase, Natasha implicitly conveyed to the group an intentional abduction that became their basis for further induction. The abductive structure became explicitly known to the group via pointing gestures, words, and rhythm, which could be considered as grade-level appropriate semiotic means of objectification. We also note that Natasha shared with the entire class another group-generated algebraically useful structure—that is, two equal rows of white squares and a dark square—that enabled the students to deal with two additional far generalization tasks. In his analysis of the patterning activity, Radford points out that the students' converted structures did not involve a transformation in representational form from the verbal to the algebraic consisting of variables, terms, and operations but reflected the use of "embodied formulas" that "instead of being expressed through letters [were] expressed through actions unfolding in space and time" (p. 7).

A further analysis of the preceding study highlights the significant role of the teacher in the social objectification of exact figural processing, which involves coordinating shape, numerical count, and figural configurations around mathematical conditions of consistency and stability in pattern generalization (cf. Carraher, Martinez, & Schliemann, 2008; Warren & Cooper, 2007). For example, Natasha effectively engaged her students in repeated inductive actions on the pattern shown in Fig. 5.22. She initially asked them to "look at the squares at the bottom … just the squares at the bottom" (p. 4). She then engaged them in a series of verification steps, as follows: "In Term 1, how many?" "Term 2?" "Term 3?" "Term 5?" "Term 6?" "Term 7?" "Term 8?" She also employed the same rhythmic pointing gestures for the top row squares.

Warren's and Cooper (2011) have also pointed out the effective use of teacher-mediated figural parsing in the context of their patterning work with Australian Year 4 students (mean age of 9 years). Their students began to perceive patterns as conveying structures with invariant parts as a consequence of the joint activity that took place between them and their teacher. We contrast this particular finding with inexact and approximate figural processing of patterns that many elementary students have been documented to manifest in some cases of patterning tasks in the absence of any formal instruction or intervention from their teachers. Some students, like David in Fig. 5.2c, Lina in Fig. 5.18, and the children in Fig. 5.19, could figurally process stages into parts. However, the parts themselves do not reflect a consistent and stable structure across the pattern stages. Some other students, like David in Fig. 5.4b, Gemiliano in Fig. 5.18, and Drake in Fig. 5.21, could also figurally process stages into parts. However, they tend to ignore the initial stages in a pattern and instead narrowly specialize on the last given stage of the pattern. Consequently, while their extended stages may appear to be consistent and stable, the stages altogether fail to be an unambiguous and a well-defined pattern.

(Exact) Figural processing that yields algebraically useful structures may also occur in objectifying situations and activities that are not fully social, that is, without assistance from, say, a teacher. This may happen in cases of patterning tasks that either have figural goodness or are causally potent. In such cases, they possess (in a distributed sense) arrangements that have evident structural features such as symmetry and repetitiveness and may be figurally parsed without much effort (Pothos & Ward, 2000; Rivera, 2011). For example, in Table 5.4, roughly 15 out of 20 second-graders in Rivera's (2010b) study obtained correct far generalizations relative to Figs. 5.14 and 5.15 patterns in the absence of formal instruction. Their constructed near and far generalizations reflect a consistent and stable interpreted structure across the given and extended pattern stages. We should note the fact that they initially experienced difficulty in (exact) figural conversion in third grade when they had to transform their verbal-based structures in arithmetical form involving the addition and multiplication operations. They overcame such difficulty when they developed a firm understanding of the meaning of multiplication. Hence, figural goodness or causal potency and relevant mathematical concepts provide powerful supporting knowledge in the absence of teacher (and classroom) intervention.[4]

Table 5.5 provides a summary of the third-grade students' pattern generalization performance on the five tasks shown in Fig. 5.24. Less than 58% of the 19 students interviewed were successful in transitioning from the specificity of their

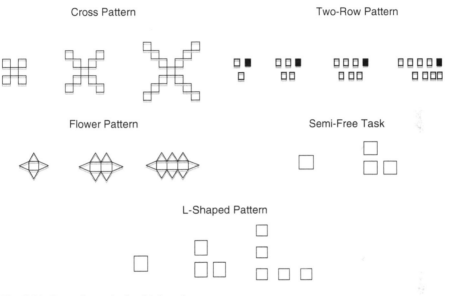

Fig. 5.24 Patterning tasks for third graders

[4] Context of the clinical interviews in third grade: The interviews took place toward the end of the school year without any intervening teaching experiment on patterns. Lack of instructional time prevented the third-grade class from exploring patterning activity. However, the author worked with the third grade teacher in ensuring that the entire third grade mathematics curriculum fostered structural and multiplicative thinking within and across the strands (i.e., number sense, algebra, statistics, data analysis, and probability, and geometry and measurement) were given the option to use the blocks to reconstruct the stages, however, they were asked to draw all the extended stages on paper. Like in the previous year, individual students were clinically interviewed on the five figural patterning tasks shown in Fig. 5.24. In each task, they were asked to: (1) construct stages 4 and 5 based on their initial interpretation of the given stages; (2) verbally describe stage 10; (3) try to transform their verbal description in arithmetical form involving whole numbers and the operations of multiplication and addition; and (4) state the total number of objects in stage 100 by using the arithmetical formula they established in (3). Concrete blocks were provided throughout the interview and drawn pictures of the pattern stages were shown one by one. The students were given the option to use the blocks to reconstruct the stages, however, they were asked to draw all the extended stages on paper.

Table 5.5 US third-grade students' performance on the pattern generalization tasks shown in Fig. 5.24 ($n = 19$)

	Near Stage 4	Near Stage 5	Far Stage 10	Far generalization expressions
Cross pattern	17	17	14	$100 \times 4 + 1$ or $4 \times 100 + 1$: 11 responses ("4 groups of 100 squares plus 1 square in the middle")
				Constructed stage 10 correctly but could not state a direct formula: 5 responses
				No structure: 2 responses
Two-row pattern	17	17	6	$2 \times 100 + 1$: 6 responses ("2 groups of 100 squares plus the shaded square")
				$100 \times 2 + 1$: 1 response ("100 groups of 2 squares plus the shaded square")
				$100 \times 2 + 1$: 2 responses ("100 top-bottom pairs of 2 squares plus the shaded square")
				Stage 10: $19 + 2 = 21$: 1 response ("Keep adding 2," see Fig. 5.22)
				No structure: 2 responses
Flower pattern	15	15	10	$2 \times 100 + 102$: 1 response ("100 triangles each on first and third rows and 102 squares in the middle row")
				$100 \times 3 + 2$: 2 responses (3 rows of 100 (squares and triangles) plus the 2 side triangles")
				$2 \times 101 + 100$: 1 response ("2 groups of 101 triangles and the 100 squares in the middle")
				Constructed stage 10 correctly but could not state a direct formula: 10 responses
Semi-free task	4	4	2	$99 \times 2 + 1$: 2 responses
				$100 + 1$: 1 response
				No structure: 15 responses
L-shaped task	11	11	5	$2 \times 99 + 1$ or $99 \times 2 + 1$: 8 responses ("2 groups of 99 squares plus the corner square")
				Constructed stage 10 correctly but could not state a direct formula: 3 responses
				$100 + 99$: 1 response ("100 squares down and 99 squares across")
				No structure: 8 responses

constructed stages and verbal-based structural descriptions to an arithmetical direct expression. Those who were unable to perform a conversion could not bring together and coordinate two different registers of representations for the same object (i.e. patterns) resulting in a conversion split. However, those who were successful in converting them could be explained by the congruent relationship between their verbally induced structures and arithmetical expressions.

Figure 5.25 illustrates three different algebraically useful structures for the Two-Row patterning task in Fig. 5.24. In all three cases, the students successfully coordinated their figural processing and conversion in a single action. Stan's generalization was the most frequent response. He immediately saw "two rows of circles

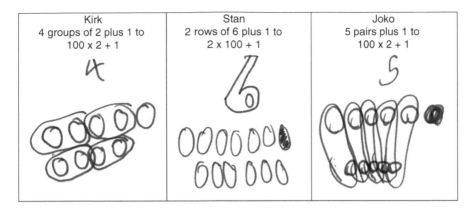

Fig. 5.25 Three different structures for the two-row patterning task in Fig. 5.24

and a dark circle" that he then conveyed arithmetically in that order, "[stage 100} there are 2 rows of 100 circles, 2×100, plus 1 for the [dark] circle at the end." The responses of Kirk and Joko reflect the manner in which they understood the concept of multiplication of whole numbers, which explains the evident use of circling groups of two objects that led them to their respective generalizations.

On the (Presymbolic and Nonsymbolic[5]) Algebraic Nature of Elementary Students' Embodied Generalizations: Gestures, Pictures, Words, Numbers, and the Emergence of Structures

Based on the foregoing discussion, elementary students are naturally drawn to expressing their incipient generalizations in several different ways and their competence does not appear to be transitional but graded due to the nature and level of complexity of a patterning task. What is certainly remarkable and impressive about children who have no formal experiences in patterning involves their disposition to choose and develop representations that they find meaningful, which conveys the embodied nature of their generalizations that are all directly tied to their developing perceptual apprehensions, operative assumptions and expectations, and sensorimotor actions on the patterns. Hence, their representations take shape in many forms through the use of gestures, pictures, words, numbers, and combinations of forms depending on their prior and ongoing experiences and context. Also, while their constructed expressions of generality oftentimes involve pictures, words, and

---

[5] In Chap. 7, we distinguish nonsymbolic and pre-symbolic algebra from symbolic algebra based on Heeffer's (2008, 2010) classification. Readers are referred to the section "Representations of Patterns in Three Contexts" (pp. 184–188) for details.

numbers, their justifications tend to be primarily gestural in nature at least prior to formal instruction. For example, David in Fig. 5.1b employed the same steady gesture as a way of expressing how he was apprehending the general shape of the given pattern stages. One consequence of formal instruction in patterning involves gesture fading in which case gestures are converted to diagrams in the form of external grouping processes such as the circling method in Fig. 5.25. The diagrams then become the basis for converting to the corresponding congruent arithmetical expressions. Suffice it to say, the graded quality of elementary students' pattern generalizations over time points to the embedded nature of at least two contexts in which such generalizations emerge with the initial context drawing quite heavily on their actual (physical) actions on the patterns and the learned context focusing on the (conceptual) relations that they extract from such actions.

While Radford (2010) in the preceding section has referred to elementary students' generalizations in patterning activity as exemplifying instances of embodied formulas, they also convey parallel forms of pre-symbolic generalizations that are either structurally iconic or indexical and nonsymbolic generalizations (Rivera, 2011). At least in the initial phase, they are structurally iconic and indexical direct expressions that resemble the structural contexts of their emergence—that is, their meanings are linked to how they are apprehended both perceptually and operatively by individual learners. The numeric terms convey the number of objects that are seen (a perceived similarity between sign and object, hence, iconic), while the overall verbal, gestural, and/or arithmetical expression with either the indicated or implicitly stated operations show the manner in which the objects are concretely and physically seen (an inferred relationship between sign and object, hence, indexical). Later, during the deductive phase of generalizing, where both the rule (established by abduction and induction) and the known instances (both given and extended stages) are used as hypotheses in order to justify a conclusion (an inferred structure that applies to all the projected stages), the expressions further evolve into structurally nonsymbolic generalizations. That is, the focus of cognitive attention is the empirically drawn rule. Students conceptually disregard the objects that comprise the stages in favor of the rule, which is determined by some (learned or social) convention, rule, code, agreement, or causality. For example, the circling process and the use of the term "m groups of n" in Fig. 5.25 have to be understood in terms of the manner in which the students interpret the meaning of multiplication.

Hence, among elementary students, psychological and pedagogical issues regarding their generalizations can be assessed on the following points that are not necessarily mutually exclusive but related:

- (*Type of relationship being inferred*) Are the generalizations structurally iconic, indexical, or nonsymbolic?
- (*Type and complexity of apprehension being manifested*) What factors support and hinder the development of structurally iconic and indexical generalizations?
- (*Context of rule being inferred*) What factors support and hinder the development of nonsymbolic structural generalizations?

Figure 5.26 captures the sense in which pattern generalization competence emerges among elementary students. Following Deacon (1997), there is a bidirec-

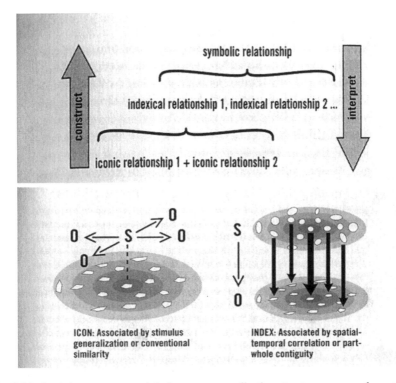

Fig. 5.26 Graded emergence model of pattern generalization structures among elementary students (adapted from Deacon, 1997, pp. 75 and 79)

tional relationship among iconic, indexical, and symbolic generalizations with the nonsymbolic generalizations with the nonsymbolic ones drawing and operating on the relevant iconic and indexical forms. Iconic representations are oftentimes the first to emerge. They are perceptually and operatively apprehended and are influenced by similarity of forms (numerical, figural, or both). Indexical representations emerge via the spatial and numerical relationships that are initially inferred on the objects. Nonsymbolic representations emerge as a logical consequence of seeing that a relationship between a particular sign and its object "*is a function of* the relationship it has" (Deacon, 1997, p. 86) with *all* the given and the projected stages in a pattern.

Arithmetical Numbers as Intuited and Tacit Variables in Algebraic Contexts

Another significant finding drawn from elementary students' ability to construct and justify incipient generalizations on certain patterns involves the manner in which they perceive the relevant numbers. That is, when they are successful in dealing with certain patterning tasks in a structural context, their reasoning manifests an implicit understanding and correct use of variables through arithmetical numbers. For example, the three students in Fig. 5.25 were clearly cognizant of their abduced structures. Hence, the use of arithmetical numbers emerged naturally during the process of induction. This situation resembles the *static geometric-solving phase* (Katz, 2007) in the history of algebra when Al-Khwarizmi's famous rhetorical-driven (i.e. verbal-based) manual for solving arithmetical problems primarily employed concrete numbers as his way of demonstrating the manner in which "he grasp[ed] the procedure of [a] solution in its entire universality" (Kvasz, 2006, p. 292). Concrete numbers to him and among those who were still oblivious to the use of variables used concrete numbers for illustrative purposes. Arithmetical numbers employed in this sense capture the context in which we use the term "nonsymbolic algebra" (Heeffer, 2008).

Referring once again to Radford's (2010) work with a small group of three Grade 2 Canadian students on the figural pattern shown in Fig. 5.22, they initially abduced an invariant structure for the pattern (i.e. two horizontal rows of squares determined by the stage number and the dark corner square) prior to performing induction involving stages 25, 50, and 500. For Radford, their emergent in-action formulas implicitly employed an *intuited variable*. Further, such formulas evolved into a "more sophisticated form of algebraic thinking" (Radford, p. 80) when the students transformed intuited variables into *tacit variables*. In Radford's study, this transition occurred when the teacher pulled out several cards with labels corresponding to stage number (e.g. 5, 15, 100, 104, etc.) that prodded the students to obtain and verbally articulate a generalization on the basis of the stipulated stage number. Rivera's (2010b) work with the US second-grade students also produced findings that were similar to Radford's (2010) study. Prior to any formal intervention and within the context of a clinical interview, Rivera asked 20 Grade 2 US students to obtain generalizations for the three figural patterns shown in Figs. 5.14–5.16. As shown in Table 5.4, between 12 and 18 of the 20 students obtained correct far generalizations for the Figs. 5.14 and 5.15 patterns and one student provided a correct far generalization in the case of the Fig. 5.16 pattern.

Hence, it seems to be the case that having an algebraically useful structure (and not just any structure for that matter) supports the emergence of arithmetical numbers as concrete variables in a nonsymbolic-algebraic context. Further, both Radford and Rivera articulated the significance of multimodality (gestures, rhythm, and language) that enabled their students to express their tacit variable-based generalizations. In Rivera's study, in particular, the students successfully generated tacit variable-based generalizations in closed forms, which they conveyed initially in a gestural-concrete mode and much later in pictorial form. The gestural-concrete mode enabled them to exhibit in-action formulas. In the pictorial mode, they were initially shown a card with a label corresponding to the stage number. Then they used a construction paper to draw the correct outcome for any far stage in the pattern that, following Radford (2010), is an indication of tacit variable-based generalizing.

The Emergence of Function Understanding via Structural Incipient Generalization

Our last remark in this chapter focuses on elementary students' understanding of functions in pattern generalization contexts. Recent research results drawn from classroom teaching experiments have shown younger children's natural capacity to construct and understand functions in context. Based on their work with prekindergarten to Grade 1 students, Blanton and Kaput (2011) note that table-based functions help students organize covarying data, which then enable them to transform the collected information from opaque (i.e. merely as a storage for ordered pairs of numbers) to transparent (i.e. "looking through to see new relationships" (p. 11)). Cooper and Warren's (2011) study with Australian Year 5 students (ages 9–10 years) also indicate their ability to "understand the workings of function machines in terms of numbers" (p. 200). Moss & London McNab's (2011) work with 7- and 8-year-old students in Canada and the USA on function machines exemplifies natural connections that students make between such machines and their understanding of multiplication that enabled them to establish and construct rules for the numbers in the machines. The authors also point out the value of designing function tables that consist of cues appearing in a nonsequential order so that students' attention are focused on covarying (vs. correspondence) relationships, which might encourage them to generate explicit (vs. recursive) rules. The studies of Carraher et al. (2008) and Vale and Pimentel (2010) conducted with Grade 3 students (ages 8–9 years) in the USA and Portugal, respectively, also employed function tables that had sequential cues. However, the dependent column consisted of arithmetical expressions instead of mere outputs that reflected an emerging structure for the pattern.

For example, in Carraher, Martinez, and Schliemann's case, the pattern generalization task had the students obtaining the maximum number of people that could sit in n number of detached square tables (one on each side). In a table provided for them to help them organize and analyze their thinking, the dependent column contained the expressions 1×4 and 2×4 that encouraged them to obtain an explicit rule for the pattern. In Vale and Pimentel's case, the pattern generalization task had their students obtaining the total number of objects that comprised a growing regular hexagon with a pair of triangular tails growing on opposite sides of the hexagon and increasing by the stage number (p. 81). The function table that was presented to them also had cues appearing in a sequential manner. However, the dependent terms reflected an emerging structure for the pattern, which took the form $1 + n + n$ or $1 + 2 \times n$, where n represents the stage number. In terms of curriculum development, Cai, Ng, and Moyer (2011) note the value accorded to functions as a big idea in the Singapore mathematics curriculum, which is introduced in Grade 2 (mean age of 8 years). At that level, students explore functional relationships in familiar numerical and figural contexts as an application of learning their multiplication facts and solving relevant multiplication problems.

Rivera's (2010b) work with the US Grade 2 students prior to formal instruction on patterns and functions also shows that some students seem to have the ability to construct functional relationships. As shown in Table 5.4, those students who were successful in constructing their far stages clearly saw and pictorially conveyed a relationship between stage number (as an input) and outcome in the absence of a function table.

In other words, the above findings indicate that having an algebraically useful structure is a minimal indicator that young children are capable of functional understanding. However, we still do not know the extent of such understanding. Rivera began to assess this issue in a clinical interview setting with the same second-grade cohort in a follow-up study that took place the following year when the students were in third grade. In his analysis, he employed the same definition of function that Carraher et al (2008) used in the context of their work with third-grade students. That is,

[a] function is a relation that uniquely associates members of one set with members of another set. More formally, a function from A to B is an object f such that every $a \in A$ is uniquely associated with an object $b \in B$. A function is therefore a many-to-one (or sometimes one-to-one) relation (Weisstein quoted in Carraher et al 2008, p. 10).

All 11 students who were successful in constructing and justifying a direct rule for the Cross Pattern in Fig. 5.24 (see Table 5.5) were asked if it was possible to generate different outcomes for the same inferred rule. Interestingly enough, all of them initially drew or constructed figures that merely changed the orientation of the original figures by rotation. Hence, in this particular figural patterning task, while the numerical outcomes for both the original and rotated figures were the same, the students saw the figures as conveying two different outcomes. Certainly with more learning, they will come to see them as equivalent.

In Chap. 6, we deal with pattern generalization studies that have been conducted with older children and adults. Readers are strongly encouraged to make comparisons between older and younger children in terms of their pattern generalization competence. For example, middle school students (ages 11 and above) tend to process patterns using a variety of numerical and recursively additive strategies. Even among adults, in fact, numerical generalizing strategies appear to be used more frequently than strategies that elementary school children in this chapter have been documented to exhibit. That is, young children's correct incipient structural generalizations are not additively recursive but additively multiplicative and functional. In other words, their use of visually drawn strategies naturally supports structural generalizations of the algebraic kind, unlike older individuals who, perhaps as a consequence of many years of training, tend to choose numerical strategies that lead to correct variable-based generalizations that they unfortunately are unable to justify in structural terms.

Chapter 6
Graded Pattern Generalization Processing of Older Students and Adults (Ages 11 and Up)

Growing Blocks Pattern Task: Blocks are packed to form pictures that form a pattern as shown below.

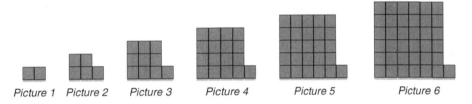

Picture 1   Picture 2   Picture 3   Picture 4   Picture 5   Picture 6

Fig. 6.1 Growing Blocks pattern

A. *How many blocks are needed to form Picture 8? How did you obtain your answer?*

B. *How many blocks are needed to form Picture 35? How did you obtain your answer?*

C. *Find a formula to calculate the number of blocks in Picture n. How did you obtain your formula?*

1. *Frank ("F"; Grade 6, 11 years old): So you add 3 every other time.*

2. *Interviewer ("JRB"): So you added 3 [blocks] to get to [Picture] 2?*

3. *F: And then you added 1, 2, 3, 4, 5 [referring to the number of blocks that were added to*
4. *form Picture 3]. And they're adding 2 and 3 every other time, so they're adding 2 and 3*
5. *to every amount that's already added.*
6. *JRB: Then how much is the next one [Picture 4] gonna be like?*

7. *F: It's gonna have 1, 2, 3, 4, 5, 6, 7 [pointing to the 7 blocks that were added in Picture*
8. *4].*

9. *JRB: Oh and I see that you're counting on here [4 blocks on the top row], here [the 2*
10. *added blocks on the fourth column], and here [the tail block].*

11. *F: Then 1, 2, 3, 4, 5, 6, 7, 8, 9 [for Picture 5]. Then 1, 2, 3, 4, 5, 6, 7, 8, 9, 10, 11 [for*
12. *Picture 6]. So for Picture 8, there's 1, 2, 3, 4, 5, 6, 7, 8, 9, 10, 11, 12, 13 [for Picture 7].*

13. *JRB: That'd be Picture 8?*

F. Rivera, *Teaching and Learning Patterns in School Mathematics: Psychological and Pedagogical Considerations*, DOI 10.1007/978-94-007-2712-0_6, © Springer Science+Business Media Dordrecht 2013

14. *F: Picture 7 [Frank then writes on paper "7 13 squares arou[nd]" (see Fig. 6.2)]. So*
15. *then if you were to add it.*

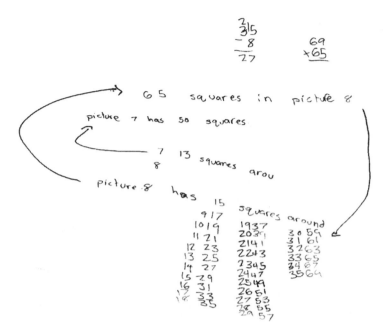

Fig. 6.2 Frank's written work on the blocks pattern in Fig. 6.1

16. *JRB: That would be added to this one [referring to Picture 6]?*

17. *F: Yes.*

18. *JRB: Okay so how many would that be altogether?*

19. *F: That would be 1, 2, 3, 4, 5, 6, 7, 8, 9, …, 34, 35, 36.*

20. *JRB: Is there another way to count that?*

21. *F: So 1, 2, 3, 4, 5, 6 [one row]. 1, 2, 3, 4, 5, 6 [another row]. So 6×6 equals 36 plus 1 equals 37.*
22. *JRB: Okay so Picture 6 has 37?*

23. *F: Yes.*

24. *JRB: Okay so how many would there be in Picture 7?*

25. *F: Plus 13 and 37 that's 50 coz 1+3 equals 4 and 3+7 equals 10, so 4 plus the 10*
26. *equals 50. [Frank then writes "picture 7 has 50 squares" (see Fig. 6.2)].*

27. *JRB: So how many would Picture 8 have?*

28. *F: So you would another round of that … 1, 2, 3, 4, 5, 6, 7, 8, 9, 10, 11, 12, 13, 14, 15.*
29. *[Frank then writes "picture 8 has 15 squares around]. So if you were to add 15 squares,*
30. *that would be 65. [Frank then writes, "65 squares in picture 8."] So how many blocks are*
31. *needed to form Picture 35? How did you obtain your answer?*

32. *JRB: That's a big jump from 8 to 35.*

33. *F: So [Frank writes,] 35 minus 8 is 27. [Fig. 6.2 shows the rest of Frank's listing*
34. *method that shows how he recursively added 2 each time from Picture 9 to Picture 35.]*

35. *JRB: So what does that 69 squares represent?*

36. *F: It represents 69 squares that Picture 35 have.*

37. *JRB: So is that 69 squares altogether?*

38. *F: Yeah. ... No, that's how many squares are around figure 35. Since figure 8 has 15*
39. *squares around it, this should be in all plus the 15 squares, that'd be 65. So, what if I*
40. *multiply? [Frank writes 69×65 and uses a calculator to multiply the two numbers].*
41. *That's 4485, four thousand four hundred eighty five squares. This may be too much.*

42. *JRB: Why would you multiply that 65 by 69?*

43. *F: Coz if there's 69 squares around it, you would have more. But if I added it, maybe 69*
44. *plus 65, 134.*

Sixth-grader Frank ignored the figural context of the pattern generalization task. He began to analyze the picture stages numerically as a recursively additive sequence. As a matter of fact, 10 out of the 28 students in Frank's class who were also interviewed employed a similar numerical process. For them, the basic rule of patterning activity was all about, in Frank's words, "figur[ing] how many [objects] are being added or subtracted in order to find the answer." How they came to such an understanding could be traced to several possible sources with patterning experiences in elementary school being the most significant factor.

In this chapter, we discuss the graded pattern generalization processing of older children and adults. Graded pattern generalization processing occurs along several routes that depend on (at the very least) the nature and complexity of a task being analyzed and various opportunities and resources that are available to them at the time of encounter. Figure 6.3 lists four documented routes based on existing research data, which we explore in further detail in the following four sections below. We note that the dashed lines in Fig. 6.3 are meant to convey the rather temporal nature of the four divisions. That is, students' graded pattern generalization processing and conversion can change in emphasis from manipulating objects to relationships (and possibly back to objects) in numerical and figural contexts. We close the chapter by discussing older students' understanding of (linear) functions as an instance of generalizing extensions but initially emerged from their experiences with patterns.

	Apprehension Processing	
Conversion	**Object dependent**	**Relationship dependent**
Numerical driven	Pattern spotting	Structural
Figural driven	Pattern spotting	Structural

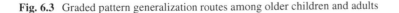

Fig. 6.3 Graded pattern generalization routes among older children and adults

Object-Dependent Numerical Processing and Conversion

Object-dependent numerical processing and conversion refers to an emerging pattern generalizing performance in which the numerical instances themselves are the primary focus of analysis with structure viewed as a consequence that may or may not be justified depending on the context of patterning activity. Rivera's (2007) clinical interviews with 42 US undergraduate elementary majors (mean age of 23.4 years) in relation to the two pattern generalization tasks shown in Fig. 6.4 in the absence of formal instruction indicate a mean of 65% in favor of this particular mode of processing and conversion. The initial and dominant mode of processing is guess and check, systematic, and otherwise, that most older children and adults tend to favor perhaps due to their prior elementary classroom experiences on patterns. Unfortunately, however, even if a generalization in the form of a converted direct formula emerges from object-dependent numerical processing, it lacks, or in many cases does not have, a strong and valid justification with many students documented as confusing justification with mere induction. For example, four students in Rivera's (2007) study produced the expressions $3n + 1$ and $5n + 1$ for the two patterns shown in Fig. 6.4 by a systematic covariational guess and check method. In the case of the

Squares Task. Consider the problem below.

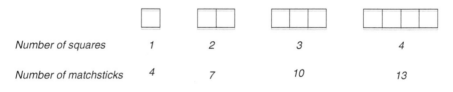

Number of squares	1	2	3	4
Number of matchsticks	4	7	10	13

a. How many matchsticks are needed to form 4 squares?
b. How many matchsticks are needed to form 5 squares?
c. How many matchsticks are needed to form n squares?

Hexagons Task. In the figure below, one hexagon takes 6 toothpicks to build, two hexagons take 11 toothpicks to build, and 3 hexagons take 16 toothpicks to build.

Number of hexagons	1	2	3	4
Number of matchsticks	6	11	16	21

a. How many matchsticks are needed to form 4 hexagons?
b. How many matchsticks are needed to form 5 hexagons?
c. How many matchsticks are needed to form n hexagons?

Fig. 6.4 Two patterning tasks (Rivera, 2007, p. 148)

expression $3n + 1$, they initially constructed a two-column table showing number of squares in the first column and number of matchsticks in the second column. Then they obtained the common difference between two consecutive rows in the second column, wrote down $3n$, and claimed that each dependent term was "always 1 more than 3 times n." A similar process was claimed in the case of the form $5n + 1$. In both contexts, none of them provided deeper explanations for the constructed formulas beyond verification through two or more examples.

Another student, GL, employed an unsystematic trial and error method in generating the direct expression $3n + 1$. He began with the expression $4n - 1$ and computed the value for $n = 1$. Because the value he obtained was 3, he then tried $4n - n$ and evaluated this expression for $n = 1$. Seeing that he needed 1 more to obtain the first term, 4, he added 1 to $4n - n$. Once again he evaluated $4n - n + 1$ and saw that it produced the correct dependent values in cases $n = 2$ and 3. When he was asked to justify his expression $4n - n + 1$, his reasoning below exemplifies what we might consider to be an instance of an *incidental structure*.

45. *Okay. Well I see here that four matchsticks equals one square. So it will just keep doubling*
46. *down to 8, but it doesn't show us here. It's not. 1, 2, 3, 4, 5, 6, 7 coz you're using that 1. So*
47. *that's 2 [referring to the two squares]. So what I've tried to do is just go through like a*
48. *shortcut and cheat coz I want 4, 8 but I know I just had to take 1 away to get 7. So now I*
49. *jumped ahead to 12. Okay but I know it's not because I have to subtract maybe one or two.*
50. *So 1, 2, 3, 4, 7, 8, 9, 10. So here I subtracted 1 [referring to the first case], here I subtracted 2*
51. *[referring to the second case]. Now with three squares, I have to subtract 3 from what*
52. *normally would make up one square. So it will be 16 subtracted by 3, 13 and I'll try that out.*
53. *Okay and here [referring to the third case] I have 10, 11, 12, 13. So what I didn't know how*
54. *to do was how to keep saying if I keep adding on squares I have to subtract that many. So*
55. *it's like taking away 1 from 8, 2 from 12, 3 from 16 ... so that's why I have this [referring to*
56. $4n - n + 1]$.

For GL, the expression $4n - n + 1$ actually involves two subgeneralizations, that is, $4n$ and $n + 1$. He knew that each square required four matchsticks, which explains the term $4n$. However, he was also aware that he had to subtract $1, 2, 3, \ldots, (n + 1)$ matchsticks in each case beginning with the second case. But he was not aware that the expressions $4n - (n + 1)$ and $4n - n + 1$ were not equivalent. In fact, he simplified the former expression and obtained $3n + 1$. He then verified that the numbers 4, 10, 13, and 16 could actually be drawn from this simplified expression. When GL was asked if he could generalize in a different way, his reasoning below shows how he numerically constructed an incorrect direct expression that he could not justify because he was not seeing its structure on the pattern.

57. *Okay it has to be a minimum of 4 matchsticks to be n squares. So ... so it's a minimum of*
58. *4 ... 4 matchsticks . . . but it could go on forever. But you need something like what we*
59. *were doing. ... So hold on. [He writes $4 + 3n$.] I just wrote that to try it out. 4*
60. *matchsticks plus 3 times n. Okay now I'm starting to think minus 1 since as I keep adding*
61. *squares on I have to keep subtracting. ... . I can see maybe 4 matchsticks but I'm*
62. *multiplying. See I don't know what the 3s are there for.*

Recent studies have also documented a similar generalizing competence among students on a variety of mathematical tasks. Orton and Orton (2004) note that in comparison with the 15-year-old UK students who participated in their patterning assessment study, a significant number of 11-year-old students who were also tested "did not

Logarithmic Properties: (a) Is it true that $\log(x+3) = \log x \cdot \log 3$ *for all x > 0? Yes* ____
No ____ *(b) Imagine that someone does not know the answer to part (a). Explain how you would convince the person that your answer to part a is correct.*

Fig. 6.5 Logarithmic property task (Senk and Thompson, 2006, p. 119)

see the underlying structure" (p. 105) and incorrectly used a numerical finite difference method in generating the succeeding terms of the doubling sequence 1, 2, 4, 8, ... When the US second-year algebra students in Senk and Thompson's (2006) study were asked to solve the problem shown in Fig. 6.5, the authors report that among the four representational strategies—numerical, symbolic, graphical, and verbal—that were available for the students to use, the most exhibited method was "numerical substitution—a strategy that often led to identifying a counterexample" (p. 125).

Research studies have also documented how object-dependent numerical processing and conversion has spawned several different correct and incorrect numerical pattern-spotting strategies with the misapplication of direct proportional reasoning (or false whole-object method (Stacey, 1989)) considered to be a very popular and frequent strategy. For example, Bishop (2000) reports that at least 22% of the 23 US Grades 7 and 8 students (ages 12–15 years) in her study basically multiplied the perimeter of the fourth shape in the pattern shown in Fig. 6.6 by 3 in order to find the perimeter of the twelfth shape. Fifteen of the 29 US Grade 6 students who participated in Becker and Rivera's (2006) study prior to a formal instruction on patterns incorrectly applied direct proportionality in dealing with stage 100 of the pattern whose initial stages are shown in Fig. 6.7. Despite being shown the typical visual model for representing the sums of consecutive odd numbers, 9 out of 15 Singapore Year 6 students (ages 11–12 years) in Yeap and Kaur's (2008) study established the sum of consecutive odd numbers from 1 to 99 by initially taking the sum of $1+3+5+7+9$ ($=25$) and then calculating the product of 25 and 11 since $9 \times 11 = 99$. In the section on Number (pp. 118–128), we note elementary students' competence in employing numeric differencing, which involves seeing recursively additive relationships among sequences of dependent terms. Among older children and adults, the same differencing strategy persists and continues to be a popular numerical strategy with several different variations. Variations of differencing involves (1) the "add 2 numbers" strategy (Fig. 6.9a), (2) the parity observation (Fig. 6.9b), and (3) relating the multiplication table (Fig. 6.9c). Tanisli's (2011) study with four Turkish Grade 5 students (mean age of 11 years) also illustrates the use of single and combined covariational (within-column) and correspondence (within-row) differencing strategies in cases involving linear function tables. Further, Hargreaves et al (2004) note the prevalent use of first- and second-order differencing among older students who dealt with both cases of linear and quadratic sequences.

Fig. 6.6 Perimeter pattern
(Bishop, 2000, p. 112)

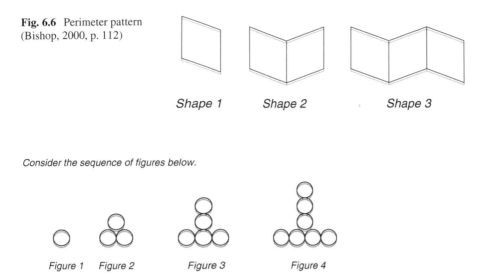

Shape 1   Shape 2   Shape 3

Consider the sequence of figures below.

Figure 1   *Figure 2*   *Figure 3*   *Figure 4*

A. How many circles would figure number 10 have in total? Explain.

B. How many circles would figure number 100 have in total? Explain.

C. You are now going to write a message to an imaginary Grade 6 student clearly explaining what s/he must do in order to find out how many circles there are in any given figure of the sequence. Message:

D. Find a formula to calculate the number of circles in the figure number "n."

Fig. 6.7 Circles pattern (Becker & Rivera, 2006, p. 97)

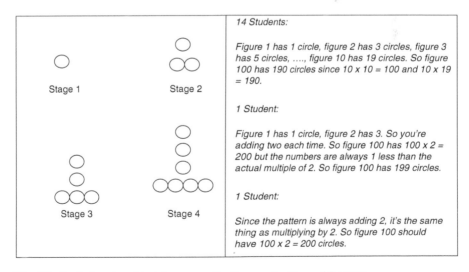

		14 Students:
Stage 1	Stage 2	*Figure 1 has 1 circle, figure 2 has 3 circles, figure 3 has 5 circles, ..., figure 10 has 19 circles. So figure 100 has 190 circles since 10 x 10 = 100 and 10 x 19 = 190.*
Stage 3	Stage 4	*1 Student:* *Figure 1 has 1 circle, figure 2 has 3. So you're adding two each time. So figure 100 has 100 x 2 = 200 but the numbers are always 1 less than the actual multiple of 2. So figure 100 has 199 circles.* *1 Student:* *Since the pattern is always adding 2, it's the same thing as multiplying by 2. So figure 100 should have 100 x 2 = 200 circles.*

Fig. 6.8 Grade 6 students' incipient generalizations on the Figure 6.7 pattern

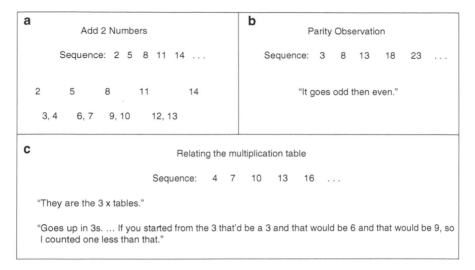

Fig. 6.9 Variations of differencing strategy involving linear sequences (Hargreaves et al., 2004)

Object-Dependent Figural Processing and Conversion

Object-dependent figural processing and conversion refers to an emerging pattern generalizing performance in which the figural instances themselves are the primary focus of analysis with structure viewed as a consequence that may or may not be justified depending on the context of patterning activity. This happens when there is no conceptual continuity between processing and conversion. For example, US seventh-grade student Anna in Rivera and Becker's (2011) study initially established the formula $D = n \times 4 + 1$ numerically (using linear differencing) for the figural pattern shown in Fig. 6.10. In justifying her direct formula, she merely circled n groups of 4 circles starting from the left and then referred to the last circle as her y-intercept. In Anna's case, because conversion occurred prior to figural processing, the objects—that is, the instances—became her primary focus of interest at the expense of a reasonably justified structure.

2. W-Dot Sequence Problem. Consider the following sequence of W-patterns below.

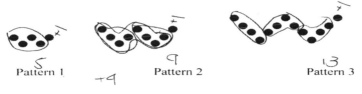

Pattern 1 $+4$ Pattern 2   Pattern 3

A. How many dots are there in pattern 6? Explain.

$$D = 6 \cdot 4 + 1$$

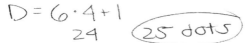

$$24 \quad \boxed{25 \text{ dots}}$$

$$D = D4 + 1$$

B. How many dots are there in pattern 37? Explain.

$$D = 37 \cdot 4 + 1$$

$$\boxed{149 \text{ dots}}$$

Fig. 6.10 Grade 7 Anna's pattern generalization of the W dot sequence

In Lannin's (2005) study, US sixth-grader Brett's thinking relative to the Cube Stickers problem shown in Fig. 6.11 shows how a reasonably justified explicit structure could emerge in an object-dependent context using a far generalization case. Brett's thinking in the interview below illustrates a conceptual continuity between his figural processing and conversion. He combined abduction and induction on the initial stages of his pattern producing a generalization that he eventually justified when he was confronted with a far generalization task. In the interview below, which took after a 10-day teaching experiment on generalization, Brett initially manifested object-dependent figural processing and conversion in lines 63–67. Then his incipient algebraically useful generalization emerged in lines 70–78 when he had to figurally process the parts for a rod of length 10.

63. *Brett (B): What I did was I multiplied [the length of the rod] by 4 and then I added 2 [to*
64. *the result]. So for [a rod of length] one I multiplied it by 4, which would be 4 and then I*
65. *added 2. So 6 stickers on the first cube. Then for the second one I did the same thing,*
66. *multiplied it by 4 and I got 8 and then I added 2. It was 10 stickers and it said it there [on*

Cube Sticker: A company makes colored rods by joining cubes in a row and using a sticker machine to place "smiley" stickers on the rods. The machine places exactly one sticker on each exposed face of each cube. Every exposed face of each cube has to have a sticker, so this length-2 rod would need 10 stickers.

1. How many stickers would you need for rods of length 1 to 10? Explain how you determined these values.
2. How many stickers would you need for a rod of length 20? of length 50? Explain how you determined these values.
3. Suppose that a particular rod needed 150 stickers. What is the length of this rod? Explain how you determined this.
4. Explain how you could find the number of stickers needed for a rod of any length. Write a formula that you could use to determine this.

Fig. 6.11   Cube sticker problem (Lannin, 2005, p. 256)

67. *his spreadsheet] too.*

68. *Interviewer (I): So you think [your rule] would for any [rod]? Do you think it would*
69. *work for [a rod of length] 10? (The interviewer showed Brett a rod of length 10)*

70. *B: (Pointing to the rod of length 10) There is 10 there, 10 there, 10 there, which is 30 and*
71.   *10 on the bottom that would be 40, 42. One on each end.*

72. *I: So you're saying 10, 10 on the top, 10 on each of the sides. So that's 3 tens. And 10 on*
73.   *the bottom.*

74. *B: Yeah.*

75. *I: So that would explain what part of this formula?*

76. *B: Multiplying by 4.*

77. *I: And then you add 2 because ...*

78. *B: Because there is 2. There is a face there and a face there [on the ends].*

Object-dependent figural processing and conversion is another variation of pattern spotting. Consequently, structures may or may not emerge but are oftentimes taken for granted. When they emerge, they may or may not be justified in a mathematically valid manner. Emergent structures in these situations are viewed as incidental and purposeful, that is, as a means of coping with the practical aspect of generalizing activity, which involves calculating particular outcomes. For example, when 71 US Grade 6 students (mean age of 11 years) in Cai and Hwang's (2002) study obtained the total number of white dots for figure 6 in the pattern shown in Fig. 6.12, about 42% of them drew the sixth figure and then counted the number of white dots. This observation contrasts with 72% of the 124 Chinese counterparts in the authors' study who employed a subtraction strategy that consisted of two values that have been inferred on two general patterns (i.e. the difference between the total number of dots and the total number of black dots). Even when the context of the problem was changed to a numerical pattern as shown in Fig. 6.13, a numerical pattern, more US Grade 6 employed an object-based strategy than their Chinese counterparts who presented structural arguments relative to the far generalization tasks. The US group "made a table or a list or noticed that each time the doorbell rang two or more guests entered than on the previous ring and so added 2s sequentially to find an answer" (Cai & Hwang, 2002, p. 410). Among the Chinese group, however, the students initially obtained a general rule indicative of a structure that then enabled them to calculate the case involving 99 guests.

Look at the figures below.

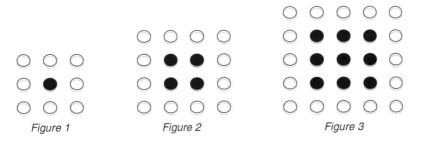

1. Draw the 4th figure.

2. How many black dots are there in the 6th figure? Explain how you found your answer.

3. How many white dots are there in the 6th figure? Explain how you found your answer.

4. Figure 1 has 8 white dots. Figure 3 has 16 white dots. If a figure has 44 white dots, which figure is this? Explain how you found your answer.

Fig. 6.12 Dots problem solving (Cai & Hwang, 2002, p. 405)

Sally is having a party. The first time the doorbell rings, 1 guest enters.
The second time the doorbell rings, 3 guests enter.
The third time the doorbell rings, 5 guests enter.
The fourth time the doorbell rings, 7 guests enter.

Keep on going in the same way. On the next ring a group enters that has 2 more persons than the group that entered on the previous ring.

1. How many guests will enter on the 10th ring? Explain how you found your answer.

2. In the space below, write a rule or describe in words how to find the number of guests that entered on each ring.

3. 99 guests entered on one of the rings. What ring was it? Explain or show how you found your answer.

Fig. 6.13 Doorbell solving task (Cai & Hwang, 2002, p. 406)

Relationship-Dependent Numerical Processing and Conversion

Relationship-dependent numerical processing and conversion refers to an emerging pattern generalizing performance in which an abduced mathematical structure is the primary focus of analysis with the relevant numerical representations viewed as providing inductive support that instantiate the relevant structural relationships. For example, Rivera's (2011) Algebra 1 students developed their understanding of the piecewise general definition of $|x|$ when they employed a number line diagram that showed what the symbol involving two vertical bars actually meant in three different situations on the line. Figure 6.14a shows eighth-grader Pam's number line representation for $|x|$ that she understood to mean the "same distance for the number x on either side of the origin."

Fig. 6.14a Pam's number line diagram of the notation $|x|$ lowercase

$$|x| = \begin{cases} x, x > 0 \\ 0, x = 0 \\ -x, x < 0 \end{cases}$$

The students then used specific examples to verify the three different situation noting, especially, the significance of the minus sign in the case when $x < 0$. Consequently, when they began to solve absolute value equations, their written solutions reflected the use of an empty number line diagram that assisted them in articulating the correct relationships between the left- and the right-hand side expressions of the equations. Pam in Fig. 6.14b continued to solve absolute value equations (and much later, inequalities) diagrammatically with the aid of an empty number line that enabled her to see the necessary relationships.

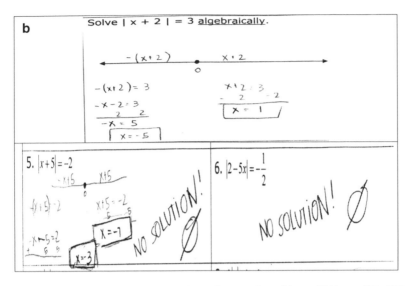

Fig. 6.14b Pam's solutions on several absolute value equations (Rivera, 2011, pp. 201–202)

Pam's written work in Fig. 6.14b involved two concepts that were undergoing generalization, namely, (1) the definition of the absolute value of a number and (2) a method for solving absolute value equations. If an object-dependent numerical processing and conversion has been employed first, the patterning process would most likely have taken an empirical route from the investigation and solution of particular examples to the construction of an intentional generalization. In a relationship-dependent numerical processing and conversion such as the top and the bottom right solutions in Fig. 6.14b, however, the pattern generalizing process oftentimes proceeds in a structural manner from an understanding of the relevant mathematical relationships to their instantiation via particular examples. Still in reference to Fig. 6.14b, Pam's thinking relative to task item 5 shifted to object-dependent numeric processing due to her interest in implementing the algorithm that she just learned. However, she also learned from task 5 why such equations had no solutions by reflecting on the conceptual definition of an absolute value of a number. Hence, in task 6, her thinking shifted to relationship-dependent processing, which enabled her to quickly conclude that the equation would yield no solution at all.

There is very little research evidence indicating the prevalent use and possible effects of relationship-dependent numerical processing and conversion. Almost all reported cases of numerical pattern generalizing situations among older children and adults, especially those that involve linear and quadratic functions, exemplify the execution of an empirical model, in particular, differencing, because it always seems to guarantee the construction of algebraically useful generalizations. Radford's (2008) reflections on his work with a small group of Grades 7 and 8 Canadian students on three generalizing tasks involving numerical patterns indicate the "reputedly difficult" nature of such numeric entities "not because of the difficulties that the students encounter in grasping [a] commonality, but because [they] tend to fail at using [the commonality] to form a direct and meaningful rule" (p. 93). For example, when four students in his study obtained a generalization for the problem "Marc saves $3 a week. He started off with $12," some of them initially failed to see the value of interpreting the commonality "$3 a week" as an indication of a multiplicative relationship. The situation apparently became worse for the students when they had to obtain a generalization for the linear pattern with the following initial four terms: 0.42, 0.75, 1.08, and 1.41 with 0.42 designated as Term 1. In this case, they had to work with "numbers [that] do not get their meaning from a concrete context … [but] must now result from abstract positional relations between numbers" (Radford, 2008, p. 88).

Küchemann's (2008) brief but interesting remark—"though we have never observed anyone doing so" (p. 2.4)—in relation to the purely numerical task below seems to appropriately sum up the current state of affairs on matters involving relationship-dependent numerical processing and conversion.

Which products of 3 consecutive numbers are multiples of 24? Explain why.

While Küchemann modeled an empirical approach using Excel in order to construct (and not necessarily justify) a generalization, he also pointed out that "the task of course can be tackled by thinking about structure from the outset" (p. 2.4). Figure 6.15a shows an Excel-induced table of cases that can help students empirically abduce observations such as "the product is a multiple of 24 when the first number is even, or when the middle number is a multiple of 8" (ibid). Figure 6.15b provides a possible structural argument that bypasses induction altogether.

Fig. 6.15a Table of values
(Küchemann, 2008, p. 2.4)

A	B	C	P=A×B×C	P/24
1	2	3	6	0.25
2	3	4	24	1
3	4	5	60	2.5
4	5	6	120	5
5	6	7	210	8.75
6	7	8	336	14
7	8	9	504	21
8	9	10	720	30
9	10	11	990	41.25
10	11	12	1320	55
11	12	13	1716	71.5
12	13	14	2184	91
13	14	15	2730	113.75
14	15	16	3360	140
15	16	17	4080	170
16	17	18	4896	204
17	18	19	5814	242.25
18	19	20	6840	285
19	20	21	7980	332.5
20	21	22	9240	385
21	22	23	10626	442.75
22	23	24	12144	506
23	24	25	13800	575
24	25	26	15600	650
25	26	27	17550	731.25
26	27	28	19656	819
27	28	29	21924	913.5
28	29	30	24360	1015
29	30	31	26970	1123.75
30	31	32	29760	1240
31	32	33	32736	1364
32	33	34	35904	1496

Fig. 6.15b Structural
argument (Küchemann,
2008, p. 2.4)

If I have three consecutive numbers, one of them must be a multiple of 3. So if one of the numbers is a multiple of 8 (e.g. 8x9x10, 7x8x9, 6x7x8, etc) I will always get a multiple of 24. I will also get a multiple of 8 (and hence of 24) if the first number is even as this means that the last number will also be even and that one of these must be a multiple of 4 (with the other a multiple of 2).

Relationship-Dependent Figural Processing and Conversion

Relationship-dependent figural processing and conversion refers to an emerging pattern generalizing performance in which an abduced mathematical structure is the primary focus of analysis with the relevant figural representations viewed as providing inductive support that instantiate the structural relationships. For example, Grant, a South African Grade 9 student in Samson and Schäfer's (2011) study, obtained the following nine equivalent pattern generalizations below relative to the task shown in Fig. 6.16a by imposing several different figural structures on the given stages.

$$3n+n-1 \qquad 3(n-1)+4+n-2 \qquad 2n+n+n-1$$
$$4n-1 \qquad n+n+n+[n-1] \qquad 2(2[n-1])+3$$
$$4(n-1)+3 \qquad n+3(n-1)+2 \qquad 3n+3(n-1)-[2n-2]$$

Figure 6.16b shows how he figurally parsed the components of stage 4 in two different ways that enabled him to produce and justify the corresponding converted direct formulas in variable form. Grant did not see the need to convert the stages in numerical form. Instead, he employed figural processing involving the operations of addition, subtraction, and multiplication. For example, the formula $T = 3n+n-1$ exemplifies the use of a combined figural multiplication and addition. Grant interpreted each stage in terms of the union of 3n edges (i.e., the total number of sides of the upward pointing triangles) and $(n-1)$ horizontal edges (i.e. the total number of segments in the top row). The formula $T = 3n+n-1$ combines figural multiplication and subtraction. In this case, Grant initially saw a common unit consisting of 4 edges, that is, an upward-pointing triangle with a horizontal edge hanging on the top vertex and parallel to the base of the triangle. He then inferred that each stage would consist of n iterations of the common unit, which explains the term 4n. However, based on the original figural constraints, the initial step in any stage involves constructing a triangle without the hanging edge, which explains the taking away of 1 (edge) in his formula.

a

Find the nth term of a pattern with the following shape numbers below.

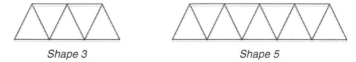

Shape 3   Shape 5

Fig. 6.16a A Grade 9 pattern generalization task with given two nonconsecutive terms (Samson, 2011, p. 37)

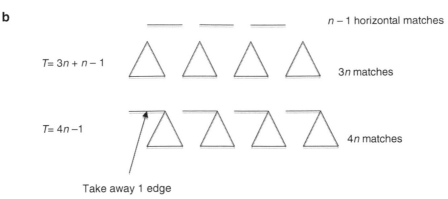

b

$T = 3n + n - 1$

$n - 1$ horizontal matches

$3n$ matches

$T = 4n - 1$

$4n$ matches

Take away 1 edge

Fig. 6.16b A Grade 9 student's justification of two equivalent direct expressions for the Fig. 6.16a Pattern Using Shape 4 (Samson, 2011)

We note that the use of a single figural operation is possible in some cases of patterning tasks. For example, some of the students in Cai and Hwang's (2002) who suggested the expression n^2 for the total number of black dots for the nth stage in the Fig. 6.12 pattern employed figural multiplication alone. Another example involves direct expression $n + n + (n + 2) + (n + 2)$ for the total number of white dots for the nth stage in the Fig. 6.12 pattern, which is a result of figural addition alone. Hence, it is possible in some cases of patterning activity to use a single figural operation in describing an emergent structure.

Recent studies have also documented other ways of exhibiting relationship-dependent figural processing and conversion. Performing intentional-driven figural action on objects has been shown to be effective and powerful in generalizing many fundamental concepts and processes in school mathematics. For example, recent technology-mediated learning tools, especially those that have a dynamic or symbolic component, have been extensively documented to support the construction and generalization of mathematical relationships (cf: Leung (2008); Rivera (2007); Ruthven, Deaney and Hennessy (2009); Todd, Lyublinskaya and Ryzhik (2010)). Even in the context of learning with manipulatives, purposeful figural actions on objects can yield meaningful generalizations and important mathematical relationships. For example, Rivera (2011) shares his experiences in his US Algebra 1 class when the students learned the concepts of least common multiple and greatest common factor mainly by physically manipulating unit cubes. In the case of the least common multiple, the students initially gathered chains of 2 and 3 unit cubes. Next they built a linear sequence of 2-chains in one row and a linear sequence of 3-chains in another row. As soon as they realized that the two rows would equal each other in length only in situations when the two numbers shared the same multiple, a figural-driven structure about common multiples emerged. The students also came to understand the least common multiple concept in terms of the first equal length between two chains, which they conceptually transferred to more complex situations such as those involving powers of the same integer, say, a^m and a^n, where $m < n$ and m and n are whole numbers. In the case of the greatest common factor, they initially constructed rectangles with areas equal to the numbers 6, 9, and 12. Next they reconfigured the rectangles in such a way that all three shared (1) a common dimension and (2) the largest common dimension. The figural process became the context in which they learned the meaning of the greatest common factor, which they used to make sense of more complex problems involving products of powers of integers, say, $a^m b^n$ and $a^n b^m$, where $m < n$ and m and n are whole numbers.

Meaningful and effective use of figural operations and actions in relationship-dependent figural processing and conversion happens in situations when learners are able to abduce and link together both invariant and variational properties or attributes of objects. When Cathy, a US Grade 7 student in Steele and Johanning's (2004) study, was asked to analyze the triangle dot problem shown in Fig. 6.17, her reasoning below indicates a clear understanding of the components in her figural stages that were changing ("the number of dots on a side") as well as those that stayed the same ("there are 3 sides in a triangle," "there are 3 corners in a triangle … [that are] shared").

79. *The reason there are only 12 dots in the triangle … and 5 dots to a side is because you don't*
80. *count the corners twice. You multiply the number of dots on a side times 3 because there are*
81. *3 sides in a triangle, and you subtract 3 because there are 3 corners in a triangle and they are*
82. *shared. So for a 13-dot triangle there will be 36 dots.* $(13.3) - 3 = 36$. *So the formula is*
83. $(N \cdot 3) - 3 = \# \text{ of dots}.$

In the diagram below is a 5-dot triangle. It is a triangle made by using 5 dots on each side. The 5-dot triangle is made using a total of 12 dots. How many dots will be used to make a 13-dot triangle? If n represents the number of dots on each side of an n-dot triangle, write an expression to represent how many total dots are in the triangle?

Fig. 6.17 Triangle dot problem (Steele & Johanning, 2004, p. 75)

We should note that in many reported cases of relationship-dependent figural processing and conversion, the numerical and figural representations appear to co-emerge in activity in a continuous manner. In such cases, both representations can be seen in a mediating role, that is, as semiotic resources that assist in the objectification of an inferred relationship or structure. For example, CG, a US undergraduate elementary major in Rivera's (2007) study, established his direct expression $4 + (n-1) \times 3$ for the squares task shown in Fig. 6.4 in the following manner below. CG's thinking reflects a co-emergence of numerical and figural data that enabled him to semiotically extrapolate an intended structure for the pattern. Figure 6.18 shows CG's written work on the hexagons task in Fig. 6.4. It shows how purposefully appropriated numerical information and arithmetical operations that he needed in his ongoing construction and justification and algebraic conversion of an emerging mathematical relationship, which he initially inferred on the available figural data.

84. *How many matchsticks are needed to form four squares? So ahm I'm looking for a pattern.*
85. *For every square you add three more. So let's see. So that would be four plus three for two*
86. *squares. Plus three more would be for three squares. So it's ten matchsticks. So you have*
87. *four. So there would be thirteen. So thirteen plus three more is sixteen ... So for three*
88. *squares, it would just be two threes. So there'd be two threes, three threes is for four*
89. *squares, and four threes for five squares. For n squares, it would just be ahm n minus 1*
90. *threes.*

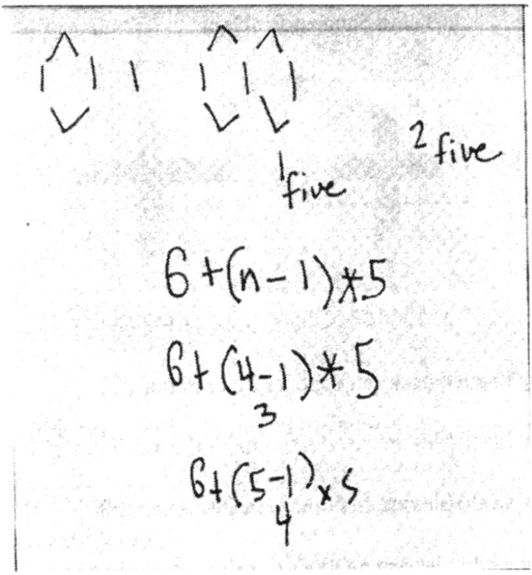

Fig. 6.18 CG's written solution on the hexagons task shown in Fig. 6.4

On The (Nonsymbolic) Algebraic Nature of Older Students' Pattern Generalizations: Variables as Situated, Induced, and Figural

Due to their earlier mathematical experiences, older children and adults oftentimes convey their generalizations with the aid of variables, where variables stand for numbers regardless of context. However, variables have been interpreted and used in at least three different ways, as follows.

- Variables as situated objects are assigned meanings that are constrained by their context of emergence.
- Variables as induced objects take the role of placeholders within or outside a structure.
- Variables as figural objects take the place of the relevant figural components and are inherently composite in nature.

Prior to a formal instruction on patterns, US sixth-grader Dung in Becker and Rivera's (2006) study employed variables in a situated manner. For example, when he obtained a pattern generalization for the Cross Pattern shown in Fig. 6.19a, he began by noting that "[for figure] 1, there's one square around it, [for figure] 2 there are two squares around it, and so 3 and so on." In obtaining the number of square tiles for figures 6 and 7, he stated in clear terms the following general process: multiply the figure number by 4 and add 1. When he converted his generalization in terms of a formula, his written work shown in Fig. 6.19b used the same variable n in four different contexts. The n in "Picture n" stood for stage number, an independent term. The n in the second line represented the number of squares appearing on each corner point of the central square. The equation $n \times 4 = n$ meant that he was performing a calculation that assigns the total number of squares on all four corner points of the central square ("$n \times 4$") to a single variable n. The n in his final step actually referred to the expression $n \times 4$ that he then added to 1 (corresponding to the central square) to find the total number of squares in all for "picture N." We are aware, of course, of the discontinuity between his initial figural processing and his converted expression, which is not an uncommon occurrence of thinking among students in a pre-instructional context.

Tiles are arranged to form pictures like the ones below.

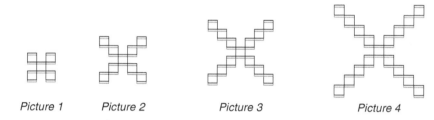

Picture 1	Picture 2	Picture 3	Picture 4

Find a formula that enables you to calculate the number of square tiles in Picture "n." How did you obtain your formula?

Fig. 6.19a　Cross pattern task (Becker & Rivera, 2006, p. 467)

Picture n=

n= how many numbers are on each …

n × 4 = n

n + 1 = how many tiles are in picture N

Fig. 6.19b　Sixth Grade Dung's variable-based generalization for the Fig. 6.19a pattern (Becker & Rivera, 2006, p. 468)

Dung's situated use of the variable n in Fig. 6.19b suggests a rather narrow interpretation in which variables behave as concrete objects rather than as unknown quantities. Radford (2001) has also noted this occurrence in his study with a group of three Canadian Grade 8 students who obtained the generalizations $(n+n)+1$ and $(n+1)+n$ for the adjacent triangular pattern in Fig. 6.20 but perceived them as being different expressions on the basis of having been drawn from two different cognitive actions.

Fig. 6.20 Two-layered circle pattern (Radford, 2001)

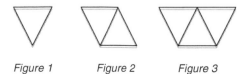

Figure 1   Figure 2   Figure 3

Variables that emerge as induced objects also behave like concrete objects. In some cases they are viewed as merely replacing the position of a stage number in some pattern, thus, a placeholder. Anna's use of the variable D in her variable expression $D4+1$ shown in Fig. 6.10 emerged through induction and it meant nothing more to her other than a convenient replacement for a number, especially noting the manner in which she justified her formula. In the absence of a meaningful structure that reflects a coordination of invariant and variant attributes of the pattern, Anna simply circled n groups of four dots beginning from the left and assigned the last dot for the constant term.

In some cases when variables are introduced as induced objects, however, an accompanying valid structural justification loads them with greater algebraic value and significance. For instance, JS, a US undergraduate elementary major in Rivera's (2007) study, constructed her direct expression $3n+1$ by numeric differencing on a table of values. In her last row of values, she introduced the variable n that substitutes for any stage number in the pattern. In justifying her expression, when she pointed out that the common difference 3 was the number that determined the "difference between one figure to the next," for her it actually meant the addition of an appropriate number of equal sets of three matchsticks, that is, $n \times 3$ (or $3n$), that enabled her to state the correct number squares in any stage of the pattern. She said:

91. *You're trying to make ahm a full square with four matchsticks, and if you already have one*
92. *side then you would be adding three more onto it depending on the number of squares that*
93. *you wanna make 'coz that's how many you're gonna put, that's how many threes you're*
94. *gonna add on.*

Variables in almost all successful accounts of figural pattern generalization appear to emerge naturally as figural objects—that is, they take the place of the relevant figural components and are inherently composite in nature and, thus, multiplicative. For example, all 9 direct expressions that ninth-grade student Grant suggested relative to the figural pattern in Fig. 6.16a employed variables in ways that captured the invariant and variant relationships in the pattern in terms of stage (shape) number. As evident in Fig. 6.16b, the variable n captures the composite essence that indicates the number of times an abduced common unit would have to be iterated or copied in order to construct a particular stage of the pattern. In the case of the formula $T = 3n + n - 1$, in particular, Grant saw the union of two common units (triangles and a horizontal row of segments), where $3n$ refers to n iteration of an upward-pointing triangle with three edges and $(n - 1)$ refers to the number of ceiling edges that are needed to connect the n triangles.

The composite essence of a variable in a figural mode can also refer to the size of the common unit itself. For example, relative to the pattern shown in Fig. 6.17, seventh-grade student Cathy in lines 79 through 83 associated her variable N with the number of dots on each side of an n-dot triangle. So, in a 5-dot triangle, $n = 5$ dots and in a 13-dot triangle, $n = 13$. She then used the same variable N in describing the structure of the growing triangle (i.e. 3 copies of N dots corresponding to the three sides of the triangle that overlap along its three vertices).

At this stage, it is worth revisiting the figural operations of addition, subtraction, and multiplication relative to the use of variables in composite form. When older children and adults exhibit multiplicative thinking on patterns, it basically means they are constructing and iterating composite units in some way. Further, in developing a formula, recursive or functional, the various figural operations convey how composite units and other related terms (e.g. constants) are combined and manipulated within an interpreted structure. In Chap. 5, we learned about findings drawn from lower elementary school children on certain patterns that indicate authentic and prevalent applications of additive thinking (i.e. seeing and counting objects as single units and not in terms of composite units). However, due to the major importance accorded to the concept of multiplication beginning in second grade (mean age of 7 years) in the elementary school mathematics curriculum, they are likely to favor figural addition and multiplication over subtraction.

We note, in particular, Rivera and Becker's (2011) 3-year longitudinal study with middle school students in the US, which shows their general preference in apprending and constructing algebraically useful structures that result from building subconfigurations, parts, or components over other structuring actions. Further, drawing on a small sample of 11 Grades 7 and 8 students (mean age of 12.5 years) from Rivera and Becker's (2011) 3-year study, Rivera (2010a) reports that when they obtained a pattern generalization for the ambiguous task shown in Fig. 6.21a, those who extended their stages according to the pattern shown in Fig. 6.21b produced generalizations that employed figural addition more frequently than figural subtraction. In Fig. 6.21c, for example, Karen figurally added two nonoverlapping composite sides and the central square ($n - 1$, $n - 1$, and 1), while Dung figurally added two nonoverlapping composite sides (a column with n squares from to top to bottom and a row with $(n - 1)$ squares).

The less popular and in many cases much harder to accomplish pattern generalizing strategies involve figural subtraction and figural actions of transformation and compensation. Figure 6.21d shows Diana's figural subtraction of the pattern in Fig. 6.21b, which involves seeing two overlapping composite sides of squares

Below are the first two stages in a growing pattern of squares.

Stage 1   Stage 2

1. Continue the pattern until stage 5.

2. Find a direct formula in two different ways. Justify each formula.

3. If none of your formulas above involve taking into account overlaps, find a direct formula that takes into account overlaps. Justify your formula.

4. How do you know for sure that your pattern will continue that way and not some other way?

5. Find a different way of continuing the pattern and obtain a direct formula for this pattern.

Fig. 6.21a An ambiguous patterning task (Rivera 2010a, 2010b)

Stage 1   Stage 2   Stage 3   Stage 4   Stage 5

Fig. 6.21b Most frequent extension of the stages shown in Fig. 6.21a (Rivera 2010a, 2010b)

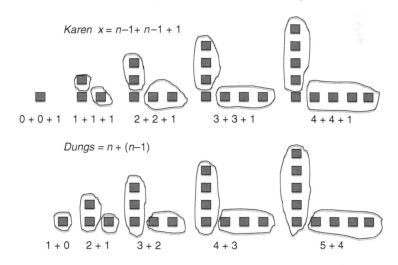

Fig. 6.21c Figural additive processing of the pattern in Fig. 6.21b (Rivera 2010a, 2010b)

having the same length n and then taking away an extra square. Figure 6.21e shows Diana's compensatory strategy for the pattern shown in Fig. 6.21b, while Fig. 6.21f shows Cherrie's combined transformation/compensation approach. Using stage 4 as a generic example, Diana initially completed the square with dimension x by x by adding squares with dimension $(x-1)$ by $(x-1)$. In her direct formula, $n = x^2 - (x-1)^2$, she then subtracted the same number of squares that she originally added to the stage. Cherrie transformed each stage in her pattern by assuming 2 columns of the same number of squares and then taking away 1 square. She reasoned as follows:

95. *So 2n, because it increases by 2, so you times it by 2 and then you minus 1. It's like a missing*
96. *block like the one in the middle [points to the missing block in stage 2], there [points to the*
97. *missing block in stage 3 after making a gesture that conveyed rotating the row of squares*
98. *into a column of squares], there [same pointing- gesturing act].*

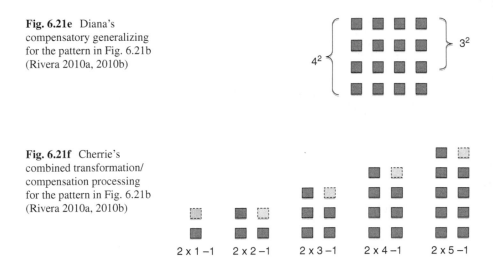

Fig. 6.21d   Diana' figural subtraction processing of the pattern in Fig. 6.21b (Rivera 2010a, 2010b)

Fig. 6.21e   Diana's compensatory generalizing for the pattern in Fig. 6.21b (Rivera 2010a, 2010b)

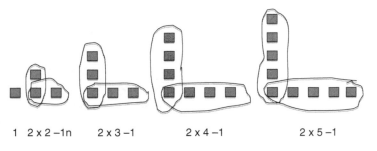

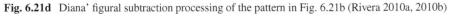

Fig. 6.21f   Cherrie's combined transformation/ compensation processing for the pattern in Fig. 6.21b (Rivera 2010a, 2010b)

Functions as Generalizing Extensions

In Rivera's (2011) Algebra 1 class, the students successfully transferred their pattern generalization skills on tasks that involve linear function modeling[1] without much effort. For example, the written work of Dariah in Fig. 6.22 employed object-dependent numeric processing and conversion, while Kent offered a relationship-dependent numeric version. Further, despite having had no formal experiences in processing such modeling tasks, the four students interpreted them based on how they approached similar tasks in pattern generalization activity. Consequently they were able to successfully deal with typical prediction problem tasks by exhibiting pattern generalization-based processes such as calculating outcomes by substitution and obtaining inputs by working backward (i.e. inverse processing).

When the students explored patterning tasks involving discrete domains, they learned to establish generalizations that was all about increasing depth by comparing inputs (stages, instances, cases, objects) drawn from the same class of objects. However, when they began to treat functions as instances of patterns, their understanding evolved in breadth, accommodating what Peirce (1960) classifies as a *generalizing extension*. That is, they expanded their pattern knowledge to include new and different classes of objects (cf. Chap. 2). Consequently, the extension also meant that they viewed the objects of functions, which involve classes of numbers beyond integers, as instantiating, and thus, subsumed under the established general structure and method that characterizes pattern generalization activity (i.e. Williams, Lombrozo, and Rehder's (2011) *subsumptive constraint*).

---

[1] Ferrini-Mundy et al (2005) point out the foundational significance of the concept of linear relationships over other relationships in students' learning of school algebra. According to the authors, linear functions: (1) are central to ideas involving direct variation, proportionality, and similarity; (2) are useful in learning about other functions, including parametric equations and families of functions; (3) lay a concrete ground for understanding concepts such as functions in general, rates of change, and relevant graphical relationships; and (4) enable the process of approximations involving nonlinear relationships (Ferrini-Mundy et al, 2005, pp. 21–23).

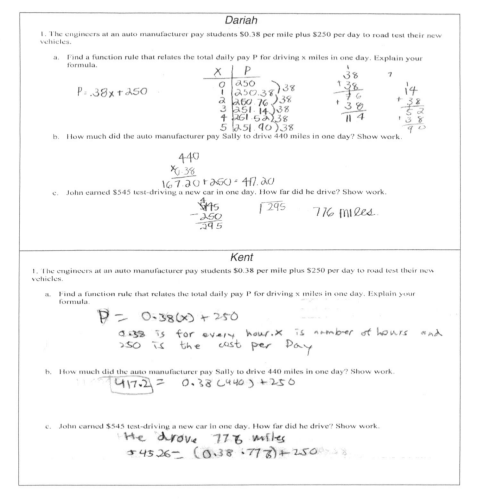

Fig. 6.22 Algebra 1 students' written work on the linear function modeling problem (Rivera, 2011, p. 195)

In the Algebra 1 class, the students conceptually grounded their understanding of functions, domain and range, the graph of linear functions, slopes of lines, and other relevant concepts and processes on their acquired mathematical experiences with linear patterns.[2] The conceptual mapping from the phase of pattern generalization to

---

[2] The concrete grounding in linear pattern generalization, in fact, enabled the students to successfully cope with the following bulleted tasks below that various research studies have documented as difficult among students who are beginning to learn linear functions.

- Forming equations for straight lines.
- Relating graphs to symbols.
- Treating the line as an object itself.
- Making qualitative judgments about graphs.
- Interpreting the meaning of the concepts involved such as slope.

the phase of generalizing extension is sumarized below, which also shows structural similarities between patterns and functions.

Generalization		Generalizing extension
Direct formula	$\longrightarrow$	Function
Stage number (positive integers)		Domain (real numbers)
Total outcome (positive integers)	$\longrightarrow$	Range (real numbers)
Discrete points in a coordinate plane	$\longrightarrow$	Continuous line (or subset of a line) in a coordinate plane
Repeating or constant, increasing, and decreasing linear patterns	$\longrightarrow$	Zero, positive, and negative slopes of lines

From the above mapping, the students' extensive experiences with linear pattern generalization provided them with every opportunity to anticipate and overcome possible processing difficulties and conversion issues when they were learning linear functions for the first time (see footnote 2). We close this chapter with a brief account of their initial dilemmas with decreasing linear patterns and how they dealt with them successfully in the context of discrete domains. The knowledge they acquired from this particular experience became useful much later when they dealt with decreasing linear functions.

When 10 of the Grade 8 Algebra 1 students participated in a clinical interview prior to a teaching experiment on pattern generalization in the previous school year, 7 of them[3] were unable to establish direct expressions for the two decreasing linear patterns shown in Fig. 6.23a and 6.23b (Rivera & Becker, 2011). While all of them were proficient in dealing with increasing linear patterns, unfortunately, many of

---

- Understanding constant functions, concepts and representations of images and preimages, and transferring from graphical to algebraic form.
- Understanding the effects of changing the y-intercept of a linear graph and whether the result is a vertical or horizontal translation.
- Interpreting graphs in terms of local and global [features and] processes.
- Creating a graph or plotting points from given data.
- Creating a symbolic representation from a graph.
- Constructing a function that represents a given graph.
- Plotting a point that follows the same pattern as the other points on tasks in which students are given a number of points lying on a straight line and an x-coordinate
- (Ferrini-Mundy et al., 2005, pp. 21–23).

[3] In Rivera and Becker (2011), the reported sample was $n = 8$ with five of them unable to establish direct formulas for the two decreasing linear patterns. The correct sample is $n = 10$. Regardless of the change in sample size, however, the number of correct generalizers was the same, that is, three of them constructed valid direct formulas.

them found it difficult to transfer the same generalizing strategy in cases involving negative differencing. Figure 6.24 shows how they dealt with the stated far generalization tasks for the pattern in Fig. 6.23a. Frank generated a long list, while Anna constructed a table of values that enumerated all the cases from stages 1 to 15.

(Losing Squares Pattern) Take a look at the three different stages in the design below.

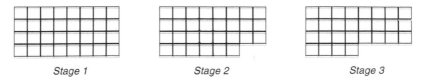

Stage 1   *Stage 2*   *Stage 3*

A. How many squares are there in stage 1? stage 2? stage 3?

B. How many squares are there in stage 10? How do you know for sure?

C. How many squares are there in stage 15? How do you know for sure?

D. Find a direct formula for the total number of squares in stage n, where n is a positive integer. If you obtained your formula numerically, what might it mean if you think about it in terms of the above pattern?

E. How many squares are there in stage 20? What might your answer mean if you think about it in terms of the above pattern?

E. For what stage number will there be no more squares left? How do you know for sure?

Fig. 6.23a Losing squares pattern generalization task

(Arrow Design Patterns) Take a look at the three different stages in the design below.

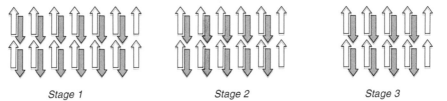

Stage 1   *Stage 2*   *Stage 3*

A. Find a direct formula for the total number of arrows in stage n, where n is a positive integer. If you obtained your formula numerically, what might it mean if you think about it in terms of the above pattern?

B. How many arrows are there in the 10th stage 10? Explain.

C. For what stage number will there be no more arrows left? How do you know for sure?

Fig. 6.23b Arrow design pattern generalization task

Frank's Listing Method

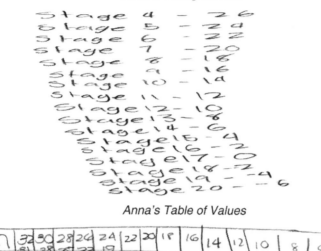

Stage 4 - 26
Stage 5 - 24
Stage 6 - 22
Stage 7 - 20
Stage 8 - 18
Stage 9 - 16
Stage 10 - 14
Stage 11 - 12
Stage 12 - 10
Stage 13 - 8
Stage 14 - 6
Stage 15 - 4
Stage 16 - 2
Stage 17 - 0
Stage 18 - -2
Stage 19 - -4
Stage 20 - -6

Anna's Table of Values

n	32	30	28	26	24	22	20	18	16	14	12	10	8	6	4
	31	28	26	22	19										
0	1	2	3	4	5	6	7	8	9	10	11	12	13	14	15

Fig. 6.24 Students' listing method relative to the losing squares pattern in Fig. 6.23a

The remaining 3 of the 10 students who were successful in constructing a direct formula had to first recall their knowledge of multiplying and adding two signed numbers. Figure 6.25 shows Tamara's written work on the pattern shown in Fig. 6.23a. From her generated table, she immediately saw that every stage after the first involves "minusing 2" squares. She then used multiplication to count the total number of squares at each stage. When she started to construct a direct formula, she was perturbed by the negative common difference. She said, "I was trying to think of, just like the last time [the previous tasks involving increasing linear patterns], I was trying to get a formula. … I was thinking of trying to do with the stage number but I don't get it." When Tamara initially multiplied −2 and a stage number, say, 1, she needed to recall how to obtain products involving a negative factor. A second dilemma that she confronted was how to obtain the same constant term that would be added to all the negative products and would match the correct output values in her table. When she successfully overcame such difficulties, they became her basis in making sense of the *Arrow Design Pattern* in Fig. 6.23b.

S	1	2	3	4	5	6	7	8	9	10	11	12	13	14	x
n	32	30	28	26	24	22	20	18	16	14	12	10	8	6	4

−2   −2   −2   −2   −2   −2   −2   −2   −2

Fig. 6.25 Tamara's table of values relative to the losing squares pattern in Fig. 6.23a

We also point out a rather unfortunate consequence of object-driven numerical processing and conversion in the case of decreasing linear patterns. In the follow-up clinical interview, none of the students could still justify their direct formulas for the decreasing pattern shown in Fig. 6.23a beyond numerical induction. That is, they merely substituted (stage) numbers and confirmed the outcomes on the corresponding tables of values. Also, they did not bother to make sense of the calculated negative values. For example, Tamara was unmindful of her answer of "−6 squares" in the case of stage 20 in Fig. 6.23a item E. Further, when they were asked to explain the relation-derived formula shown in Fig. 6.26 item C, which was not included in the original task shown in Fig. 6.23a, they once again confused numerical induction verification with justification. Of course these difficulties and issues were pursued and dealt with the following year in the Algebra 1 class before the students began their formal study of linear functions.

To sum up, the phase of generalizing extension basically broadened and mapped the students' current knowledge of pattern generalization to include other classes of (abstract) objects (e.g. rational numbers, negative numbers, decimal fractions, irrational numbers). The metonymic relationship that emerged between patterns and functions helped them cope with the tasks listed under footnote 2.

(Losing Squares Pattern) Take a look at the three different stages in the design below.

(Same figural cues shown in Figure 6.23a.)

Stage 1   Stage 2   Stage 3

A. Complete the table below.

n	1	2	3	10	15
S					

B. Find a direct formula for the total number of squares in stage n, where n is a positive integer. If you obtained your formula numerically, what might it mean if you think about it in terms of the above pattern?

C. Mario's direct formula is $S = 32 - 2(n - 1)$. Is he correct? Why or why not? If he is correct, how might he be thinking about his formula?

D. How many squares are there in stage 20? What might your answer mean if you think about it in terms of the above pattern?

E. For what stage number will there be no more squares left? How do you know for sure?

Fig. 6.26   Modified task involving the losing squares pattern in Fig. 6.23a

In Chap. 7, we discuss ways in which algebra, which Kaput (2008) considers as "play[ing] the key role across K-12 mathematics" (p. 15), can be grounded in pattern generalization activity. Consequently the development of algebraic generalization is also a graded phenomenon, which involves states of presymbolic, nonsymbolic, and symbolic processing and conversion, reflective of the conceptual changes that occurred in the history of the subject. We also deal with the following points: (1) the different contexts of pattern generalization activity and the kinds of algebraic generalizations they generate; (2) the relationship between arithmetical thinking and context-based structural thinking; (3) the grounding of symbolic algebra, functions, and models in presymbolic and nonsymbolic algebraic contexts; and (4) the graded nature of pattern generalization.

Chapter 7
Patterns and Graded Algebraic Thinking

Various empirically-driven pattern generalization studies in different parts of the globe have research goals that map with the following four standards for mathematical practice below, taken from the *US Common Core Standards* (National Governors Association Center for Best Practices, Council of Chief State School Officers (NGACBP/CCSSO), 2010). While individual studies appear to have a narrow focus in terms of the kinds of patterns that are pursued, the basic practical intent is the same, which involves developing effective ways of democratizing access to the fundamental structures of mathematics. Patterns are ubiquitous in both mathematical and everyday contexts, and the main activity across context oftentimes pertains to the discernment, construction, and justification of an interpreted structure. Even the closure is almost the same, which involves the formation of meaningful and mathematically valid categories, concepts, labels, and methods. Fundamental differences are expected, of course, which can be explained in terms of what counts as meaningful. For example, the four standards below reflect a view of meaningfulness drawn from the values of the larger mathematics community. Consequently, patterns in the school mathematics curriculum are good things to think with for as long as they encourage students to engage in abstract, quantitative, model-driven, structural, and regularity thinking. Further, because students' ways of expressing outcomes vary depending on grade level, it makes sense to view them as positions or locations on a continuum of objects from figural on one end to algebraic on the other end of the continuum. For instance, many young children's incipient generalizations on patterns are pictorial and structural (Chap. 5), while older students' versions appear to be algebraic and structural (Chap. 6). Certainly, variables ought to be interpreted along the same object-continuum as well, which we discuss in the next section in terms of nonsymbolic and symbolic algebraic thinking.

2. Reason abstractly and quantitatively. Mathematically proficient students make sense of quantities and their relationships in problem situations. They bring two complementary abilitals to bear on problems involving quantitative relationships: the ability to decontextualize—to abstract a given situation and represent it symbolically and manipulate the representing symbols as if they have a life of their own, without necessarily attending to their referents—and the ability to contextualize, to pause as needed during the manipulation

F. Rivera, *Teaching and Learning Patterns in School Mathematics:*
Psychological and Pedagogical Considerations, DOI 10.1007/978-94-007-2712-0_7,
© Springer Science+Business Media Dordrecht 2013

process in order to probe into the referents for the symbols involved. Quantitative reasoning entails habits of creating a coherent representation of the problem at hand; considering the units involved; attending to the meaning of quantities, not just how to compute them; and knowing and flexibly using different properties of operations and objects.

4. Model with mathematics. Mathematically proficient students can apply the mathematics they know to solve problems arising in everyday life, society, and the workplace. In early grades, this might be as simple as writing an addition equation to describe a situation. In middle grades, a student might apply proportional reasoning to plan a school event or analyze a problem in the community. By high school, a student might use geometry to solve a design problem or use a function to describe how one quantity of interest depends on another. Mathematically proficient students who can apply what they know are comfortable making assumptions and approximations to simplify a complicated situation, realizing that these may need revision later. They are able to identify important quantities in a practical situation and map their relationships using such tools as diagrams, two-way tables, graphs, flowcharts and formulas. They can analyze those relationships mathematically to draw conclusions. They routinely interpret their mathematical results in the context of the situation and reflect on whether the results make sense, possibly improving the model if it has not served its purpose.

7. Look for and make use of structure. Mathematically proficient students look closely to discern a pattern or structure. Young students, for example, might notice that three and seven more is the same amount as seven and three more, or they may sort a collection of shapes according to how many sides the shapes have. Later, students will see 7×8 equals the well remembered $7 \times 5 + 7 \times 3$, in preparation for learning about the distributive property. In the expression $x^2 + 9x + 14$, older students can see the 14 as 2×7 and the 9 as $2 + 7$. They recognize the significance of an existing line in a geometric figure and can use the strategy of drawing an auxiliary line for solving problems. They also can step back for an overview and shift perspective. They can see complicated things, such as some algebraic expressions, as single objects or as being composed of several objects. For example, they can see $5 - 3(x - y)^2$ as 5 minus a positive number times a square and use that to realize that its value cannot be more than 5 for any real numbers x and y.

8. Look for and express regularity in repeated reasoning. Mathematically proficient students notice if calculations are repeated, and look both for general methods and for shortcuts. Upper elementary students might notice when dividing 25 by 11 that they are repeating the same calculations over and over again, and conclude they have a repeating decimal. By paying attention to the calculation of slope as they repeatedly check whether points are on the line through (1, 2) with slope 3, middle school students might abstract the equation $(y - 2)/(x - 1) = 3$. Noticing the regularity in the way terms cancel when expanding $(x - 1)(x + 1)$, $(x - 1)(x^2 + x + 1)$, and $(x - 1)(x^3 + x^2 + x + 1)$ might lead them to the general formula for the sum of a geometric series. As they work to solve a problem, mathematically proficient students maintain oversight of the process, while attending to the details. They continually evaluate the reasonableness of their intermediate results (NGACBP/CCSSO, 2010).

Representations of Patterns in Three Contexts: Presymbolic, Nonsymbolic, and Symbolic Algebraic Generalizations

Mathematical Practice 2 in the above list describes the distinguishing features between contextualized and decontextualized mathematical activity. Extended to the pattern generalizing process, context-based activity disposes learners to check in with the relevant referents, while decontextualized activity encourages them to reflect on the corresponding symbolic representations alone. The distinction is compatible with the two definitions of algebra that Heeffer (2008, 2010) has referred to as nonsymbolic algebra and symbolic algebra. He writes:

> Let us call (nonsymbolic) algebra *an analytical problem-solving method for arithmetical problems in which an unknown quantity is represented by an abstract entity*. There are two crucial conditions in this definition: *analytical*, meaning that the problem is solved by considering some unknown magnitudes hypothetical and deductively deriving statements so that these unknowns can be expressed as a value, and an *abstract entity* that is used to represent the unknowns. This entity can be a symbol, a figure, or even a color .... More strictly, symbolic algebra is *an analytical problem-solving method for arithmetical and geometrical problems consisting of systematic manipulation of a symbolic representation of the problem*. Symbolic algebra thus starts from a symbolic representation of a problem, meaning something more than a shorthand notation (Heeffer, 2010, pp. 88–89).

For Heeffer, pre-sixteenth century algebra was nonsymbolic (i.e. arithmetical and figural). Drawing on Hoyrup's (2002) reinterpretation of the early Babylonian problem texts that were all arithmetical in context, the algebraic techniques employed at that time were all conveyed through "geometrical constructions rather than formulas or equations" (Heeffer, 2008, p. 151). That is, in Babylonian (and Arabic) algebra, formulas and equations were absent despite the fact that the authors of the clay cuneiform tablets grasped the abstract nature of the unknowns and exhibited procedures that were all analytical. However, when the Italian mathematicians toward the end of the sixteenth century began to focus on (systems of) equations and their structures, that marked the beginning of a shift toward symbolic algebra, especially noting the successful integration of letter variables as notations for unknowns.

The 20 or so years of research on patterns across cohorts of learners reflect the prevalence of presymbolic and nonsymbolic forms of algebraic generalizations. Young children, especially, are drawn to employ gestures or verbally describe their figural (re)construction of parts that comprise a known stage in their emerging pattern. They repeat the explicit actions over several more stages in the pattern until they feel certain that they are able to grasp a stable rhythm or essence of their interpreted structures. Successful (re)constructions are analytical, that is, they are structural in the sense that they employ abduction, induction, and deduction. Further, there is oftentimes an implicit understanding of the relevant unknowns that enables the students to engage in conceptual projection and prediction involving any far stage in the pattern. Among older children and adults, while they are able to grasp the essence of their algebraic generalizations in variable terms, many of their direct formulas remain rooted in presymbolic and nonsymbolic phases. In light of the available empirical evidence, such variables in students' direct formulas do not usually evolve beyond their practical role in the conversion process. In fact, they rarely use them to construct "a higher level of abstraction" that could potentially yield "new mathematical objects" that "are abstractions of abstractions of abstractions" (Derbyshire, 2006, pp. 5–6). Certainly, this initial constraint in pattern generalization activity should not be viewed negatively considering its significant role in the development of structural thinking and other long-term benefits that have been noted in various research reports.

In practical terms, students' structural competence in presymbolic and nonsymbolic algebraic generalization can motivate them to learn the structures of symbolic algebra, which is the typical content of beginning and advanced algebra in today's schools. Hence, in *Teaching and Learning Patterns in School Mathematics*, which is also the title of this book, we implicitly acknowledge this limitation but favorably recommend their use for all other reasons with easy access to structures being the most valuable. In presymbolic and nonsymbolic algebraic contexts, variables in pattern generalization contexts are viewed as structure-driven quantities. This label helps us later when we discuss and compare them with the algebraic quantities that comprise symbolic algebra.

Elementary students who produce presymbolic and nonsymbolic algebraic generalizations on figural and numerical patterns model what we classify as context-based structural thinking since the construction and justification of such generalizations do not stray far from their referents. The terms in students' direct expressions are, in fact, arithmetical quantities—"numbers with units" (Parker & Baldridge, 2004, p. 167)—that require them to attend to their meanings, especially when calculations are performed on them. A similar observation holds in the case of older students and adults who tend to produce more nonsymbolic than symbolic algebraic generalizations, which is an effect of learning about variables and their many uses in the earlier grades. Hopefully, of course, more pattern generalization experiences will deepen their conceptions of the meaning of variables from one that sees them as playing a mere replacement role (a placeholder) in a general formula relative to a particular pattern to one that considers them as an abstract signpost for all generalities across different types of patterns and domains. Patterns range from the arithmetical (e.g., figural and numerical sequences of numbers and objects) to the algebraic (e.g., matrices, functions, motions, curves, abstract algebra concepts).

The presymbolic, nonsymbolic, and symbolic contexts of algebraic generalizations indicate that students' conceptions of variables will also undergo changes from the concrete to the abstract. Both arithmetical- and figural-based variable generalizations are structural, which means that the converted formulas convey relationships between the elements in the patterns over the elements themselves (cf. Osserman, 1981). Further, appropriating Dörfler's (2008) characterization of the two views of algebraic notation, which he traces to the British Algebraic School (de Morgan, Boole, etc.), arithmetically and figurally conceived variables are *referential,* that is, they are generalized numbers that emerge from arithmetical laws and certain kinds of numerical arithmetical experiences. Further, appropriating Kvasz (2006), the referential grounding is *perspectivist* in nature since they are constructed expressions that capture "pictures of reality seen from a particular point of view" (p. 288). Hence, because figural and arithmetical variables belong to the realm of our common perceptions of quantities, the manner in which we manipulate them refers to and is validated in a relevant external world.

Algebraic generalizations, and algebra for that matter, work with symbols that are abstract and decontextualized, that is, as noted in *Mathematical Practice 2* above, "they have a life of their own, without necessarily attending to their referents." The (general) symbols encompass concepts and processes. For example, *Mathematical*

Practice 8, which involves looking for and expressing regularity in repeated reasoning, addresses the emergence of symbolic algebraic generalizations when reflection deemphasizes the particularity of the given objects in favor of the underlying general concepts and methods that unite them in some regular manner. Thus, variables in symbolic algebra emerge as universal quantities, and the meaningful ones tend to arise genetically from arithmetic- and figural-based structural thinking. When developed in this continuous manner, they can be (easily) manipulated by employing "operations and rules [that] are similar to those in common arithmetic, founded upon the same principles" (Maclaurin (1748, p. 1) quoted in Katz, 2007, p. 185). Further, the generalities in all symbolic algebraic generalizations can be applied to all relevant classes of objects, unlike nonsymbolic and pre-symbolic algebraic generalizations that tend to focus on the specificity of a single class of objects.

Hence, when specific algebraic techniques (such as principles related to solving equations) operate on symbolic algebraic generalizations alone, they convey the view that we are at the same time attending to all the relevant classes of objects and situations that we grasp and assume in their entire universality. In Dörfler's (2008) terms, algebraic notations have an *operative* nature, that is, they are objects that are structural effects of "the rules of algebra themselves … [as] signs without a referent but to be manipulated according to agreed upon rules" (pp. 144–145). Further, in Kvasz's (2006) sense, they are *projective* rather than perspectivist in which case the relevant structures, and not necessarily everyday reality and visual experiences, are the ones that are driving the representations. Symbolic algebra in the projective phase splits "the bond between language and reality" (Kvasz, p. 299) with the eventual construction of "formal objects [that are] constructed from symbols, [and] independent of any realistic context in which they are supposed to be interpreted" (ibid). This strong characterization of symbolic algebra should help clarify why, in this book, we have fundamentally associated pattern generalization competence mainly along the lines of structural thinking. While patterns without a doubt support growth in structural thinking, they may or may not lead us to symbolic algebraic thinking in the sense just described.

Considering the distinctions noted in the preceding paragraphs, students' use of variables in several reported empirical accounts of pattern generalization activity is an effect of structural thinking (versus symbolic algebraic thinking). For example, the variables that are used to express the different ways of obtaining the total number of students that can sit around any number of tables in the pattern shown in Fig. 7.1 are derived effects of, borrowing from Gentner (2010), structural alignment and processing, which then enable the projection of inferences on the unknown. Alignment and matches between stages or instances in a pattern produce structurally consistent (one-to-one) correspondences yielding justifiable projections and a general representation of stable and regular features in variable form. But, in light of the preceding discussion, the pattern generalization conversion phase is presymbolic or nonsymbolic and structural. Certainly the patterning task can be used to help students transition to symbolic algebraic thinking. If and when this happens, the context is removed and replaced by an activity that might involve systematically transforming or operating on the unknowns through the application of the properties of equality.

A further reflection on the thinking that is involved relative to the task shown in Fig. 7.1 leads us to note that when students employ either substitution to find the number of students that can sit in 56 tables or working backward to determine the number of trapezoid tables that can sit 56 students, the particular numerical processes necessitate the application of arithmetical operations. All the projection and prediction tasks are primarily consequences of structural thinking that depend on the given conditions of the arithmetic situation. A symbolic algebraic mindset, however, emerges when they begin to either perform transformation techniques on the symbolic representations or subsume such representations (i.e., direct formulas) as instances of (linear) functions over domains larger than the set of positive integers. In either situation, variables transform into what Lagrange refers to as *algebraic quantities*, that is, formal analytic expressions "whose identit(ies) merely depend on [them] being expressed by their appropriate expressions, and [are] then to be conceived as nothing but a *relatum* of the net of relations corresponding to the operations that the very expression[s] represent" (Ferraro & Panza, 2012, p. 108).

Fig. 7.1 Table and chairs task (Moss & Beatty, 2006, pp. 461–462)

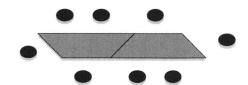

Patterns in the Elementary School Mathematics Curriculum: The Emergence of Presymbolic and Nonsymbolic Structural Generalizations in Arithmetical Contexts

Pattern generalization is undoubtedly a unifying theme in the elementary school mathematics curriculum. It is clear that the relevant goal of mathematical activity involves helping students develop structural thinking that yields, at the very least, presymbolic and nonsymbolic algebraic generalizations. For instance, first-grade students learn a benchmarking structure that can generate all addition facts involving numbers up to 20 in a systematic manner following a compensation action strategy. Figure 7.2 shows how to construct all addition facts for the number 6 beginning with the number sentence $6+0=6$. Young children use a ten frame in order to start benchmarking by 5, which explains the sentence $5+1=6$. Then they produce the remaining addition facts for 6 by taking away a circle chip in one column and adding the chip to the other column. They do that repeatedly until all the distinct number sentences are generated. In some cases students use their hands instead of a ten frame to perform the same sequence of actions just described.

A similar benchmarking structure takes place in the case of numbers bigger than 10 in which case students learn to benchmark by 10 possibly using unifix cubes in the case of relatively large numbers. The underlying processing that is associated with the benchmarking structure clearly involves systematic compensation. When translated in algebraic form, the pattern generalization activity involving addition number fact generation can be expressed as finding whole number values for x and y such that $x+y=n$, where n stands for the targeted sum. The abstract entities can be whole numbers or objects (e.g., apples, bananas, erasers) and the targeted analytical method may involve a systematic application of compensation. Considering the mathematical proficiency of elementary students, the algebraic activity can either be presymbolic or nonsymbolic. In the presymbolic algebraic phase, the action of generating addition facts is tied to how they manipulate whole numbers. In the nonsymbolic algebraic phase, the arithmetical representations can be seen as individual inferences of deductively drawn actions that they consistently exhibit across any value based on their experiences on the chip activity.

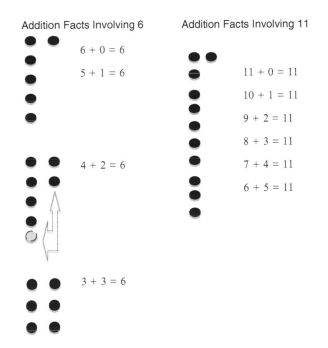

Fig. 7.2 Generating addition facts to 20 by benchmarking to 5 and 10 in Grades 1 and 2 by benchmarking to 5 and 10

Another instance of structural thinking in the first and second grade school mathematics curriculum involves the use of a math triangle model that helps students establish a relationship between an addition fact and its corresponding subtraction facts. In Fig. 7.3, for instance, first grade students can see that the addition sentence *15 + 10 = 25* has two distinct subtraction facts. In second grade, they can use the same math triangle model to generate multiplication facts and their corresponding division facts (Fig. 7.4). Once again, the gradedness of algebraic thinking should be evident in the way they deal with numbers in such a structural context.

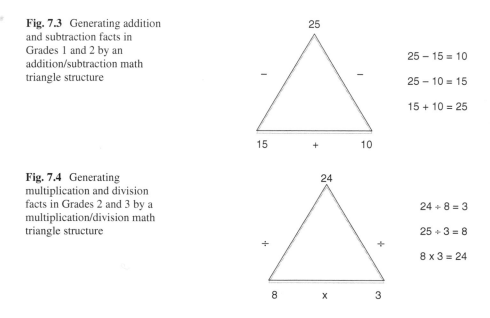

Fig. 7.3 Generating addition and subtraction facts in Grades 1 and 2 by an addition/subtraction math triangle structure

25

25 − 15 = 10

25 − 10 = 15

15 + 10 = 25

15   +   10

Fig. 7.4 Generating multiplication and division facts in Grades 2 and 3 by a multiplication/division math triangle structure

24

24 ÷ 8 = 3

25 ÷ 3 = 8

8 x 3 = 24

8   x   3

Numbers also increase in complexity from single digit whole numbers to multi-digit integers, and the nature of complexity can be approached using a well-defined structure called place value, which is the conceptual story underlying the construction and understanding of numbers in the elementary school mathematics curriculum. Place value means that the value of a digit in an explicitly well-defined numeration scheme is determined by its position relative to the number. Parker and Baldridge (2004) describe the place value process in our decimal system as follows, which becomes the students' structuring basis for implementing the operations of composition (ungrouping and ungrouping) and transformation (adding, subtracting, multiplying, and dividing) involving two or more numbers.

1. One forms bundles of 1, 10, 100, 1,000, etc.
2. If necessary one rebundles to ensure that there are at most 9 bundles of each denomination.
3. One counts the number of bundles of each denomination and records that number in the appropriate position (Parker & Baldridge, 2004, p. 8).

Figure 7.5 illustrates US third-grade student Mark's structural approach involving rectangles, squares, sticks, and circles that enabled him to conceptually grasp the underlying place value processing that he needed to perform the operations of addition and subtraction involving regrouping of digits. The same structural approach can, in fact, be consistently applied to all whole numbers. We especially note the emergence of Mark's numerically driven structure for dividing multidigit numbers by a single-digit factor as shown in Fig. 7.6. Through repeated experiences with the visual representations involving division, Mark's converted numerical division processing eventually captured in an economical manner how he actually perceived the underlying general method across particular instances of numbers.

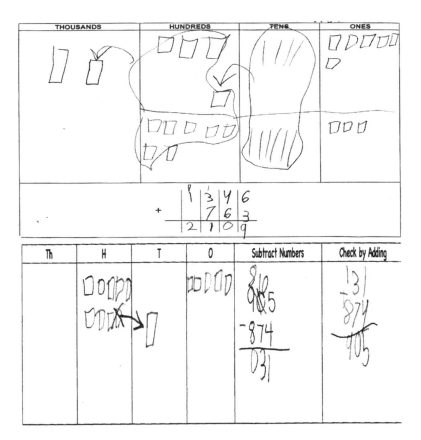

Fig. 7.5 Adding and subtracting numbers using place value math drawings (Fuson, Kalchman, & Bransford, 2005; Rivera, 2011)

The preceding presymbolic and nonsymbolic structures convey relationship-based representations that emerged in arithmetical activity. The essence of the students' generalities is evident in the forms, notations, expressions, and equations that reflect only the essential details. In Fig. 7.6, for example, Mark's converted numerical algorithm for division deemphasized the visual representations that accompanied his initial processing. It exemplifies a type of nonsymbolic algebraic generalization in which a stable numerical method has been deduced. A presymbolic algebraic generalization also employs an analytical method, however, it is intricately

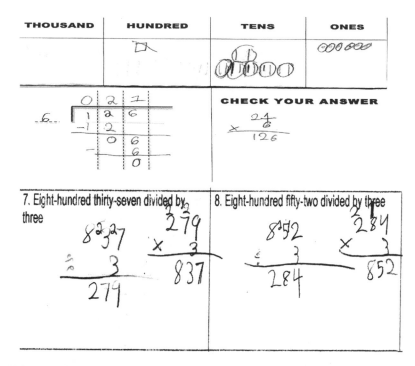

Fig. 7.6 Grade 3 student Mark's division structure from visual to numerical structures

linked to the particular conditions of the relevant instances that support inductive processing within an abductive constraint. Further, both visual and numerical steps indicate a clear consistent structural alignment between the two representations.

Hence, when elementary students extend their pattern-based understanding of place value in the upper grades to include larger numbers (e.g., trillions) and smaller numbers (e.g. decimals), structural algebraic thinking may remain presymbolic or nonsymbolic. From the point of view of Mathematical Practice 4, which involves modeling with mathematics, number fact and place value structures emerge from applying mathematics to (especially conceptually rich) situations that necessitate systematic processes for counting objects, which also means that they are always directly linked to their concrete referents whose structures are characterized as referential and perspectivist in nature (Fig. 7.7).

(Stem) What number or expression goes in the box too make this number sentence true?

$$35 + 6 = 35 + \square \qquad\qquad 3 + 5 = \square \times 2$$

A. 2 + 2   B. 2 x 2   C. 2 + 3   D. 2 x 3   A. 3   B. 4   C. 5   D. 6

Fig. 7.7 Sample released algebra and functions item tasks on the California Assessment for Grades 3 and 4 students (California Department of Education, 2009)

Many elementary school textbook problems and assessments classify the tasks shown in Fig. 7.7 as algebraic since (1) there is an unknown variable represented by a box that needs to be determined and (2) a general process is involved that requires the analysis of a correct relationship from a pool of possible values or expressions. In such cases of arithmetical tasks, they can be analyzed algebraically in either presymbolic, nonsymbolic, or symbolic terms. Third and fourth grade students can solve for the unknown values by employing relational thinking (e.g. since both the left and the right hand side of the equation on the left of Fig. 7.7 has 36 as an addend, then they only need to consider which expression in the choices would equal 6). They can also either draw place value sticks and circles (e.g. the visuals in Fig. 7.5) or use chips or other concrete objects (fruits, pencils, animals, etc.) to help them determine the unknown value. Another reasonable presymbolic algebraic strategy involves manipulating the numbers based on the definitions of the operations involved (e.g. $3 + 5 = 8$, so what number $\times 2$ yields 8 means the missing factor has to be 4, the answer). A nonsymbolic algebraic strategy involves the application of the multiplication property of equations (e.g. $3 + 5 = 8$, so dividing both sides of the equation by 2 means that the missing unknown number ought to be 4). The algebraic strategies exemplify how numbers, operations, and unknowns can be interpreted in different ways depending on how students view the nature of algebraic activity from the specificity of a given context to the generality of a method for manipulating the relevant objects.

The fourth-grade tasks shown in Fig. 7.8 exemplify symbolic algebraic problems that involve evaluating an expression and an equation in an arithmetical context. While the appropriate grade-level domain is limited to the set of rational numbers, the variables over time will come to represent different mathematical objects in other domains (e.g. complex numbers, functions, series, matrices, etc.) before fully transitioning to their final status as algebraic quantities. Such quantities are still manipulated like numbers in arithmetical contexts. The only difference is that the process of manipulation is expected to also apply to all applicable generalities across domains.

In sum, we note how: arithmetic is inherently structural and algebraic; algebra is inherently arithmetical; structures are inherently relational; and the most meaningful and powerful mathematical relations are inherently general(izable). The unifying process in all pattern generalization activity in the elementary school mathematics curriculum foregrounds the symmetrical and genetic relationship that exists between arithmetic and algebra.

What is the value of the expression below if $a = 3$?

$$15 - (a + 8)$$

A. 4   B. 12   C. 20   D. 26

The letters S and T stand for numbers. If $S - 100 = T - 100$ which statement is true?

A. $S = T$ B. $S > T$ C. $S = T+100$

D. $S > T + 100$

Fig. 7.8 Sample released algebra and functions item tasks on the California Assessment for Grade 4 students (California Department of Education, 2009)

Patterns in the Middle and High School Mathematics Curriculum and Beyond: The Emergence of Symbolic Algebraic Structures in Presymbolic and Nonsymbolic Algebraic Contexts

One important strand of symbolic structures in the middle and high school mathematics curriculum pertains to the classical algebraic concepts and processes involving equations and inequalities. In the *US Common Core Standards: Mathematics* (NGACBP/CCSSO, 2010), the stipulated high school course *Algebra* covers these topics with an explicit recommendation toward understanding their underlying (syntactical) structures. Birkhoff (1977) characterizes classical algebra in the following manner below.

> The most essential idea [of classical algebra] consists in replacing each verbal statement about numerical quantities by a symbolic equation, whose terms can be rearranged and combined by well-established general laws to give a sequence of equivalent, but, hopefully, simpler equations. The original equation can be considered as "solved" when the unknown quantity has been isolated on one side of the equality symbol =, on the other side of which is some expression involving only the known quantities (Birkhoff, 1977, p. 464).

In several chapters we discussed in some detail recent research investigations on figural pattern generalization that document students' natural abilities to construct and justify different, but equivalent, direct expressions and formulas on well-defined patterns. The Table and Chairs Pattern in Fig. 7.1, for example, can engender the construction of the direct formulas $S(n) = 2 + n \times 3$, $S(n) = 2 + 3n$, and $S(n) = 1 + 3(n-1) + 4$, where the variable S refers to the total number of students that can sit in n trapezoid-shaped tables based on the constraints stated in the arithmetical problem. The formulas can then be used to talk about differences between expressions and equations, including basic syntactical structures and terminologies that are needed to write algebraic expressions and equations. The presymbolic algebraic contexts can provide the concrete ground that prepares students to the follow up symbolic algebraic activity, which involves systematically manipulating the established symbolic representations as algebraic quantities. Being mindful of the initial patterning context, the symbolic algebraic process of simplifying expressions also has meaning and significance because it can be checked against the reality of the nonsymbolic phase that enabled different but equivalent ways of seeing and expressing structures yield different equivalent ways of expressing them. Further, the problem of determining the exact number of trapezoid tables that can sit a given number of students can be used to talk about what it means to solve equations. We also note the additional patterning activities shown in Figs. 7.9 and 7.10 that can motivate the study of linear systems of equations and quadratic equations, respectively. Certainly, objects in patterns need not be confined to figural representations. Numerical patterning tasks can also be used such as the one shown in Fig. 7.11. In the US Common Core Standards for Algebra, there is a recommendation to use spreadsheets and computer algebra systems as additional ways of "experiment[ing] with algebraic expressions, perform[ing] complicated algebraic manipulations, and understand[ing] how algebraic manipulations behave" (NGACBP/CCSSO, 2010, n.p.).

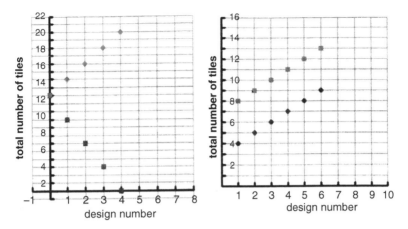

Fig. 7.9 Patterning activities involving linear systems of equations (Charles Dana Center, 2004; Reprinted with the permission of the Dana Center)

Suppose that n straight lines are drawn on a plane such that no two lines are parallel and no three are concurrent. What is the maximum number of regions into which the plane can be divided by the n straight lines?

Fig. 7.10 Patterning activity involving a quadratic equation (Barnes & Gordon, 1987, p. 8)

Paul, Judy, and Sam are discussing patterns arising from the sum of a multiple of 3 and a multiple of 6. They propose their own ideas, as follows:

(a) Paul says that the sum of a multiple of 3 and a multiple of 6 must be a multiple of 3. Do you agree or disagree with Paul's idea? Explain your answer.
(b) Judy says that the sum of a multiple of 3 and a multiple of 6 must be a multiple of 6. Do you agree or disagree with Judy's idea? Explain your answer.
(c) Sam says that the sum of a multiple of 3 and a multiple of 6 must be a multiple of 9. Do you agree or disagree with Sam's idea? Explain your answer.

Fig. 7.11 A numerical patterning activity (Lin, Yang, & Chen, 2004, p. 237)

Two other strands in the high school mathematics curriculum that are strongly linked to symbolic algebraic structures pertain to concepts and processes involving functions and models. In the *US Common Core Standards: Mathematics* (NGACBP/ CCSSO, 2010), the strands *Functions* and *Models* are separately discussed from the *Algebra* strand. However, symbolic algebraic structures can provide the underlying conceptual foundation that can link and unify all three strands. As a matter of fact, Mesa (2004) notes that among the five or so different mathematical practices that are associated with the topic of functions in 24 middle school mathematics textbooks in 15 countries, symbolic algebraic relationships often receive the most attention. This unique and special relationship between functions and symbolic algebra is clearly described in the two paragraphs below.

> *Expressions can define functions, and equivalent expressions define the same function. Asking when two functions have the same value for the same input leads to an equation; graphing the two functions allows for finding approximate solutions of the equation. Converting a verbal description to an equation, inequality, or system of these is an essential skill in modeling.*
>
> *Determining an output value for a particular input involves evaluating an expression; finding inputs that yield a given output involves solving an equation. Questions about when two functions have the same value for the same input lead to equations, whose solutions can be visualized from the intersection of their graphs. Because functions describe relationships between quantities, they are frequently used in modeling. Sometimes functions are defined by a recursive process, which can be displayed effectively using a spreadsheet or other technology (NGACBP/CCSSO, 2010, n.p.).*

The preceding symbolic algebraic characterization of functions treats quantities in general terms. Further, they do not merely refer to or represent quantities but make sense within a rule or a system of relations that emerges as a result of manipulating some relevant operations (cf. Ferraro & Panza, 2012). Modeling activity can then be implemented in order to endow them with meaning and significance as students begin to establish structural relationships. For example, in the following US Common Core Standard in mathematics for Grade 4 stated below, we learn in clear terms and for the very first time this beginning relationship between symbolic algebra, functions, and modeling in the context of patterning activity.

> *Generate a number or shape pattern that follows a given rule. Identify apparent features of the pattern that were not explicit in the rule itself. For example, given the rule "Add 3" and the starting number 1, generate terms in the resulting sequence and observe that the terms appear to alternate between odd and even numbers. Explain informally why the numbers will continue to alternate in this way (NGACBP/CCSSO, 2010, n.p.).*

Hence, the nonsymbolic algebraic usefulness of pattern generalization applies to functions, which is likely going to provide a meaningful route and easy access to the relevant symbolic algebraic structures. Further, since pattern generalization in the nonsymbolic algebraic phase assumes a broader view of the concept of variables—that is, one that operates within the context of functional relationships—the classical consequence of viewing variables as (single) unknowns to be determined by analytical methods is treated as a special case of this broader view. If students are able to develop this broader view early in their mathematical experiences with patterns, that might help resolve difficulties and interferences such as holding a narrow view of variables as unknowns especially in problem situations that necessitate the construction and justification of multiple answers (cf. Malisani & Spagnoio, 2009).

The Graded Shape of Pattern Generalization

In this book, we explored and illustrated a graded perspective on pattern generalization. We hope that it incites further discussion and empirical research, especially considering the possibility that it can sufficiently explain converging, diverging, and idiosyncratic actions in figural and numerical processing and conversion of objects in an emerging pattern that is always interpreted in context. Reported transition accounts are interesting and insightful, and we do not seek to dismiss them but rather subsume them under a more encompassing perspective. Further, we note that the real conditions of acquiring pattern generalization skills (even among experts) do not in many cases reflect what we gain from simple and predictable accounts of permanent shifts, which many teachers are likely to claim on the basis of their daily experiences with their students in their own classrooms. Among individual students, in fact, dealing with pattern generalization tasks oftentimes requires making "generalizations in the wild" (in a Hutchinean sense) in which case conditions are not usually ideal but contingent on opportunities and resources that are available to them. In the context of well conceived teaching experiments, especially, it is frequently the case that pattern generalization tasks are designed so that students in joint purposeful activity with each other and with their teacher experience continuous "delicate shifts of attention" (Mason, 1989) from the processing to the conversion phase. On regular instruction days, however, pattern generalization, like any other mathematical skills, is performed rather routinely with teachers drawing on the strength of their students' prior knowledge and inferential abilities and students focusing on aspects in patterns that they find interesting and meaningful at the moment. Discontinuities are, thus, considered frequent and normal.

Suffice it to say, teachers in everyday classroom situations always work with students who analyze pattern generalization tasks in an unproductive manner in which case the complexity of what they interpret to be sensible in a collection of objects cannot be conveniently grasped, processed, and converted in algebraic terms. Without a doubt, transition models of pattern generalization thinking provide important information that help teachers and students deal with certain types of patterns. However, graded pattern generalization processing underscores the complex and "executory rather than rule-driven" nature of students' emergent thinking across task in terms of the choices and actions they pursue and the consequences they generate.

References

Adler, J. (2008). Introduction: Philosophical foundations. In J. Adler & L. Rips (Eds.), *Reasoning: Studies of human inference and its foundations* (pp. 1–34). New York, NY: Cambridge University Press.

Ainley, J., Wilson, K., & Bills, L. (2003). Generalizing the context and generalizing the calculation. In N. Pateman, B. Dougherty, & J. Zilliox (Eds.), *Proceedings of the 27th international conference of the Psychology of Mathematics Education (PME)* (Vol. 2, pp. 9–16). Honolulu, Hawai'i: PME.

Alvarez, G., & Cavanagh, P. (2004). The capacity of visual short-term memory is set both by visual information load and by number of objects. *Psychological Science, 15*(2), 106–111.

Anderson, K., Casey, B., Thompson, W., Burrage, M., Pezaris, E., & Kosslyn, S. (2008). Performance on middle school geometry problems with geometry clues matched to three different cognitive styles. *Mind, Brain, and Education, 2*(4), 188–197.

Ansari, D. (2010). Neurocognitive approaches to developmental disorders of numerical and mathematical cognition: The perils of neglecting development. *Learning and Individual Differences, 20*, 123–129.

Arzarello, F. (2008). The proof in the 20th century. In P. Boero (Ed.), *Theorems in schools: From history, epistemology, and cognition in classroom practices* (pp. 43–64). Rotterdam: Sense Publishers.

Barnes, M., & Gordon, S. (1987). *Mathematical induction*. Sydney, Australia: Mathematics Learning Centre.

Bastable, V., & Schifter, D. (2008). Classroom stories: Examples of elementary students engaged in early algebra. In J. Kaput, D. Carraher, & M. Blanton (Eds.), *Algebra in the early grades* (pp. 165–184). New York, NY: Erlbaum.

Becker, J., & Rivera, F. (2005). Generalization strategies of beginning high school students. In H. Chick & J. Vincent (Eds.), *Proceedings of the 29th conference of the International Group for the Psychology of Mathematics Education* (Vol. 4, pp. 121–128). Melbourne: PME.

Becker, J., & Rivera, F. (2006). Establishing and justifying algebraic generalization at the sixth grade level. In J. Novotna, H. Moraova, M. Kratka, & N. Stehlikova (Eds.), *Proceedings of the 30th Conference of the International Group for the Psychology of Mathematics Education* (Vol. 4, pp. 465–472). Prague, Czechovslovakia: Charles University.

Bereiter, C. (1991). Implications of connectionism for thinking about rules. *Educational Researcher, 20*(3), 10–16.

Bhatt, R., & Quinn, P. (2011). How does learning impact development in infancy? The case of perceptual organization. *Infancy, 16*(1), 2–38.

Birkhoff, G. (1977). Current trends in algebra. In S. Montgomery, E. Ralston, S. R. Gordon, G. Janusz, M. Schacher, & M. Smith (Eds.), *Selected papers on algebra* (pp. 463–485). Washington, DC: The Mathematical Association of America.

F. Rivera, *Teaching and Learning Patterns in School Mathematics:*
Psychological and Pedagogical Considerations, DOI 10.1007/978-94-007-2712-0,
© Springer Science+Business Media Dordrecht 2013

Bishop, J. (2000). Linear geometric number patterns: Middle school students' strategies. *Mathematics Education Research Journal, 12*(2), 107–126.

Blanton, M., & Kaput, J. (2004). Elementary grades students' capacity for functional thinking. In M. Hoines & A. Fuglestad (Eds.), *Proceedings of the 28th conference of the International Group for the Psychology of Mathematics Education* (Vol. 2, pp. 135–142). Bergen, Norway: PME.

Bodanskii, F. (1991). The formation of an algebraic method of problem solving in primary school children. In V. Davydov (Ed.), *Soviet studies in mathematics education: Psychological abilities of primary school children in learning mathematics* (Vol. 6, pp. 275–338). Reston, VA: National Council of Teachers of Mathematics.

Britt, M., & Irwin, K. (2011). Algebraic thinking with and without algebraic representation: A pathway for learning. In J. Cai & E. Knuth (Eds.), *Early algebraization: A global dialogue from multiple perspectives* (pp. 137–160). Netherlands: Springer.

Brown, J. R. (1997). Proofs and pictures. *British Journal for the Philosophy of Science, 48*, 161–180.

Cai, J., & Hwang, S. (2002). Generalized and generative thinking in US and Chinese students' mathematical problem solving and problem posing. *The Journal of Mathematical Behavior, 21*, 401–421.

Cai, J., Ng, S. F., & Moyer, J. (2011). Developing students' algebraic thinking in earlier grades: Lessons from China and Singapore. In J. Cai & E. Knuth (Eds.), *Early algebraization: A global dialogue from multiple perspectives* (pp. 25–42). New York: Springer.

California Department of Education. (2009). STAR released item questions. Sacramento, CA: Author.

Cañadas, M., & Castro, E. (2007). A proposal of categorization for analyzing inductive reasoning. *PNA, 1*(2), 67–78.

Carey, S. (1985). *Conceptual change in childhood*. Cambridge, MA: MIT.

Carpenter, T., Franke, M., & Levi, L. (2003). *Thinking mathematically: Integrating arithmetic and algebra in elementary school*. Portsmouth, NH: Heinemann.

Carpenter, T., & Levi, L. (2000). *Developing conceptions of algebraic reasoning in the primary grades*. Madison, WI: National Center for Improving Student Learning and Achievement in Mathematics and Science.

Carraher, D., Martinez, M., & Schliemann, A. (2008). Early algebra and mathematical generalization. *ZDM, 40*, 3–22.

Carraher, D., Schliemann, A., & Brizuela, B. (1999). *Bringing out the algebraic character of arithmetic*. Paper presented at the 1999 AERA Meeting, Montreal, Canada. Available at http://www.earlyalgebra.terc.edu.

Carraher, D., Schliemann, A., Brizuela, B., & Earnest, D. (2006). Arithmetic and algebra in early mathematics education. *Journal for Research in Mathematics Education, 37*(2), 87–115.

Cavanagh, P., & He, S. (2011). Attention mechanisms for counting in stabilized and in dynamic displays. In S. Dehaene & E. Brannon (Eds.), *Space, time, and number in the brain: Searching for the foundations of mathematical thought* (pp. 23–35). New York: Academic.

Center, C. D. (2004). *Ensuring teacher quality: Algebra I*. Austin, TX: The University of Texas.

Chua, B., & Hoyles, C. (2010). Generalization and perceptual agility: How did teachers fare in a quadratic generalizing problem? *Research in Mathematics Education, 12*(1), 71–72.

Chua, B., & Hoyles, C. (2011). Secondary school students' perception of best help generalizing strategies. In: *Proceedings of the Seventh Congress of the European Society for Research in Mathematics Education (CERME)*. Rzeszow, Poland: CERME. Retrieved December 23, 2011, from http://www.cerme7.univ.rzeszow.pl/WG/3/CERME7_WG3_Chua.pdf.

Clements, D., & Sarama, J. (2009). *Learning and teaching early math: The learning trajectories approach*. New York, NY: Erlbaum.

Condry, K., & Spelke, E. (2008). The development of language and abstract concepts: The case of natural number. *Journal of Experimental Psychology. General, 137*(1), 22–38.

Cooper, T., & Warren, E. (2011). Years 2 to 6 students' ability to generalize: Models, representations, and theory for teaching and learning. In J. Cai & E. Knuth (Eds.), *Early algebraization: A global dialogue from multiple perspectives* (pp. 187–214). Netherlands: Springer.

Davydov, V. V. (1990). Type of generalization in instruction: Logical and psychological problems in the structuring of school curricula. In J. Kilpatrick (Ed.), *Soviet studies in mathematics education* (Vol. 2). Reston, VA: National Council of Teachers of Mathematics.

Davydov, V. (2008). *Problems of developmental instruction: A theoretical and experimental psychological study* (P. Moxhay., Trans.). New York, NY: Nova Science Publishers.

Deacon, T. (1997). *The symbolic species: The co-evolution of language and the brain*. New York: W. W. Norton & Company.

Dehaene, S. (1997). *The number sense*. New York, NY: Oxford University Press.

Dehaene, S., & Cohen, L. (1995). Two mental calculational systems: A case study of severe acalculia with preserved approximation. *Neuropsychologia, 29*, 1045–1074.

Derbyshire, J. (2006). *Unknown quantity: A real and imaginary history of algebra*. Washington, DC: Joseph Henry Press.

Dörfler, W. (1991). Forms and means of generalization. In A. Bishop & S. Mellin-Olsen (Eds.), *Mathematical knowledge: Its growth through teaching* (pp. 63–85). Netherlands: Kluwer.

Dörfler, W. (2008). En route from patterns to algebra: Comments and reflections. *ZDM, 40*(1), 143–160.

Dreyfus, H. (1979). *What computers still can't do*. New York, NY: MIT.

Dreyfus, H. (1988). The Socratic and Platonic basis of cognitivism. *Artificial Intelligence and Society, 2*, 99–112.

du Sautoy, M. (2008). *Symmetry: A journey into the patterns of nature*. New York, NY: HarperCollins Publishers.

Duval, R. (1998). Geometry from a cognitive point of view. In C. Mammana & V. Villani (Eds.), *Perspectives in the teaching of geometry for the 21st century* (pp. 29–83). Boston: Kluwer.

Duval, R. (1999). Representation, vision, and visualization: Cognitive functions in mathematical thinking. In F. Hitt & M. Santos (Eds.), *Proceedings of the 21st North American PME Conference* (pp. 3–26). Cuernavaca, Morelos, Mexico: PMENA.

Eco, H. (1983). Horns, hooves, insteps: Some hypotheses on three types of abduction. In U. Eco & T. Sebeok (Eds.), *The sign of three: Dupin, Holmes, Peirce* (pp. 198–220). Bloomington, IN: Indiana University Press.

Ellis, A. (2007). Connections between generalizing and justifying: Students' reasoning with linear relationships. *Journal for Research in Mathematics Education, 38*(3), 194–229.

Empson, S., & Levi, L. (2011). *Extending children's mathematics: Fractions and decimals*. Portsmouth, NH: Heinemann.

Feigenson, L. (2011). Objects, sets, and ensembles. In S. Dehaene & E. Brannon (Eds.), *Space, time, and number in the brain: Searching for the foundations of mathematical thought* (pp. 13–22). New York: Academic.

Feigenson, L., & Carey, S. (2003). Tracking individuals via object-files: Evidence from infants' manual search. *Developmental Science, 6*, 568–584.

Ferraro, G., & Panza, M. (2012). Lagrange's theory of analytical functions and his ideal purity of method. *Archive for History of Exact Sciences, 66*, 95–197.

Ferrini-Mundy, J., Floden, R., McCrory, R., Burrill, G., & Sandow, D. (2005). *Knowledge for teaching school algebra: Challenges in developing an analytic framework*. Paper presented at the American Education Research Association. Montreal, Quebec, Canada.

Fischbein, E. (1993). The theory of figural concepts. *Educational Studies in Mathematics, 24*, 139–162.

Fuson, K., Kalchman, M., & Bransford, J. (2005). Mathematical understanding: An introduction. In M. S. Donovan & J. Bransford (Eds.), *How students learn: History, mathematics, and science in the classroom* (pp. 217–256). Washington, DC: National Research Council.

Gal, H., & Linchevski, L. (2010). To see or not to see: Analyzing difficulties in geometry from the perspective of visual perception. *Educational Studies in Mathematics, 74*, 163–183.

Garcia, M., Benitez, A., & Ruiz, E. (2010). Using multiple representations to make and verify conjectures. In P. Brosnan, D. Erchick, & L. Flevares (Eds.), *Proceedings of the 32nd annual meeting of the North American Chapter of the International Group for the Psychology of Mathematics Education* (Vol. 6, pp. 270–278). Columbus, OH: Ohio State University.

Garcia-Cruz, J., & Martinón, A. (1998). Levels of generalization in linear patterns. In A. Olivier & K. Newstead (Eds.), *Proceedings of the 22nd conference of the International Group for the*

Psychology of Mathematics Education (PME) (Vol. 2, pp. 329–336). Stellenbosch, South Africa: PME.

Gentner, D. (2010). Bootstrapping the mind: Analogical processes and symbol systems. *Cognitive Science, 34*, 752–775.

Glenberg, A., de Vega, M., & Graesser, A. (2008). Framing the debate. In M. de Vega, A. Glenberg, & A. Graesser (Eds.), *Symbols and embodiment: Debates on meaning and cognition* (pp. 1–10). New York: Oxford University Press.

Goldstone, R., Son, J., & Byrge, L. (2011). Early perceptual learning. *Infancy, 16*(1), 45–51.

Gopnik, A., & Wellman, H. (1994). *Mapping the mind: Domain specificity in cognition and culture*. Cambridge, MA: Cambridge University Press.

Goswami, U. (2011). Inductive and deductive reasoning. In U. Goswami (Ed.), *The Wiley-Blackwell handbook of childhood cognitive development* (pp. 399–419). Malden, MA: Wiley-Blackwell.

Griffiths, T., Chater, N., Kemp, C., Perfors, A., & Tenenbaum, J. (2010). Probabilistic models of cognition: Exploring representations and inductive biases. *Trends in Cognitive Sciences, 14*, 357–364.

Harel, G. (2001). The development of mathematical induction as a proof scheme: A model for DNR-based instruction. In S. Campbell & R. Zazkis (Eds.), *Learning and teaching number theory: Research in cognition and instruction* (pp. 184–212). Westport, CT: Greenwoood Press.

Harel, G., & Tall, D. (1991). The general, the abstract, and the generic in advanced mathematics. *For the Learning of Mathematics, 11*, 38–42.

Hargreaves, M., Threlfall, J., Frobisher, L., & Shorrocks-Taylor, D. (2004). Children's strategies with linear and quadratic sequences. In A. Orton (Ed.), *Pattern in the teaching and learning of mathematics* (pp. 65–83). UK: Continuum International Publishing Group.

Heeffer, A. (2008). The emergence of symbolic algebra as a shift in predominant models. *Foundations of Science, 13*, 149–161.

Heeffer, A. (2010). Learning concepts through the history of mathematics: The case of symbolic algebra. In K. François & J. P. Van Bendegem (Eds.), *Philosophical dimensions in mathematics education* (pp. 83–103). Dordrecht, Netherlands: Springer.

Heid, K., & Blume, G. (Eds.). (2008). *Research on technology and the teaching and learning of mathematics*. New York, NY: Information Age Publishing.

Hershkowitz, R. (1998). About reasoning in geometry. In C. Mammana & V. Villani (Eds.), *Perspectives on the teaching of geometry for the 21st century* (pp. 29–37). Boston: Kluwer.

Hibben, J. (1905). *Logic: Deductive and inductive*. New York: Charles Scribner's Sons.

Hill, C., & Bennett, D. (2008). The perception of size and shape. *Philosophical Issues, 18*, 294–315.

Holland, J., Holyoak, K., Nisbett, R., & Thagard, P. (1986). *Induction: Processes of inference, learning, and discovery*. Cambridge, MA: MIT.

Hoyrup, J. (2002). *Lengths, widths, surfaces: A portrait of old Babylonian algebra and its kin*. Heidelberg, Netherlands: Springer.

Israel, R. (2006). Projectibility and explainability or how to draw a new picture of inductive practices. *Journal for General Philosophy of Science, 37*, 269–286.

Iwasaki, H., & Yamaguchi, T. (1997). The cognitive and symbolic analysis of the generalization process: The comparison of algebraic signs with geometric figures. In E. Pehkonnen (Ed.), *Proceedings of the 21st annual conference of the Psychology of Mathematics Education* (Vol. 3, pp. 105–113). Finland: Lahti.

Josephson, J. (2000). Smart inductive generalizations are abductions. In P. Flach & A. Kakas (Eds.), *Abduction and induction: Essays on their relation and integration* (pp. 31–44). Netherlands: Kluwer.

Josephson, J., & Josephson, S. (1994). *Abductive inference: Computation, philosophy, technology*. New York, NY: Cambridge University Press.

Kaput, J. (1995). Long term algebra reform: Democratizing access to big ideas. In C. Lacampagne, W. Blair, & J. Kaput (Eds.), *The algebra initiative colloquium* (Vol. 1, pp. 33–49). Washington, DC: U.S. Department of Education.

Kaput, J. (2008). What is algebra? What is algebraic reasoning? In J. Kaput, D. Carraher, & M. Blanton (Eds.), *Algebra in the early grades* (pp. 5–18). New York, NY: Erlbaum.

Kaput, J., Carraher, D., & Blanton, M. (2008). *Algebra in the early grades*. New York, NY: Erlbaum.

Katz, V. (2007). Stages in the history of algebra with implications for teaching. *Educational Studies in Mathematics, 66*, 185–201.

Kleinberg, J. (2011). What can huge data sets teach us about society and ourselves? In M. Brockman (Ed.), *Future science: Essays from the cutting edge* (pp. 72–87). New York: Vintage Books, Random House Inc.

Kline, M. (1980). *Mathematics: The loss of certainty*. New York: Oxford University Press.

Knuth, E. (2002). Proof as a tool for learning mathematics. *Mathematics Teacher, 95*(7), 486–490.

Küchemann, D. (2008). *Looking for structure*. London: Dexter Graphics.

Küchemann, D. (2010). Using patterns generically to see structure. *Pedagogies, 5*(3), 233–250.

Kvasz, L. (2006). The history of algebra and the development of the form of its language. *Philosophia Mathematica, 14*, 287–317.

Lannin, J. (2005). Generalization and justification: The challenge of introducing algebraic reasoning through patterning activities. *Mathematical Thinking and Learning, 7*(3), 231–258.

Le Corre, M., & Carey, S. (2007). One, two, three, four, nothing more: An investigation of the conceptual sources of the verbal counting principles. *Cognition, 105*, 395–438.

Lee, L. (1996). An initiation into algebra culture through generalization activities. In C. Bednarz, C. Kieran, & L. Lee (Eds.), *Approaches to algebra: Perspectives for research and teaching* (pp. 87–106). Dordrecht, Netherlands: Kluwer.

Lee, L., & Freiman, V. (2004). Tracking primary students' understanding of patterns. In D. McDougall & J. Ross (Eds.), *Proceedings of the 26th annual conference of the North American Chapter of the International Group for the Psychology of Mathematics Education (PMENA)* (Vol. 2, pp. 245–251). Toronto, Canada: PMENA.

Leung, A. (2008). Dragging in a dynamic geometry environment through the lens of variation. *International Journal of Computers for Mathematical Learning, 13*(2), 135–157.

Lin, F., Yang, K., & Chen, C. (2004). The features and relationships of reasoning, proving, and understanding proof in number patterns. *International Journal of Science and Mathematics Education, 2*, 227–256.

Lipton, J., & Spelke, E. (2005). Preschool children master the logic of number word meanings. *Cognition, 20*, 1–10.

Luck, S., & Vogel, E. (1997). The capacity of visual working memory for features and conjunctions. *Nature, 390*, 279–281.

Luria, A. (1976). *Cognitive development: Its cultural and social foundations*. Cambridge, MA: Harvard University Press.

MacGregor, M., & Stacey, K. (1992). A comparison of pattern-based and equation-solving approaches to algebra. In B. Southwell, K. Owens, & B. Perry (Eds.), *Proceedings of the 15th annual conference of the Mathematics Education Research Group of Australasia (MERGA)* (pp. 362–371). Brisbane, Australia: MERGA.

Malisani, E., & Spagnoio, F. (2009). From arithmetical thought to algebraic thought: The role of the variable. *Educational Studies in Mathematics, 71*, 19–41.

Maslow, A. (1970). *Motivation and personality*. New York: Harper & Row.

Mason, J. (1989). Mathematical abstraction as the result of a delicate shift of attention. *For the Learning of Mathematics, 9*(2), 2–8.

Mason, J. (2002). Generalization and algebra: Exploiting children's powers. In L. Hegarty (Ed.), *Aspects of teaching secondary mathematics: Perspectives on practice*. London: Routledge Falmer.

Mason, J., & Johnston-Wilder, S. (2004). *Fundamental constructs in mathematics education*. London: Routledge Falmer.

Mason, J., Stephens, M., & Watson, A. (2009). Appreciating mathematical structures for all. *Mathematics Education Research Journal, 21*(2), 10–32.

McClelland, J. (2010). Emergence in cognitive science. *Topics in Cognitive Science, 2*, 751–770.

McClelland, J., Botvinick, M., Noelle, D., Plaut, D., Rogers, T., Seindenberg, M., et al. (2010). Letting structures emerge: Connectionist and dynamical systems approaches to cognition. *Trends in Cognitive Science, 14*, 348–356.

McClelland, J., & Rogers, T. (2003). The parallel distributed processing approach to semantic cognition. *Nature Reviews Neuroscience, 4*, 310–322.

Mesa, V. (2004). Characterizing practices associated with functions in middle school textbooks: An empirical account. *Educational Studies in Mathematics, 56*, 255–286.

Moss, J., & Beatty, R. (2006). Knowledge building in mathematics: Supporting collaborative learning in pattern problems. *International Journal of Computer-Supported Collaborative Learning, 1*, 441–465.

Moss, J., & London McNab S. (2011). An approach to geometric and numeric patterning that fosters second grade students' reasoning and generalizing about functions and co-variations. In J. Cai & E. Knuth (Eds.), *Early algebraization: A global dialogue from multiple perspectives* (pp. 277–302). New York: Springer.

Mulligan, J., & Mitchelmore, M. (2009). Awareness of pattern and structure in early mathematical development. *Mathematics Education Research Journal, 21*(2), 33–49.

Mulligan, J., Prescott, A., & Mitchelmore, M. (2003). Taking a closer look at young students' visual imagery. *Australian Primary Mathematics, 8*(4), 175–197.

Mulligan, J., Prescott, A., & Mitchelmore, M. (2004). Children's development of structure in early mathematics. In M. J. Hoines & A. B. Fuglestad (Eds.), *Proceedings of the 28th conference of the International Group for the Psychology in Mathematics Education*. Bergen, Norway: Bergen University College.

Murphy, G., & Medin, D. (1985). The role of theories in conceptual coherence. *Psychological Review, 92*, 289–316.

Nathan, M., & Kim, S. (2007). Pattern generalization with graphs and words: A cross-sectional and longitudinal analysis of middle school students' representational fluency. *Mathematical Thinking and Learning, 9*(3), 193–219.

National Governors Association Center for Best Practices, Council of Chief State School Officers. (2010). *Common core state standards: Mathematics*. Washington, DC: Author.

Newell, A., & Simon, H. (1976). Computer science as empirical inquiry: Symbols and search. *Communications of the ACM, 19*(3), 113–126.

Norman, D. (1986). Reflections on cognition and parallel distributed processing. In J. McClelland & D. Rumelhart (Eds.), *Parallel distributed processing: Explorations of the microstructure of cognition* (Vol. 2, pp. 531–546). Cambridge, MA: MIT.

Norton, A., & Hackenberg, A. (2010). Continuing research on students' fraction schemes. In L. Steffe & J. Olive (Eds.), *Children's fractional knowledge* (pp. 341–352). New York, NY: Springer.

Noss, R., Healy, L., & Hoyles, C. (1997). The construction of mathematical meanings: Connecting the visual with the symbolic. *Educational Studies in Mathematics, 33*, 203–233.

Orton, A., & Orton, J. (2004). Pattern and the approach to algebra. In A. Orton (Ed.), *Pattern in the teaching and learning of mathematics* (pp. 105–120). UK: Continuum International Publishing Group.

Osserman, R. (1981). Structure vs. substance: The fall and rise of geometry. *The Two-Year College Mathematics Journal, 12*(4), 239–246.

Otte, M. (2011). Evolution, learning, and semiotics from a Peircean point of view. *Educational Studies in Mathematics, 77*(2–3), 313–329.

Paavola, S. (2011). Diagrams, iconicity, and abductive discovery. *Semiotica, 186*(1/4), 297–314.

Papic, M., Mulligan, J., & Mitchelmore, M. (2009). The growth of mathematical patterning strategies in preschool children.

Papic, M., Mulligan, J., & Mitchelmore, M. (2011). Assessing the development of preschoolers' mathematical patterning. *Journal for Research in Mathematics Education, 42*(3), 237–268.

Parker, T., & Baldridge, S. (2004). *Elementary mathematics for teachers*. Okemos, MI: Sefton-Ash Publishing.

Pedemonte, B. (2007). How can the relationship between argumentation and proof be analyzed? *Educational Studies in Mathematics, 66*, 23–41.

Pedemonte, B., & Reid, D. (2011). The role of abduction in proving processes. *Educational Studies in Mathematics, 76*, 281–303.

Peirce, C. (1869). Grounds of validity of the laws of logic: Further consequences of four incapacities. *The Journal of Speculative Philosophy, 2*, 193–208.

Peirce, C. (1934). *Collected papers of Charles Saunders Peirce: Volume 5*. Cambridge, MA: Harvard University Press.

Peirce, C. (1960). *Collected papers of Charles Saunders Peirce: Volumes I and II*. Cambridge, MA: The Belnap Press of Harvard University Press.

Pillow, B., Pearson, R., Hecht, M., & Bremer, A. (2010). Children's and adults' judgments of the certainty of deductive inference, inductive inferences, and guesses. *Journal of Genetic Epistemology, 171*(3), 203–217.

Pinel, P., Dehaene, S., Riviere, D., & Le Bihan, D. (2001). Modulation of parietal activation by semantic distance in a number comparison task. *NeuroImage, 14*, 1013–1026.

Pizlo, Z., Sawada, T., Li, Y., Kropatsch, W., & Steinman, R. (2010). New approach to the perception of 3D shape based on veridicality, complexity, symmetry, and volume. *Vision Research, 50*, 1–11.

Plaut, D., McClelland, J., Seindenberg, M., & Patterson, K. (1996). Understanding normal and impaired word reading: Computational principles in quasi-regular domains. *Psychological Review, 103*(1), 56–115.

Polya, G. (1957). *How to solve it*. Princeton, NJ: Princeton University Press.

Polya, G. (1973). *Induction and analogy in mathematics: Volume I of mathematics and plausible reasoning*. Princeton, NJ: Princeton University Press.

Pothos, E., & Ward, R. (2000). Symmetry, repetition, and figural goodness: An investigation of the weight of evidence theory. *Cognition, 75*, 65–78.

Prusak, N., Hershkowitz, R., & Schwarz, B. (2012). From visual reasoning to logical necessity through argumentative design. *Educational Studies in Mathematics, 79*, 19–40.

Radford, L. (1999). The rhetoric of generalization: A cultural semiotic approach to students' processes of symbolizing. In O. Zaslavsky (Ed.), *Proceedings of the 23rd conference of the International Group for the Psychology of Mathematics Education (PME)* (Vol. 4, pp. 89–96). Technion-Israel Institute of Technology, Israel: PME.

Radford, L. (2000). Students' processes of symbolizing in algebra: A semiotic analysis of the production of signs in generalizing tasks. In T. Nakahara & M. Koyama (Eds.), *Proceedings of the 24th conference of the International Group for the Psychology of Mathematics Education (PME)* (Vol. 4, pp. 81–88). Hiroshima University, Japan: PME.

Radford, L. (2001a). Signs and meanings in students' emergent algebraic thinking: A semiotic analysis. *Educational Studies in Mathematics, 42*, 237–268.

Radford, L. (2001b). Factual, contextual, and symbolic generalizations in algebra. In M. V. D. Hueuvel-Panhuizen (Ed.), *Proceedings of the 25th conference of the International Group for the Psychology of Mathematics Education (PME)* (Vol. 4, pp. 81–88). Freudenthal Institute, Utrecht University, Netherlands: PME.

Radford, L. (2003). Gestures, speech, and the sprouting of signs: A semiotic-cultural approach to students' types of generalization. *Mathematical Thinking and Learning, 5*(1), 37–70.

Radford, L. (2006). Algebraic thinking and the generalization of patterns: A semiotic perspective. In S. Alatorre, J. Cortina, M. Saiz, & A. Mendez (Eds.), *Proceedings of the 28th annual meeting of the North American Chapter of the International Group for the Psychology of Mathematics Education (PME)* (Vol. 1, pp. 2–21). Universidad Pedagogica Nacional, Mexico: PME.

Radford, L. (2008). Iconicity and contraction: A semiotic investigation of forms of algebraic generalizations of patterns in different contexts. *ZDM, 40*, 83–96.

Radford, L. (2010). The eye as a theoretician: Seeing structures in generalizing activities. *For the Learning of Mathematics, 30*(2), 2–7.

Radford, L., Bardini, C., & Sabena, C. (2007). Perceiving the general: The multisemiotic dimension of students' algebraic activity. *Journal for Research in Mathematics Education, 38*(5), 507–530.

Read, S., & Marcus-Newhall, A. (1993). Explanatory coherence in social explanations: A parallel distributed processing account. *Journal of Personality and Social Psychology, 65*(3), 429–447.

Rivera, F. (2007). Accounting for students' schemes in the development of a graphical process for solving polynomial inequalities in instrumented activity. *Educational Studies in Mathematics, 65*(3), 281–307.

Rivera, F. (2010a). Visual templates in pattern generalization. *Educational Studies in Mathematics, 73*, 297–328.

Rivera, F. (2010b). Second grade students' preinstructional competence in patterning activity. In M. Pinto & T. Kawasaki (Eds.), *Proceedings of the 34th conference of the International Group for the Psychology of Mathematics Education (PME)* (Vol. 4, pp. 81–88). Belo Horizante, Brazil: PME.

Rivera, F. (2011). *Toward a visually-oriented school mathematics curriculum: Research, theory, practice, and issues (Mathematics Education Library Series 49)*. New York, NY: Springer.

Rivera, F., & Becker, J. (2009). Algebraic reasoning through patterns. *Mathematics Teaching in the Middle School, 15*(4), 212–221.

Rivera, F., & Becker, J. (2011). Formation of pattern generalization involving linear figural patterns among middle school students: Results of a three-year study. In J. Cai & E. Knuth (Eds.), *Early algebraization: A global dialogue from multiple perspectives (advances in mathematics education)* (Vol. 2, pp. 323–366). New York: Springer.

Rivera, F., & Becker, J. (Eds.). (2008). From patterns to generalization: Development of algebraic thinking. *ZDM, 40*(1), 1–161.

Rogers, T., & McClelland, J. (2004). *Semantic cognition: A parallel distributed processing approach*. Cambridge, MA: Bradford Book.

Rogers, T., & McClelland, J. (2008). Précis of semantic cognition: A parallel distributed processing approach. *The Behavioral and Brain Sciences, 31*, 689–749.

Rumelhart, D. (1989). The architecture of mind: A connectionist approach. In M. Posner (Ed.), *Foundations of cognitive science* (pp. 133–159). Cambridge, MA: MIT.

Ruthven, K., Deaney, R., & Hennessy, S. (2009). Using graphing software to teach about algebraic forms: A study of technology-supported practice in secondary school mathematics. *Educational Studies in Mathematics, 71*, 279–297.

Samson, D. (2011). Capitalizing on inherent ambiguities in symbolic expressions of generality. *Australian Mathematics Teacher, 67*(1), 28–32.

Samson, D., & Schäfer, M. (2009). An analysis of the influence of question design on learners' approaches to number pattern generalization tasks. In M. Schäfer & C. McNamara (Eds.), *Proceedings of the 17th annual Meeting of the Southern African Association for Research in Mathematics, Science, and Technology Education (SAARMSTE)* (Vol. 2, pp. 516–523). Grahamstown, South Africa: SAARMSTE.

Samson, D., & Schäfer, M. (2011). Enactivism, figural apprehension, and knowledge objectification: An exploration of figural pattern generalization. *For the Learning of Mathematics, 31*(1), 37–43.

Schliemann, A., Carraher, D., & Brizuela, B. (2007). *Bringing out the algebraic character of arithmetic: From children's ideas to classroom practice*. New York, NY: Erlbaum.

Schweitzer, K. (2006). Teacher as researcher: Research as a partnership. In S. Smith & M. Smith (Eds.), *Teachers engaged in research: Inquiry into mathematics classrooms, grades pre-k-2* (pp. 69–94). Greenwich, CT: Information Age Publishing.

Schyns, P., Goldstone, R., & Thibaut, J.-P. (1998). The development of features in object concepts. *The Behavioral and Brain Sciences, 21*, 1–54.

Senk, S., & Thompson, D. (2006). Strategies used by second-year algebra students to solve problems. *Journal for Research in Mathematics Education, 37*(2), 116–128.

Shtoff, V. (1966). *Modeling and philosophy*. Moscow: Leningrad.

Smith, L. (2002). *Reasoning by mathematical induction in children's arithmetic*. Oxford, UK: Elsevier Science Ltd.

Stacey, K. (1989). Finding and using patterns in linear generalizing problems. *Educational Studies in Mathematics, 20*, 147–164.

Stacey, K., & MacGregor, M. (2001). Curriculum reform and approaches to algebra. In R. Sutherland, T. Rojano, A. Bell, & R. Lins (Eds.), *Perspectives on school algebra* (pp. 141–154). Dordrecht, Netherlands: Kluwer.

Stavy, R., & Babai, R. (2008). Complexity of shapes and quantitative reasoning in geometry. *Mind, Brain, and Education, 2*(4), 170–176.

Steele, D., & Johanning, D. (2004). A schematic-thoeretic view of problem solving and development of algebraic thinking. *Educational Studies in Mathematics, 57*, 65–90.

Steels, L. (2008). The symbol grounding problem has been solved, so what's next? In M. de Vega, A. Glenberg, & A. Graesser (Eds.), *Symbols and embodiment: Debates on meaning and cognition* (pp. 223–244). New York: Oxford University Press.

Strevens, M. (2008). *Depth: An account of scientific explanation.* Cambridge, MA: Harvard University Press.

Swafford, J., & Langrall, C. (2000). Grade 6 students' preinstructional use of equations to describe and represent problem situations. *Journal for Research in Mathematics Education, 31*(1), 89–112.

Tabach, M., Arcavi, A., & Hershkowitz, R. (2008). Transitions among different symbolic generalizations by algebra beginners in a computer intensive environment. *Educational Studies in Mathematics, 69*(1), 53–71.

Tanish, D. (2011). Functional thinking ways in relation to linear function tables of elementary school student. *The Journal of Mathematical Behavior, 30*, 206–223.

Tanisli, D. (2011). *Functional thinking ways in relation to linear function tables of elementary school students, 30*(3), 206–223.

Tanisli, D., & Özdas, A. (2009). The strategies of using generalizing patterns among primary school 5th grade students. *Educational Sciences: Theory & Practice, 9*(3), 1485–1497.

Taylor-Cox, J. (2003). Algebra in the early years? *Young Children, 58*(1), 15–21.

Thagard, P. (1978). Semiosis and hypothetic inference in C. S. Peirce. *Versus Quaderni Di Studi Semiotici, 19*(20), 163–172.

Thagard, P. (1989). Explanatory coherence. *The Behavioral and Brain Sciences, 12*, 435–467.

Thelen, E., & Smith, L. (1994). *A dynamic systems approach to the development of cognition and action.* Cambridge, MA: MIT.

Todd, P., Lyublinskaya, I., & Ryzhik, V. (2010). Symbolic geometry software and proofs. *International Journal of Computers for Mathematical Learning, 13*(2), 135–157.

Triadafillidis, T. (1995). Circumventing visual limitations in teaching the geometry of shapes. *Educational Studies in Mathematics, 15*, 151–159.

Vale, I., & Pimentel, T. (2010). From figural growing patterns to generalization: A path to algebraic thinking. In M. Pinto & T. Kawasaki (Eds.), *Proceedings of the 34th conference of the International Group for the Psychology of Mathematics Education (PME)* (Vol. 4, pp. 241–248). Belo Horizante, Brazil: PME.

van den Heuvel-Panhuizen, M. (Ed.). (2008). *Children learn mathematics: A learning-teaching trajectory with intermediate attainment targets for calculation with whole numbers in primary school.* Rotterdam, Netherlands: Sense.

Varzi, A. (2008). Patterns, rules, and inferences. In J. Adler & L. Rips (Eds.), *Reasoning: Studies of human inference and its foundations* (pp. 282–290). New York, NY: Cambridge University Press.

Vinner, S. (2011). The role of examples in the learning of mathematics and in everyday thought processes. *ZDM Mathematics Education, 43*, 247–256.

Vygotsky, L. (1962). *Thought and language.* Cambridge, MA: MIT.

Wallis, G., & Bülthoff, H. (1999). Learning to recognize objects. *Trends in Cognitive Sciences, 3*(1), 22–31.

Warren, E., & Cooper, T. (2007). Repeating patterns and multiplicative thinking: Analysis of classroom interactions with 9-year-old students that support the transition from the known to the novel. *Journal of Classroom Interaction, 41*(2), 7–17.

Watson, A. (2009). Thinking mathematically, disciplined noticing, and structures of attention. In S. Lerman & B. Davis (Eds.), *Mathematical action & structures of noticing* (pp. 211–222). Rotterdam, Netherlands: Sense Publishers.

Williams, J., & Lombrozo, T. (2010). The role of explanation in discovery and generalization: Evidence from category learning. *Cognitive Science, 34*, 776–806.

Williams, J., Lombrozo, T., & Rehder, B. (2011). Explaining drives the discovery of real and illusory patterns. In L. Carlson, C. Hölscher, & T. Shipley (Eds.), *Proceedings of the 33rd annual conference of the Cognitive Science Society* (pp. 1352–1357). Austin, TX: Cognitive Science Society.

Wilson, K., Ainley, J., & Bills, L. (2005). Naming a column on a spreadsheet: Is it more algebraic? In D. Hewitt & A. Noyes (Eds.), *Proceedings of the Sixth British Congress of Mathematics Education* (pp. 184–191). Warwick, UK: BCME.

Yeap, B. H., & Kaur, B. (2008). Elementary school students engaging in making generalization: A glimpse from a Singapore classroom. *ZDM, 40*, 55–64.

Yerushalmy, M., & Maman, H. (1988). *The Geometric Supposer as the basis for class discussion in geometry.* Haifa, Israel: University of Haifa Laboratory of Computers for Learning.

Yerushalmy, M. (1993). Generalization in geometry. In J. Schwartz, M. Yerushalmy, & B. Wilson (Eds.), *The geometric supposer: What is it a case of?* (pp. 57–84). Hillsdale, NJ: Erlbaum.

Yevdokimov, O. (2008). Making generalizations in geometry: Students' views on the process. In O. Figueras, J. L. Cortina, S. Alatorre, T. Rojano, & A. Sepulveda (Eds.), *Proceedings of the joint meeting of PME 32 and PMENA XXX* (Vol. 4, pp. 193–200). Morelia, Mexico: Cinvestav-UMSNH and PME.

Zazkis, R., Liljedahl, P., & Chernoff, E. (2008). The role of examples in forming and refuting generalizations. *ZDM, 40*, 131–141.

Author Index

F. Rivera, *Teaching and Learning Patterns in School Mathematics:*
Psychological and Pedagogical Considerations, DOI 10.1007/978-94-007-2712-0,
© Springer Science+Business Media Dordrecht 2013

Subject Index

F. Rivera, *Teaching and Learning Patterns in School Mathematics:*
Psychological and Pedagogical Considerations, DOI 10.1007/978-94-007-2712-0,
© Springer Science+Business Media Dordrecht 2013

Printed by Publishers' Graphics LLC
MLSI130514.15.17.32